Economic Development in Africa

Economic Development in Africa

International Efforts, Issues and Prospects

Edited by Olusola Akinrinade and J. Kurt Barling

 Pinter Publishers, London

First published in Great Britain in 1987 by
Pinter Publishers Limited
25 Floral Street, London WC2E 9DS

British Library Cataloguing in Publication Data

Economic development in Africa.
    1. Africa—Economic condition—1960—
    I. Akinrinade, Olusola   II. Barling, J. Kurt
    330.96′0328   HC800

    ISBN 0-86187-909-0

Library of Congress Cataloging-in-Publication Data

Economic development in Africa.

    Bibliography: p.
    Includes index.
    1. Economic assistance—Africa.   2. Africa—
Economic conditions—1960— .   I. Akinrinade, Olusola.
II. Barling, J. Kurt.
HC800.E275   1987   338.98   87-15296
ISBN 0-86187-909-0

Typeset by Florencetype Ltd, Kewstoke, Avon
Printed by Biddles of Guildford Ltd.

Contents

List of tables

List of abbreviations

AAPSO	Afro-Asian People's Solidarity Organization
ACCT	Agence Pour la Coopération Culturelle et Technique also known by the acronym (AGECOOP)
ACP	African, Caribbean and Pacific (Countries)
ADB	African Development Bank
ADELF	Association des Ecrivains de Langue Française
AfDB	African Development Bank
AIPLF	Association Internationale des Parlementaires de Langue Française
ANC	African National Congress
APPER	African Priority Programme for Economic Recovery
ASEAN	Association of Southeast Asian Nations
AUPELF	Association des Universités Partièllement ou Entièrement de Langue Française
BIS	Bank for International Settlements
BLS	Botswana, Lesotho, Swaziland
CAP	Common Agricultural Policy
CBI	Caribbean Basin Initiative
CCC	Commodity Credit Corporation
CCCE	Caisse Centrale de Coopération Economique
CCP	Common Commercial Policy
CCT	Common Commercial Tariff
CEAO	Communauté Economique de l'Afrique de l'Ouest
CEPGL	Economic Community of the Great Lakes Countries
CET	Common External Tariff
CFA	Communauté Financière Africaine (West Africa), Coopération Financière en Afrique Centrale
CFTC	Commonwealth Fund for Technical Cooperation
CG	Consultative Groups

CKD	Completely Knocked Down
CPTA	Commonwealth Programme for Technical Assistance
CSFP	Commonwealth Scholarships and Fellowships Plan
DAC	Development Assistance Committee (OECD)
DBSA	Development Bank of South Africa
DG	Directorate-General
EAC	East African Community
EC	European Community
ECA	Economic Commission for Africa (UN)
ECE	Economic Commission for Europe (UN)
ECLA	Economic Commission for Latin America (UN)
ECOSOC	Economic and Social Council (UN)
ECOWAS	Economic Community of West African States
EDF	European Development Fund
EIB	European Investment Bank
EXIMBANK	Export Import Bank
FAC	Fonds d'Aide et Coopération
FAO	Food and Agricultural Organisation (UN)
FPRD	Food Production and Rural Development Division (Commonwealth)
FRELIMO	Frente de Libertaçao de Moçambique
G24	Group of 24 (Industrialized Countries)
GATT	General Agreement on Tariffs and Trade
GDI	Gross Domestic Investment
GDP	Gross Domestic Product
GNP	Gross National Product
GRIP	Guaranteed Recovery of Investment Principle
GSP	Generalized System of Preferences
GSS	General Scholarship Scheme (India)
HSRC	Human Sciences Research Council (South Africa)
IDA	International Development Agency
IDEP	African Institute for Economic Development and Planning
IDS	Institute for Development Studies (Sussex University)
IDU	Industrial Development Unit
IFC	International Finance Corporation
ILO	International Labour Organization
IMF	International Monetary Fund
IRES	Institut de Recherches Economiques et Sociales
LDC	Less Developed Countries (OECD)

LIBOR	London Interbank Offered Rate (Reference point for syndicated bank loans)
LIC	Low Income Countries (World Bank)
LLDC	Least Developed Countries (OECD)
LPA	*Lagos Plan of Action*
MFA	Multifibre Arrangement
MIC	Middle Income Countries
MIGA	Multilateral Investment Guarantee Agency
MNR	Movimento Naçional de Resistência
MPLA	Movimento Popular de Liberatçao de Angola
MULPOC	Multilateral Programming and Operational Centres
MYRA	Multiyear Rescheduling Agreement
NAM	Non-Aligned Movement
NGO	Non-Governmental Organization
NIC	Newly Industrializing Countries
NIEO	New International Economic Order
NIMEXE	Nomenclature of goods for the external trade statistics of the community and statistics of trade between member states (EC)
NNPC	Nigerian National Petroleum Corporation
NTB	Non-Tariff Barriers
OAU	Organization of African Unity
OCAM	Organisation Commune Africaine et Mauricienne
ODA	Official Development Assistance (UK)
ODA	Overseas Development Administration (UK)
ODM	Ministry of Overseas Development
OECD	Organization for Economic Cooperation and Development
OPEC	Organization of Petroleum Exporting Countries
OSAS	Overseas Service Aid Scheme (UK)
PSD	Programme Spécial de Développement
PTA	Preferential Trade Area
RIN	Rassemblement pour l'Indépendence Nationale
RMA	Rand Monetary Area
SACU	South African Customs Union
SADCC	Southern African Development Coordination Conference
SBDC	Small Business Development Corporation
SCAAP	Special Commonwealth African Assistance Plan
SWAPO	South West Africa People's Organization

TAG	Technical Assistance Group (Commonwealth)
TBVC	Transkei, Bophuthwatswana, Venda and Ciskei
TCDC	Technical Cooperation among Developing Countries
TMA	Tripartite Monetary Area
UDEAC	Union Douanière et Economique de l'Afrique Centrale
UDF	United Democratic Front
UK	United Kingdom
UN	United Nations
UNCTAD	United Nations Conference on Trade and Development
UNDATs	United Nations Interdisciplinary Development Advisory Teams
UNDP	United Nations Development Programme
UNECA	United Nations Economic Commission for Africa
UNEP	United Nations Environment(al) Programme
UNESCO	United Nations Educational, Scientific and Cultural Organisation
UNFPA	United Nations Fund for Population Activities
UNHCR	United Nations High Commissioner for Refugees
UNICEF	United Nations Children Fund
UNIDO	United Nations Industrial Development Organisation
USAID	United States Agency for International Development
VER	Voluntary Export Restraint
WFP	World Food Programme
WHO	World Health Organisation
ZANU	Zimbabwe African National Union
ZAPU	Zimbabwe African People's Union

Acknowledgements

This volume was inspired by the Africa research workshop set up in Spring 1986 in the Department of International Relations at the London School of Economics and Political Science by James Mayall and Dennis Austin. Our association with this forum has helped to stimulate and channel the ideas presented in this volume, providing an informed basis for scholarship.

We would like to thank the contributors for making this collection of essays possible, in the belief that readers will profit from their labours. We have greatly appreciated their responsiveness to our suggestions as well as their good humour in the pursuance of pressing deadlines. These colleagues have provided us with valuable insights and information. We would also like to thank Dolores Cooke for the loan of her typing skills at such short notice.

The work for this volume has been carried out while the Editors have been funded with scholarships given by the London School of Economics and Political Science and the Economic and Social Research Council (UK) respectively.

Any opinions, findings or recommendations expressed in this volume, needless to say, are those of the editors and contributing authors and do not represent the views either of the London School of Economics and Political Science or the Economic and Social Research Council.

Olusola Akinrinade
J. Kurt Barling
London, June 1987

1 Editors' introduction

J. Kurt Barling and Olusola Akinrinade

Over the last three decades the development problematic has exercised the talents of some of the best scholars without any degree of consensus being reached between the varied conceptualizations of 'development'; either in terms of what we should identify as development, or how we should measure this phenomenon. This volume does not pretend to aspire to the reconciliation of these different convictions.

The chapters in this book need, however, to be located within the context of the debate on development in general and African development in particular. Therefore in this introduction we sketch a brief historiography of the different conceptualizations of 'development', by examining its meaning for the three principal 'schools of thought' associated with the development debate and we briefly address the question of the measurement of economic development. We also look at the evolution of the development debate within the context of sub-Saharan Africa itself and how this has been reflected in the various development strategies.

THE CONCEPT OF DEVELOPMENT

Since the end of the Second World War a more readily identifiable international political economy has emerged. During the inter-war years underdevelopment did not exist *per se*. That is to say, the term had not been subjected to any rigorous theorizing. The prevailing *laissez faire* wisdoms during this period, by process of assumption, suggested that comparative advantage and the international division of labour would automatically lead to a process of economic growth in the less developed countries and colonies.[1] However, as the decolonization process gathered momentum and a 'Third World'[2] began to emerge, formal changes took place in the structure of relations between states. As individual states acceded to sovereign status, political power within these newly created states was relinquished by the colonial authorities in favour of the representatives of the former colonized peoples.

Whilst the reality of this newly acquired membership of the international community, tended to be a significant degree of political equality, it soon became evident that economic inequality would persist, unless changes could be made to the manner in which economic exchanges between the 'North' and the 'South' were realized. This economic dilemma gave rise to claims that the decolonization process had only managed to reach a half-way house, or in more radical circles that the new relationships were simply manifestations of 'neo-colonialism'. This evident imbalance between the economic and the political provoked a good deal of serious academic discourse and scholars began to examine the political and economic relationships between the industrialized countries and the rest of the world.

During the 1950s, when the development issue first surfaced in international debate,[3] relations between the industrialized 'North' and developing 'South' were expected to be largely cooperative, and this was very much reflected in the way 'development' was conceptualized. Structural-functionalists like Lipset[4] and Almond and Coleman[5] began to write of the political development of states, in terms of the development of their governmental institutions, to resemble those associated with liberal democracy. This was juxtaposed by the work of economists like Lewis[6] and Rostow[7] who began to write about the notion of economic growth and development. Development according to these scholars assumed, firstly, that the developing countries should aspire to Westernization; secondly, that the West provided an established model of *the* 'developed state'; and finally, that this form of development would provide the building blocks for the emergence of a homogeneous world culture, based broadly upon the West's culture (or perhaps, the 'American way of life'). The 'ideological' content of this conceptualization was therefore essentially humanitarianism based on the Western value system. This concept of development was as such identified with capitalist social relations and the so-called economic 'backwardness' was seen as a product of the isolation of the developing countries from the world economy. This 'backwardness', it was argued, could easily be remedied by greater global economic integration. This form of development drew a contrast between the process of development in the industrialized and developing countries, as well as a contrast between the developing countries and an idealized process of development which would lead to both a 'maximum utilization of resources' and 'the most rational allocation of surplus'.

Underdevelopment was as such the direct antithesis of this concept. This conceptualization can clearly be seen to be a product of two distinct political issues. Firstly, the Cold War concerns of the West (i.e., the containment of communism) and, secondly, a response to the social problems posed by decolonization and the Nationalists' radical development strategies.[8] These two concerns were of course interrelated.

This original theorizing, following the *laissez faire* tradition, is now largely scorned. These theorists took development as a given 'state of nature' and were *ipso facto* uncritical of the concept itself. Moreover, they relied on ahistorical analyses, failing to acknowledge that development could be different under specific historical conditions. Finally, this group of scholars failed to identify the possible implications of domestic social structures, as well as the nature of the dominant relations between North and South. This rendered their concept essentially descriptive and static.

This *laissez faire* conceptualization was subjected to two broad levels of critique from the beginning of the 1960s. On the one hand, there were those scholars who essentially agreed with the fundamentals of this school but who undertook a more rigorous theorizing of the concept of development. This *liberal critique* is also often referred to as the *internal critique*. The alternative *Marxist critique* or *external critique* broke entirely with the earlier concept.

The liberal re-evaluation focused on the one hand, with writers like Bairoch[9] and Freyssinet,[10] on further developing historical and regionally specific analyses of underdevelopment. However, it also involved a broader critique of the fundamental question underlying the thesis outlined by Rostow and the other 1950s liberals—i.e., how could development be promoted in the underdeveloped Third World? On the other hand Hirschmann,[11] Perroux[12] and Myrdal[13] pioneered attempts to examine the need for the internal transformation of the social structures of developing societies (hence internal critique). They began to draw attention to what they saw as the necessity of development planning on the level of the national economy, organizing development around certain key axes of growth. The basic premise in this line of logic was that the developing economies were largely uncoordinated, with a series of structural mismatches on both the economic and social levels.

These mismatches produced a plethora of constraining resource gaps in the production and consumption processes. Developing states were analysed as having dual economies—a traditional subsistence economy alongside a modern industrial economy—and this was considered to create a fundamental mismatch, inevitably retarding economic development.

While the capitalist sector remained the means to achieving growth, industrialization was the key to this growth pattern. Indeed most liberal theorists suggested that the rural economy should only perform a secondary role as an outlet for capital products and a supplier of manpower. This secondary role also implied a *de facto* subordination of food production for consumption to production for export currency earning. Furthermore, it was argued that responsibility lay with the domestic authorities to provide a domestic climate conducive to attracting foreign capital (this more often than not implied social stability and a non-communist orientation).

Industrialization provided the framework for integrating and co-ordinating the differentiated sectors of the developing economy, as well as a means of changing rigid domestic social structures. Industrialization would achieve this on three fronts. Firstly, by acting as the engine of growth; secondly, by providing the means to develop infrastructure and restructure the agricultural sector; and finally, it could provide the opportunity to capitalize on the migration of peoples from rural to urban areas by providing secure employment in the growth industries.[14] In this way the *internal critique* attempted to take into account the social costs of development, given its emphasis on the process of economic growth. It tried to project the 'human face' of growth in an attempt to confront and seek remedies to the perceived implications of social conflict which were to be unleashed by rapid decolonization and economic development. In many respects this internal critique dominated the practical application of development strategies during the first United Nations Development decade.

As already suggested the 1960s also produced an alternative *radical critique* of the *laissez faire* concept, originating from the Marxist 'schools of thought'. This critique focused upon the external factors hindering development in the Third World (hence external critique). For example, it pointed to the dominant position of the industrialized world over the international political economy and its alleged use of this position to exploit the developing world. This critique differed from the internal critique, not only in its analysis, but more fundamentally it sought to answer a different kind of question. Whereas the latter took underdevelopment as the original position and then sought to discover a means of emerging from this predicament, the external critique sought to answer the question: can capitalism promote development or does it necessarily produce underdevelopment? In this sense it was a theory less of development but of underdevelopment, seeking to demonstrate that the latter condition was a product of capitalist penetration. The evolution of this critique can be linked to the anti-colonial and neo-colonial debates at the turn of the 1960s. In most respects the dichotomy produced by these two fundamentally different questions asked by the liberal and Marxist critiques has remained the locus of debate ever since.

Writers like Amin,[15] Franck,[16] Prebisch, Wallerstein[17] and Emmanuel[18] set about demolishing the notion of comparative advantage and development, suggesting alternatively that international specialization was a function of imperialism and that underdevelopment was essentially a means of maintaining the *dependency* links between South and North.

Prebisch played a key role in developing the *dependencia* school, which argued for a strategy of import substitution and industrialization. The assumption here was that in an international environment in which political domination was significantly reduced, economic development was essentially conditioned by internal factors of organization and planning.[19] Franck is more critical and suggested that 'economic development' and underdevelopment are opposite sides of the same coin. Both are the necessary result and contemporary manifestion of internal contradictions of the world capitalist system'. This linked in with his analysis of the world system in terms of a *centre and periphery*, the peripheralized developing world being the exploited party in an 'unequal exchange'.

Wallerstein's *World System Analysis* added a historical analysis of how this centre–periphery relationship evolved as a means of structuring the world political economy. He suggests that the international division of labour, although constantly changing (i.e., the location of the centre and the periphery constantly changes), is essentially a product of the structuring of the world economy in the sixteenth century.

These three levels of the radical critique see the state as the central mechanism for promoting growth, as the primordial agency in organizing the redistribution of resources through its central role in planning within the domestic political economy. Some writers like Amin have gone so far as to advocate that the only manner in which foreign domination can be completely eradicated is through the pursuance of a totally autarkic strategy, promoting the concept of *self-development*.

The importance of class analysis within this critique implies that, unlike liberal writers who have developed their theories with the precise objective of minimizing social conflict, a degree of social conflict is a necessary condition for achieving a socialist order without classes.

This radical critique, although naturally challenged by liberal critics, has also been subjected to substantial internal divisions, often a product of its own ambiguities.[20] This has resulted in so-called 'neo-Marxist' re-evaluations. Although the Marxist critique, represented above, discounts the value of political independence and regards centre–periphery relations as generally exploitative, writers like Warren[21] have suggested that power relations between North and South, which naturally affect exploitation and manifestations of domination, have in fact been altered since independence. In particular the previous monopoly of imperialist political power was severed during the decolonization process. Furthermore, Warren has argued that not only did the imperialists positively favour development strategies as an effective means of preventing revolution during the decolonization period, but also, and more controversially, that the interests of the imperialist powers are not directly served by the maintenance of underdevelopment in the Third World, since the classic imperialist division of labour is slowly being broken down. A further element of this re-evaluation is developed by Leys,[22] who argues that the internal class structures of developing societies are not principally a result of foreign interventions, rather the development of the domestic industrializing society.

Whilst the *external critique* or theories of underdevelopment have provided a justification for the logic of socialism, it is difficult to see how they confront the question of what development actually is (other than the antithesis of under-development). This critique tends to focus upon 'Utopian questions of desirability', rather than upon whether development is a scientific and political possibility. We may observe that many developing country governments and the authorities of the international organizations used the external critique during the late 1960s and 1970s as an instrument of rhetoric, as a way of justifying their demands for international reform (particularly in the name of national independence) without actually using it as a doctrine of execution. In this sense it is interesting to note a type of dual-track application of the development concept. On the one hand, the *external critique* being used as a justifying rhetorical mechanism and, on the other, the *internal critique* being used as a mechanism of practical application; courting the notion of dependence for political ends whilst using the liberal concept to achieve economic results.

This brief conceptual discussion seems to suggest a rather obvious but basic conclusion. The concept of development is controversial and the phenomenon of economic development extremely complex. It is impossible to state objectively, for example, what 'an *optimal* exploitation' might be. The concept of development is in this sense primarily evaluative.

This ambiguity exacerbates the scholar's problem of finding an adequate indicator to measure this development.[23] There is a whole range of different quantifiable variables to assess levels of economic development (for example: GDP per capita, output per worker or manhour, levels of nutrition, infant mortality, life expectancy, underemployment and unemployment, price and interest rate stability, etc.) and any given set of variables must be *ipso facto* selective as well as subjective. On the international level it is clearly not possible to consider all the aspects of the dynamic development process and thereby predict (guessing apart) with any degree of accuracy, the future capacity of a given economy.

Nevertheless, there are broadly speaking three distinct areas of the economy that are looked at when assessing levels of economic development: the production of goods and services; the standard of living of the population; changes in the productive capacity of an economy to provide the necessary goods and services in the future.

Considering these three fields, along with the numerous variables that are available, suggests that we need to make a sectoral approach to quantitative analysis if we are to establish appropriate indicators for international comparisons. Having said this, on an international comparative level, aggregate GDP (and its derivatives, GDP per capita, annual percentage change in GDP, etc.) remains one of the most useful of indicators.[24] With the use of purchasing power parities, for example, at any given period of time GDP per capita can provide a measure of the relative performance levels of various national economies.[25]

Development, however, should not merely be seen as a reflection of material production or potentialities of production, it also refers to the entire process of change that may result from the efforts undertaken to raise the productivity of the economy as well as the standard of living of the population. As we have seen, the social aspects of development are part and parcel of much contemporary conceptualization of the development problematic. Accelerated growth cannot take place in a static political and social framework. It requires concomitant policies to adapt the social structure and encourage broader participation of people in the political and economic processes. In Africa in particular, the changing nature of social organization threatens traditional social and political practices, and the resulting conflicts of interests and values has often led to action which runs counter to the desire for rapid economic development. Growth necessitates compromise, as it cannot ensure the preservation of existing social structures; indeed growth implies the very transformation of these structures.

Development must be a matter of fusing social and economic objectives, not only for an increase in production but in order to ensure considerable structural and social transformations, as well as a resource redistribution, resulting in improvements that benefit the entire community.

The African concern for development[26]

Within the space of a single generation African countries found themselves transformed into independent states with the full responsibilities associated with the status of statehood. One of the principal concerns for the majority of African governments on the attainment of independence was the rapid fulfilment of economic expectations. There is now a greater sense of awareness among the peoples of these states as to what to expect from their governments. Popular expectations of the material benefits of independence, created to a large extent by the nationalists themselves in the years of the anti-colonial struggle and the utterances of political leaders in the period after, demand at least partial fulfilment. Independence had been projected, not merely as an end in itself, but as a means towards attaining the good things of life that had been denied to people during the years of the anti-colonial struggle. People had become conscious of their poverty, and through the utterances of their political leaders were convinced that something could be done about it. Moreover, the very legitimacy of the authorities has been constantly challenged on the basis of their economic performance. Indeed over the years, many African governments have been removed from office as a result of poor levels of economic performance and their failure to halt the descent into poverty of their citizens.

Naturally, the government leaders are aware of the need to satisfy the rising expectations of their citizens. In the process they seek to protect and diversify state economies and foreign trade patterns; they seek to educate and provide employment for their citizens; they seek to overcome the problems of development that are not only responsible for the weakness of their states in the international system but also a possible future source of domestic instability. The awareness on the part of governments of the need to develop their economies has led to efforts to harness both international and internal elements contributing to development. Their efforts are usually given expression in development plans which often draw upon external expertise. Development planning became fashionable for nearly all African countries and most produced programmes which, in nearly all cases, contained exaggerated expectations. Realizing the objectives of most of these development plans was dependent not just on resources available within the state but to a great extent on external contributions. This is so because underdevelopment, the principal characteristic of most African economies, manifests itself not only in terms of material insufficiency and popular dissatisfaction, but also in the means to overcome them. Most African governments have never been shy of seeking development assistance when drafting their development plans; in fact, in many cases, it is usually stated that achieving certain elements of these plans is dependent on the availability of foreign assistance.

For much of the 1960s African states pursued, with varying degrees of vigour, their various development plans. Although in most cases the states continued, at least at the theoretical level, to give increasing importance to the utilization of internal resources for the purposes of development, the paths followed by these states differed substantially and essentially fell into two distinct groups. One group of countries opted for direct governmental participation in and ownership of the most important branches of their industry.[27] The other group adopted an almost opposite approach, preferring to put their trust in private ownership and private management rather than public administration.[28] However, by the early 1970s, African states were reassessing their economic performance and the impact of their various development strategies. Both the system of state control and that of private enterprise were already showing evidence of inadequacy. The most determined defenders of private enterprise could hardly overlook the great weaknesses of the African entrepreneur on the one hand and the unconcealed profiteering of many foreign firms on the other. At the same time those governments which opted for state control of the 'commanding heights' of the economy were also facing growing difficulties including marketing problems, and capital and skilled manpower shortages. Almost all of the African countries had witnessed stagnation in economic output; were suffering from worsening balances of payments brought about by deteriorating terms of trade; were facing increasing payments for the import of high-level skills, capital goods, spare parts and equipment, raw material inputs, marketing, shipping and insurance services; were labouring under widespread unemployment and mass poverty. African governments slowly came to a painful conclusion that past policies were neither viable nor sustainable if the objectives of self-reliance, eradication of mass poverty, reduction of mass unemployment, equitable distribution of the benefits of development and economic growth, along with equitable participation in international decision-making processes were to be pursued and achieved.[29] 'Capitalists' and 'socialists' were arriving at common grounds on certain key issues. For example, by then people rarely questioned the need for foreign capital investment[30] or the need for economic diversification.

The global economic recessions of the early and late 1970s, combined with poor levels of economic performance, stepped up the need for a reassessment of development strategies. This was to lead to a series of conferences and consultations with the participation of both academics and practitioners in the field of development. There were a number of sectoral conferences including the Conference of African Ministers of Industry, the Conference of African Ministers of Trade, and the Conference of African Ministers of Transport, Communication and Planning. The proposals worked out at these conferences formed the basis of the recommendations made by African Ministers responsible for economic development and planning to the Assembly of Heads of State and Government of the OAU meeting in Monrovia in 1979, which then adopted the programme dubbed the *Monrovia Strategy for the Economic Development of Africa*—simply referred to as the Monrovia Strategy. It is the Monrovia Strategy which introduced the notions of self-reliance and self-sustainment into development debates on a continental level in Africa.[31] It was realized that the development performance of most African states had been disappointing over the past decade and, more importantly, that the prospects for the future were gloomy. Furthermore, the failure of the demands for a New International Economic Order (NIEO) implied that the solution to the African problem—indeed to that of most Third World countries—did not lie in a restructured international economic system.

The acute nature of the crisis, as highlighted by the Monrovia Strategy, implied immediate action. The first economic summit of the Organization of African Unity in Lagos in April 1980 convened to devise a plan for the implementation of the Strategy. It was this economic summit that produced the *Lagos Plan of Action*.[32] The chief elements of the LPA centred around its endorsement of the African objective of attaining a more self-reliant and more economically integrated continent by the year 2000. It underscores the importance of involving all *agents* of development and change—private and public enterprises, chambers of commerce, agriculture, industry and mines, universities and other institutions of learning and research—in the *process* of economic development and growth.[33] The importance of regional economic cooperation and integration as necessary instruments for pursuing the objectives of national collective self-reliance is now recognized. In the light of this, it spells out clearly steps to be taken for strengthening economic cooperation and integration efforts. While recognizing the importance of external assistance, OAU Heads of State and Government were convinced that 'outside contributions should only supplement our own efforts, and they should not be the mainstay of our development'.[34] Although it contains recommendations for meeting short-term and medium-term needs, in its intention to transform the productive basis of the African economy, the LPA has more to offer on long-term recommendations. The recommendations to a great extent reflect the pillars on which both the Monrovia Strategy and the LPA were based. These are as follows:

(1) the deliberate promotion of an increasing measure of national self-reliance;
(2) the acceleration of internally located and relatively autonomous processes of growth and diversification and the achievement of a self-sustained development process;
(3) the democratization of the development process;
(4) the progressive eradication of mass poverty and unemployment and a fair and just distribution of income and the benefits of development among the populace;
(5) the acceleration of the process of regional economic integration through cooperation.[35]

The *Lagos Plan of Action* was presented to the eleventh Special Session of the UN General Assembly in September 1980 and has since become an integral part of the International Development Strategy for the Third United Nations Development Decade.[36]

In 1979 the African Governors of the World Bank addressed a joint memorandum to the Bank's President expressing their alarm about the gloomy economic prospects for the nations of sub-Saharan Africa as projected by the IBRD's *World Development Report* (1979). They requested the Bank to prepare 'a special paper on the economic development problems of these countries and an appropriate programme for helping them'. The response to that request was the 1981 report entitled *Accelerated Development in Sub-Saharan Africa: An Agenda for Action* (The Berg Report).[37] The Berg Report endorses the long-term objectives of African development expressed in the LPA, but emphasizes that for these objectives to be attained by the year 2000—the target year indicated in the LPA—immediate steps must be taken to 'reverse the stagnation and possible decline of per capita incomes which are projected for the 1980s'.[38] Thus, for the most part, the report 'deals with short- to medium-term responses to Africa's current economic difficulties. It focuses on how growth can be accelerated and how the resources to achieve the longer-term objectives set by the African governments can be generated, with the support of the international community'.[39]

In essence, it will be seen that the two reports (the LPA and the Berg Report) are complementary. Both recognize that Africa has enormous economic potential that awaits fuller development. The African governments have recognized the importance not only of international assistance but also of self-sustained development. However, in the years that have followed these reports, it has not appeared as if the sub-Saharan states have come any closer to achieving many of their objectives. If anything, as we enter the late 1980s the economic crisis continues to worsen. By the middle of the decade, the debt crisis had assumed alarming proportions with most economies remaining static in growth terms. African states were, once again, set to take their case to the international forum.

In 1984, after recovering from the political crisis which had beset the organization towards the end of the 1970s, the OAU was able to concentrate its attention on the economic problems of the continent, and the 1985 summit saw the adoption of an Economic Charter which seriously reappraised the LPA in the light of the worsening economic conditions.[40] A direct result of this charter was a Special Session of the UN General Assembly devoted to the problems of African development between 27 May and 1 June 1986. The basis of discussions at the Special Session was the *African Priority Programme for Economic Recovery* (APPER), a well-documented programme which highlighted costs as well as the expected level of foreign financial assistance. APPER was compiled under the auspices of both the OAU and the UN Economic Commission for Africa (ECA) and draws substantially from the LPA. The UN Special Session was regarded as a partial success, in as much as an increased willingness was displayed on the part of African states not only to accept that part of the problem was of their own making—in the process playing down the much orchestrated 'consequences of colonialism'—but also to declare their readiness to try out some of the recommendations suggested by the Western countries. To put these measures into effect the Special Session adopted the *United Nations Programme of Action for African Economic Recovery and Development 1986–1990.*

While the African states recognized the importance of self-reliance, committing themselves to implementing deep-seated economic re-forms—laying considerable emphasis on the food and agricultural sector—they also continued to demand a greater contribution to the cause of African development from the advanced countries. Under the terms of the UN Programme, the international community pledges support for fresh African initiatives being undertaken to promote food production, build up agricultural industries and related infrastructure, reverse the effects of drought and desertification, and develop human resources through 'radical changes' in the educational system. The cost of APPER was estimated at US$128 billion (1986 prices). For their part the African states undertook to mobilize US$82.5 billion, while calling upon the international community to provide an additional US$9 billion annually for the five years to 1990. At the time of writing it is a year since the UN Special Session. Given the lack of tangible developments during this period, it is clear that the principal 'achievement' of the Special Session was the recognition of the problem—a discussion of the malady rather than a cure. Western countries are already being reproached for not fulfilling their own part of the bargain, even though signs are that the African countries are implementing capitalist econ-omic solutions to their problems, as the West has so vigorously recommended. A meeting has been called under the auspices of the UN/ECA to be held in Nigeria (Abuja), in June 1987 to review progress made in implementing the resolutions of the Special Session. The importance of such a meeting cannot be over-emphasized at this point in time.

In the quarter-century that has constituted the years of African independence, African countries have not only recognized their own problems of development but also the need for collective efforts and international assistance. Most of the states, at least in theory, now recognize the need for more economic cooperation. Cooperation is recognized as being necessary, among other things, in the fields of food supply, infrastructure, education and industrial settlements. The inadequacies of national markets are recognized along with the need to develop inter-African trade. The Monrovia Strategy and the LPA are generally recognized as manifestations of the common will to develop. However, both are crystallizations of a trend which gradually came to the fore in the early and mid-1970s. This trend had seen the adoption of the African Convention for Cooperation and the African Cultural Charter, both in 1975. The states started off at independence by addressing their problems individually and adopting various approaches to solving them with little or no cooperation. Undeniably, most of the states placed prime importance on self-reliance. The Arusha Declaration of 1967 in Tanzania, emphasizing the need to harness internal resources for the purposes of development is a good example of this phenomenon. However, to a great extent, these states did not share their experiences in tackling development problems with each other, because of the political desire to remain 'independent' and develop through self-help. Efforts at intra-African economic cooperation as a route towards attaining greater levels of integration were slow to be conceived. Ironically, it is their frustrations with the problems that independence has brought that has rekindled the collective African spirit and also highlighted the need for all types of internationally concerted action.

Organization of this volume

The principal concern of this book is with the contributions of the international environment to the development process in Africa. It takes into consideration efforts conceived within bilateral, multilateral and regional frameworks. While all of the authors do not come to the same conclusion on the necessary paths to be taken to achieve greater levels of economic development in Africa, they do agree on the central consideration—the need for greater efforts on the part of the developed and developing world to improve the prospects currently entertained.

J. Kurt Barling in his chapter on aid and African development, considers the influence of external financial and technical assistance on the development process and looks at the prospects for the continued use of these resources and sees promise in the methods of policy dialogue and increased coordination. The efforts at regional cooperation and their prospects for development are examined in the following three chapters. *S.A. Olanrewaju* and *Toyin Falola* look at the economic and political problems faced by ECOWAS in the attempt to pursue development through integration in the West African sub-region. The sub-regional approach and the moves in this direction by the United Nations through its sub-regional organization, the Economic Commission for Africa, as a means to promoting and facilitating economic cooperation in Africa, appear in the account by *Ekei U. Etim*. Regional security problems have plagued the path of development in Southern Africa, and the perennial link between problems of regional security and economic development in the region is the subject of the contribution by *Scott Thomas*.

The next four chapters consider various aspects of multilateral approaches that have been undertaken to counter the development problem. The contribution of the European Community through the Lomé Conventions is discussed by *Christopher Stevens*, while he makes it clear that poor coordination between the internal and external policies of the community diminishes its overall effectiveness. The role of the Commonwealth in assisting the development of the former British colonies in Africa is the topic of the chapter by *Olusola Akinrinade*. He explores the promotion of technical cooperation through the CFTC and the manner in which it uses resources available within developing countries themselves. *Kaye Whiteman* looks at the emergence of efforts to merge the notions of culture and development. Using the example of La Francophonie, he argues that this link, although only a recent development, has as yet to make a considerable impact. The increasing interest given to important South–South cooperation and the contribution this could make to the development efforts in Africa is considered by *Mark S.C. Simpson*, using the example of African exchanges with Brazil.

The final chapter examines the paralysing impact of the now generally recognized debt crisis on the African development process. *Matthew*

Martin argues that a precondition for the regeneration of the development process in Africa is an international solution to the debt problems encountered by virtually all of sub-Saharan Africa, whether within the London or Paris clubs or through the World Bank and its affiliates.

Notes

1. Here we see that the idea of 'development' was synonymous with the idea of 'economic growth'.
2. The first use of this term is credited to Professor Alfred Sauvy, who in 1952, at the beginning of the Cold War, used it to distinguish between the two superpower blocs and those declared neutral and non-aligned states. In general the term now has a broader meaning.
3. See for example one of the first reports on the issue commissioned by the United Nations from a Group of Experts, *Measures for the Economic Development of Under-developed Countries* (New York, United Nations, 1951).
4. Lipset, S.M., *Political Man* (London, Heinemann, 1959).
5. Almond, G.A. & Coleman, J.S. (eds), *The Politics of the Developing Areas* (London, Oxford University Press, 1960).
6. Lewis, W.A., *The Theory of Economic Growth* (London, Allen & Unwin, 1955).
7. Rostow, W.W., *The Stages of Economic Growth: A Non-Communist Manifesto* (Cambridge, Cambridge University Press, 1961).
8. 'Radical' in the strict sense of the word, to denote a fundamental break with the immediate past.
9. Bairoch, P., *Diagnostic de l'Evolution Economique du Tiers-Monde depuis 1900* (Paris, Gauthier-Villars, 1967).
10. Freyssinet, J., *Le Concept de Sous-Développement* (Paris, Mouton, 1966).
11. Hirschmann, A.O., *The Strategy of Economic Development* (New Haven, Yale University Press, 1958).
12. Perroux, F., *L'Economie des Jeunes Nations* (Paris, Presses Universitaires de France, 1962).
13. Myrdal, G., *Economic Theory and Underdeveloped Regions* (London, Duckworth, 1957).
14. This strategy was not without its problems. See Barling, J.K., Chapter 2, pp. 34–5.
15. Amin, S., *Imperialism and Unequal Development* (New York, Monthly Review Press, 1977); Amin, S., *Unequal Development: An Essay on the Social Formations of Peripheral Capitalism* (New York, Monthly Review

Press, 1977); Amin, S., *Accumulation on a World Scale* (2 volumes) (New York, Monthly Review Press, 1978).

16. Franck, A.G., *Capitalism and Underdevelopment in Latin America* (Harmondsworth, Middx, Penguin, 1971).

17. Wallerstein, I., *The Modern World System: Capitalist Agriculture and the Origins of the European World-Economy in the Sixteenth Century* (London and New York, Academic Press, 1974).

18. Emmanuel, A., *Unequal Exchange: A Study in the Imperialism of Trade* (London, New Left Books, 1972).

19. Developed during his term at the head of the UN Economic Commission for Latin America, Prebisch's thesis quite obviously bears theoretical similarities to the internal critique.

20. For a good discussion of these divisions see Phillips, A., 'The Concept of Development', *Review of African Political Economy*, No.8, Jan-April 1977, pp. 7-20.

21. Warren, B., 'Imperialism and Capitalist Industrialisation', *New Left Review*, No.81, September-October, 1977, pp. 3-44.

22. Leys, C., *Underdevelopment in Kenya: The Political Economy of Neo-Colonialism, 1964-71* (London, Heineman, 1975).

23. Here the reader needs to be aware of the confusion often made between 'levels of development' and 'rates and direction of economic growth'.

24. A recent study by the International Price Statistics Section of the United Nations Statistical Office, has derived a method of improving the accuracy of a 'Real Gross Domestic Product' indicator for international comparisons. See Summers, R. and Heston, A., 'Improved International Comparisons of Real Product and its Composition, 1950-80', *Review of Income and Wealth*, Series 30, No.2, June 1984. The Editors are grateful to Mark E. Schaffer for clarifying this issue.

25. Summers and Heston, op. cit., while purchasing power parities are theoretically ideal, their adequate computation does require a greal deal of data. Also see statistical appendices, pp. 250–3.

26. Also refer to statistical appendices, pp. 250–3.

27. These included principally, Guinea, Tanzania and, for some time, Mali and Egypt.

28. In this group were, among others, states like Kenya, Côte d'Ivoire, Nigeria and Liberia.

29. '*Accelerated Development in Sub-Saharan Africa: An Assessment by the OAU, ECA and ADB Secretariats*' (ECA Edited Version) *Africa Development*, Vol.7, No.3, 1982, p. 110.

30. Voss, J. (ed.), *Development Policy in Africa* (Bonn–Bad Godesberg: Verlag Neue Gesellschaft GmbH, 1973), p. 10.

31. Adedeji, Adebayo and Shaw, Timothy, M., 'Introduction', in Adedeji, A. and Shaw, T.M., (eds), *Economic Crisis in Africa* (Boulder, Co.: Lynne

Rienner Publishers, 1985), p. 2.

32. *The Lagos Plan of Action for the Implementation of the Monrovia Strategy for the Economic Development of Africa*, adopted by the Second Extraordinary Assembly of the OAU Heads of State and Government, Devoted to Economic Matters (Lagos, Nigeria: 28-9 April, 1980).

33. Accelerated Development in Sub-Saharan Africa: An Assessment by the OAU, ECA and ADB Secretariats, op. cit., p. 111.

34. *The Lagos Plan of Action*, op. cit., para. 14(iii).

35. Adedeji, A., 'The Monrovia Strategy and the *Lagos Plan of Action*: Five Years After', in Adedeji and Shaw, *Economic Crisis in Africa*, op. cit., p. 15.

36. *Accelerated Development in Sub-Saharan Africa: An Assessment by the OAU, ECA and ADB Secretariats*, op. cit., p. 109.

37. World Bank, *Accelerated Development in Sub-Saharan Africa: An Agenda for Action* (Washington, D.C.: 1981).

38. Ibid., p. v.

39. Ibid., p. 1.

40. *West Africa*, No. 3641, 25 May 1987, p. 995.

2 Aid and African development

J. Kurt Barling*

Introduction

Over the past thirty years, since the beginning of the decolonization process, one of the most hotly debated issues in the context of the African political economy, has been the influence of external financial and technical resources on the pace and depth of the development process. In particular, political interest has always been sensitive over the impact of foreign aid or Official Development Assistance (ODA) on this process.[1] In relation to ODA, the general question most frequently posed seem to have been: is ODA working? That is, has ODA made (and will it continue to make) a significant contribution to the economic and social development of Africa?[2]

A number of studies conducted over this thirty-year period have suggested that the causal relationship between ODA and development has indeed been a positive one. The central theme of the Pearson report (1969) was that increased public concessional finance *should* build on the successes of the 'aid effort' already identified: this had enabled the developing world to both accelerate its short-term growth prospects and aim for a degree of self-sustaining growth by the close of the century.[3] The Brandt Commission reports (1980 and 1983) endorsed these earlier conclusions in terms of the global 'North–South' divide,[4] while the Berg report (1981), focusing specifically upon the African context, was largely positive in its findings presented to the World Bank.[5] The Brandt and Manley report (1985) accepted the notion that the potential

* I am grateful to the Economic and Social Research Council (UK) for their financial support extended through my current doctoral research programme.

of ODA had not as yet been 'unleashed', but that if activated could make a significant contribution to the development process, particularly in the Low Income Countries (LICs).[6] The more recent Cassen report (1986) concluded that: 'Most aid . . . succeeds in its developmental objectives . . . contributing positively to the recipient countries' economic performance . . . not substituting for activities which would have occurred anyway . . . Its performance varies by country and by sector . . . and there is a substantial fraction of aid that does not work.'[7] The important message in this document is that 'accelerated development' can only be achieved by an increase in a regular and guaranteed flow of external resources, a significant proportion of which should take the form of public concessional finance or ODA. These reports have one essential characteristic in common—they all assume a given moral predilection. This moral constant stems from a belief that the 'North' *should* share a proportion of its accumulated wealth with the 'South'.[8]

There are other studies which have interpreted the causal relationship between ODA and development as purely negative.[9] These studies tend to fall into two categories and appear to form a paradoxical 'alliance' between, on the one hand, a fairly vociferous group of socialists and on the other, liberal *laissez-faire* economists against the use of ODA. The socialists have interpreted the use of aid as an instrument of neocolonialism, that is, essentially an exploitative instrument used to foster the dependency of the *developing* South on the *developed* North.[10] The liberal *laissez-faire* economists have suggested that ODA has a negative impact on economic growth and well-being and indeed that it is probably even inimicable to the whole notion of self-reliance as envisaged, for example, by those inspired by the principles outlined in the Arusha Declaration.[11] The adopted champion of this particular interpretation, Lord Bauer, has suggested that 'development depends on personal and social factors and not on handouts'.[12] Some studies indeed share some of the reservations expressed by both of these interpretations and to a large degree exercise a 'well-educated' assessment of the role of ODA.[13]

However, in spite of these varying interpretations in the literature, we can make a preliminary observation at this point that ODA has not lived up to the broad expectations generated by the rapid process of *political* decolonization in the 1960s. Aid to accelerate growth and modernization has not reduced the gap between the 'rich' North and the 'poor' South. Neither has it reduced similar asymmetries between the 'richer' and 'poorer' South. Turning from the general level of the aid and development debates to the specific context of Africa, the growing awareness of these limitations has led to a threefold response.[14] Firstly, there has been a call for a greater volume of aid. Secondly, efforts are being made to improve the quality and management of the aid disbursed, adequately captured by the concepts of 'policy dialogue' and 'coordination'. Thirdly, there has been a significant effort within Africa to initiate development strategies associating the notion of self-reliance with development. For example, the *Lagos Plan of Action* (1980) under the auspices of the Organization of African Unity (OAU) has made a particular contribution to the re-orientation of these strategies.

This chapter has three objectives: firstly, to survey past aid and development efforts;[15] secondly, to examine these past efforts and isolate what can be broadly identified as their successes and limitations; and thirdly, to examine the responses of those governmental actors (recipients and donors) within the 'aid system' to overcome past limitations as well as establish some of the prospects for ODA in the current agenda-setting environment and giving an idea of the prospects for aid in African development.[16]

The role of development aid in Africa

African decolonization spurned a new stage in the growth of post-war foreign aid disbursements. Prior to this period the aid debate had been dominated, firstly, by the concerns for rebuilding Europe through the European Recovery Programme (Marshall Aid) and secondly, by strategic concerns generated by the Cold War environment (economic and military aid).[17] The new developmental emphasis of foreign aid grew out of development programmes undertaken prior to independence, particularly in the French and British African empires.

The leaders of the newly independent African states sought to achieve unprecedented growth levels and foreign aid was a vital resource to be used to promote this effort. For many of these leaders, growth was synonymous with development and in turn development was taken to by synonymous with modernization. Furthermore, the level of modernization was associated with the levels of industrialization achieved. ODA was seen as a critical external resource, which could fill a series of 'gaps' that were potential retardants to the African development process. Three priority gaps were identified; a savings gap which would limit the available resources for investment; a foreign exchange gap which would minimize possibilities for importing technology; and a skills gap, leaving a shortage of skilled manpower to manage the projected intensive modernization process.

Foreign aid was therefore identified as a means of filling these gaps, thereby acting as a catalyst for the 'take off' point to rapid economic growth.[18] Given this conception of ODA, all that was required from foreign aid was a supplement for the projected shortfalls in capital or technical resources. In terms of the expectations of the likely achievement of this aim in the 1960s, the first United Nations Development Decade (announced by the General Assembly in 1961) was characterized by excessive optimism.

In the donor countries, these early developmental concerns led to the establishment of aid ministries or administrations[19] as well as efforts among donors to establish normative standards in the operationalization of the aid process. The chief institutional product of these latter efforts was the Development Assistance Committee (DAC) of the Organization for Economic Cooperation and Development (OECD) set up in 1961.[20] In many of the recipient countries the new governments established centralized planning agencies to assist in the mobilization of the necessary resources for development as well as planning for the distribution of these resources once acquired. In retrospect it would seem that this period was largely a 'period of illusion', for donors and recipients alike, illusions fuelled by the high expectations raised by models of development. In particular the assumption that economic rationality would provide a basis for 'automaticity' in the system of aid disbursement, severely underestimated the political nature of the entire aid process.

By the end of the first development decade most of the single factor approaches to development began to lose credibility. This was reflected in a considerable shift away from the emphasis on 'gaps' in the use of foreign aid resources, focusing instead on the efficiency of the operating methods of the donor and recipient institutions of development. This reorientation took account of the important fact that the aid process was indeed dynamic.[21] It also acknowledged that the paths to development were different in different areas, not only different in Africa from South-East Asia for example, but different within the African continent itself. These latter distinctions were clearly exemplified by the different approaches to development adopted by countries even in close geographical proximity, such as Kenya and Tanzania or Ghana and Côte d'Ivoire. Ghana and Côte d'Ivoire, for example, chose two radically different paths to development. Ghana chose a socialist and independent path; Côte d'Ivoire chose a path that kept its very close links with the former French *métropole* and followed a decidedly more liberal approach to economic management. These differences showed that political choices had a greater impact on the nature of the development path than economic 'rationality'.

The non-fulfilment of the high expectations of the 1960s led to a considerable degree of pessimism shrouding the aid debate in Africa during the late 1970s. It brought with it a reassessment on the part of many Africans of the possibilities of an independent path to self-sustaining growth.[22] For example, it was recognized that many Western concepts such as 'performance conditioning' or 'achievement motivation' were insufficient or perhaps even inappropriate to the African economic and cultural environment.[23] In particular ODA had been more frequently orientated towards macro-economic schemes, which had meant that the resources had sometimes been misused or poorly allocated, principally because the necessary resources were not available for governments to choose their priorities. Another familiar problem associated with the macro-level had been the practice of recipients drawing up a 'shopping list' of development projects or development programmes to be funded by prospective donors, with the express intention of obtaining the maximum volume of aid possible, without due regard to its most efficient usage. This 'fungibility' of resources often added to the problem of efficient resource distribution.[24]

Bilateral and multilateral aid to Africa

It has already been suggested that many African aid programmes in the 1960s resulted from the decolonization process. In many respects the aid programmes of France, the United Kingdom and Belgium were a direct continuation of the development efforts already under way in the colonies during the 1950s. The predominance of the African colonies in the Belgian and French empires and the importance given by the British to the African Commonwealth countries meant that a large proportion of their respective aid budgets was orientated towards Africa. The importance of the Yaoundé conventions linking the EEC to Africa reinforced the bias of the Belgian and French programmes. The Cold War desire to consolidate zones of influence also led to large amounts of United States' aid being channelled to areas of key strategic interest, of which Africa was one. The Truman Point Four Program and

Public Law 480 on the use of US food surpluses for aid purposes helped give Africa a higher profile in USAID (US Agency for International Development).[25]

In addition, other European nations joined in the aid effort. By 1960 the Federal Republic of Germany had established a considerable capital and technical assistance programme to Africa. The Scandinavian countries also began to take a more active role in aid disbursement. Canada's External Aid Office (later to become the Canadian International Development Agency in 1968) and Japan's Overseas Economic Cooperation Fund also added to the efforts of the aid-donor community.

The Soviet Union and the other states of Eastern Europe were less involved in this Northern aid effort, often suggesting that it was the express duty of the former imperial powers to compensate for the hardship caused to the indigenous peoples during the colonial period. Like the Chinese aid programme to Africa, the Eastern European efforts largely revolved around large infrastructural and industrial projects or provided logistic support to certain regimes or movements. The Aswan Dam project in Egypt was funded by the Soviets, whilst the Tanzam railway linking Tanzania with Zambia was constructed with the assistance of the Chinese. The Soviets offered assistance to Sekou Touré's Guinea for a considerable time after the sudden French withdrawal in 1958, whilst Mugabe's ZANU resistance movement received help from the Chinese.[26]

In addition to these accumulative bilateral disbursements, the role of multilateral aid in the African context increased in importance in the 1960s. This growth is identifiable on two levels: firstly, the level of disbursements grew within the UN system; and, secondly, the role of the World Bank and its affiliates underwent a considerable transformation. I shall examine the World Bank group first.

After the largely successful role fulfilled by the World Bank in the reconstruction of post-war Europe through Marshall Aid, the institution found it had a surplus capacity of funds, which could be put to good use in the context of the developing world's drive for accelerated development. Although its role as a loan mechanism was felt to be less relevant to the African than the Asian context, the establishment of its soft-loan affiliate, the International Development Agency (IDA) in 1960 meant that more loans were made more affordable for the Low Income Countries (LICs), which we have already seen predominated in Africa.[27] In addition to these global institutions, the African Development Bank was also established in 1964 to generate funds to be used to support the economic development of Africa.

The United Nations' system was by far the most influential international network of multilateral institutions to be distributing capital and technical assistance to Africa during the 1960s. Drawing upon the resources provided by the special funds,[28] the specialized agencies[29] participated in a broad range of projects and programmes, in addition to the limited technical assistance operations already carried out by the special funds. With the establishment of the Economic Commission for Africa a new regional level of coordination within the UN structure was made available, to coordinate efforts between the member countries as well as provide advice and technical expertise in scientific, educational and economic fields.[30] As we have already seen, by the end of the 1960s there had been a shift from an emphasis on the resource of foreign aid to an emphasis on the institutions of development. This naturally produced an increasingly critical attitude towards those institutions associated with the development process thus far. Indeed the UN system was not spared from this criticism and the in-house Jackson Report published in 1969 was highly critical of the efficiency of the whole UN system in promoting development particularly in the LICs.[31]

In spite of these bilateral and multilateral aid efforts, the limited growth of most African economies in the 1960s threw into sharp relief the marginality of aid in the whole process of development. This realization in turn led to a period of prolonged disillusionment. The 1970s produced a number of responses as a direct result of this disillusionment. Disappointed donors began to pin the blame for the perceived failure on the mismanagement of economic policies by the recipient governments, rather than, for example, the inadequate model-building of the donor community. In order to deal with this, the Second United Nations Development Decade (1970s), started with donor emphasis in project and programme appraisal shifting towards qualitative and not quantitative assessments, in order to determine the developmental effectiveness of aid.

There was moreover a re-evaluation of the nature of the development process as well as the assumed objectives of this process as accepted in the 1960s. Any such re-evaluation was bound to have an impact on the perceived role of the foreign aid resource. Perhaps most significantly, it was more adequately appreciated that the development process was generational, and that because of the planning cycles in individual countries there was a considerable 'aid lag', that meant there would be a lengthy delay before any realistic assessments of any given unit of aid could be undertaken. This combination of factors led to a fundamental re-orientation of the aid debate and as a corollary redefined the developmental objectives of the aid resource.

Whereas modernization and industrialization had become the bywords of the development debate during the 1960s, the 1970s saw a re-orientation towards the perceived 'basic needs' of the recipient community. This basic needs orientation was of particular importance in the African context, as it was fuelled by a desire to alleviate what Robert McNamara referred to as 'absolute poverty'.[32] Large industrial programmes were increasingly seen to be incompatible with the level of human suffering experienced by a large percentage of the African population. To a large extent the various 'trickle-down' theories, which had suggested that modernization through industrialization would produce spin-off benefits for the poorer members of the community, were largely discredited (it does appear that these theories were in many respects self-serving). Further to the desire to alleviate poverty the new basic needs approach sought to promote social equity as well as to ensure that there was more employment of manpower. It also sought to redress the balance between the rural–urban divide that had been exacerbated in many parts of Africa due to the bias implicit in the 1960s modernization drive. In essence then, the basic needs approach along with the emphasis on the quality and appropriateness of aid, re-politicized the aid and development debates: there now appeared to be a certain legitimacy in donors having a say in changing the political conditions in the LICs (effectively any talk of redistribution, talks of political priorities). The dual problem of 'aid lag' and provision of 'basic needs' called for a greater geographical redistribution of ODA to the LICs, as well as laying a greater emphasis on technical as opposed to capital aid.

The economic crises of the 1970s meant, on the one hand, that most sub-Saharan African states had an increasingly greater need for external resources whilst, on the other, the same crises undermined aid in the context of the domestic political agendas of the Northern countries. Essentially we need to consider three major crises: the oil or energy crises of 1973 and 1978–9; the consequential recession in the developed world that led to the implementation of anti-inflationary policies; and the food crisis that began in 1973.[33]

The two waves of the oil crisis, which took the price of oil from US$1.80 a barrel in 1971 to US$34.00 a barrel in 1982, posed a hitherto unimaginable constraint on the development prospects of the non-oil producing countries. It threatened the assumed fundamental pre-requisite for modernization, economic growth. The inability to compensate for massive rises in oil-related import costs, with increased revenue from export earnings, prompted severe balance of payments' crises. The poorest countries, the LICs, were hardest hit by this increase as they were unable to fund these rapidly accumulated deficits by increased borrowing on the world's commercial credit markets, unlike many of the Middle Income Countries (MICs). The combined deficits of the non-oil producing African countries as a consequence rose dramatically from US$305 million in 1970 to US$3,310 million in 1984.[34]

The resultant slow-down in growth, particularly for the LICs, damaged the prospects for renewed growth and development in terms of the original conception of modernization, and even put a question mark over their ability to maintain existing levels of real per capita income. For example, the draining of the foreign exchange reserves, forced a reduction in oil-related import levels and led to decreased levels of energy consumption. This in turn led to an overall down-turn in production and consumption. For the LICs, and therefore most of Africa, any hope of growth relied on ODA.

The second crisis to affect the African continent was the recession in the North. The anti-inflationary policies of developed countries' governments, like cutting overall government expenditure, led to depressed demand and a fall in price for most commodities supplied by many of the African states. This trend was merely exacerbated by the monocultural base of many of the African economies, particularly those poorer ones which had been unable to diversify production patterns after independence. The resulting increase in borrowing and the rise in the value of the US dollar led to the overall increase in the debt burden.[35]

The third major crisis to afflict Africa was perhaps potentially the most far-reaching. In essence it was a problem that was virtually left untouched by the early emphases of modernization. In the rush to industrialize, resources for agricultural development were sorely lacking. It became increasingly clear that Southern food production was unable to keep pace with the rapidly expanding population. Prior to 1973 the gap between food needs and food production plus foreign exchange available to import staple foods was filled by Northern surplus production. A series of droughts and floods, along with the serious mismanagement of farm policies in some Northern states, led to a rise in world food prices.[36]

Unlike their counterpart countries in Asia most African countries did not experience a 'Green Revolution', and by the late 1970s and early 1980s the food crisis in Africa had become worse. This was largely an outcome of growing population, economic policies that effectively discouraged food production by offering too low a price to producers, and poor soil management, which had resulted in severe environmental degradation.

By the beginning of the 1980s, then, the need for ODA in Africa had been exacerbated by these three crises. It provided a substantial share of GNP in the majority of African states, and an even larger share of investment funding for longer-term expansion. In the African LICs, ODA provided virtually the only source of capital to finance long-term projects, as they could not benefit from credit from the private banking sector or trade preferences established by many of the developed countries. By 1985 total ODA to Africa amounted to around US$9.5 billion or 29.7 per cent of total aid disbursed to the developing countries. This figure had clearly been affected by the basic needs emphasis of the late 1970s. The figures given in Table 2.1 illustrate that Africa had benefited from a significant increase in the total aid it received, as well as from a slightly higher proportion of total aid disbursements, as did the LICs as a whole.

Table 2.1 Changes in the distribution of ODA 1979-85

	1979		1981		1983		1985	
Country Group	Amount*	%	Amount	%	Amount	%	Amount	%
LIC	11,850.2	41.3	12,988.0	39.6	12,610.2	43.2	14,486.5	45.1
LLDC	5,628.2	19.6	6,408.4	19.5	6,509.6	22.3	7,669.1	23.9
Africa[†]	6,888.7	24.0	8,137.9	24.8	7,934.8	27.2	9,533.3	29.7
China and India	1,366.7	4.7	2,387.1	7.3	2,412.4	8.3	2,409.6	7.5
MIC	11,166.6	38.9	12,720.1	38.8	10,778.2	36.9	11,315.0	35.2
Unallocated	4,302.8	15.0	4,727.3	14.4	3,400.7	11.6	3,938.3	12.2
Total	28,686.3	100.0	32,822.5	100.0	29,201.5	100.0	32,149.5	100.0

Source: *Geographical distribution of financial flows to developing countries 1982/1985* (Paris, OECD, 1987).

* Millions of $US.
† Africa south of the Sahara.

Nevertheless, in terms of overall ODA disbursements, the LICs in general and Africa in particular, only marginally benefited from any geographical redistribution. This would suggest that these poorer recipients were in fact unable to attract more ODA resources and that most donors remained tied to the original conceptions of modernization, as well as being constrained by obligations already entered into.[37]

In spite of this marginal shift in distribution on a global level by the mid-1980s, the 'basic needs' strategies have provided little evidence of effectiveness at the national level. That is to say, by the mid-1980s they seem to have made no significant impact on the redistribution of income within the recipient countries.

These trends led to further concentration on the 'quality' of the 'aid cycle': that is, monitoring the implementation of a funded project; evaluation of project results; and reporting on the sustainability of the project in question. However, the level of crisis in many African countries, particularly the LICs, has led to a shift away from the project emphasis to programmes in collaboration with the World Bank; this has often been undertaken within the negotiating framework of the aid consortium.

But what of the aid actually disbursed? The second part of this chapter looks at the successes and limitations experienced in the disbursement of aid and then outlines the principal prospects for the aid resource.

Successes and limitations of ODA in the African development process

How do we measure success or failure?

Having established some of the causes of the major economic crises afflicting sub-Saharan Africa, outlined the depth of these crises and illustrated the subsequent response of the donor 'aid community' (note the figures given in Tables 2.1 and 2.2), it is quite apparent that the *expectations* raised by the 1960s were largely unfulfilled by the end of the 1970s. Indeed in many of the African LICs, if we consider population growth along with the reduction in production and consumption, growth rates in real terms were actually negative.

In considering the impact of a resource such as ODA on development, one cannot fail to be struck by the enormous amount of policy

choices and problems that need to be examined. A further methodological problem is the lack of authoritative evidence on the correlation
between aid and growth, the fundamental determinant of development.[38] Superimposed on this problem is the difficulty of assessing
whether, in view of insufficient evidence, aid policies have been
beneficial or harmful. This needs more authoritative work in a broad
range of case studies. What we can do here is to highlight the constraints
on ODA in the development process and examine its prospects.

As we have already seen, the Cassen report (1986) suggested that
overall, ODA has a positive impact. In particular ODA is seen to effect
economic performance, and in general in the LICs it has not been used
as a resource to substitute for activities that would have happened
anyway. Although aid has clearly not worked in all its applications, too
much past analysis has centred on aid as a single factor element in
development. It is, however, quite clear that where the relief of poverty
is concerned, where general governmental redistributive priorities are
concerned, or even the bias towards industrial as opposed to agricultural
production is concerned, the domestic policies of the recipient government are as important as the resources which they will then assign to
implement these policies. In this respect ODA is a contingent factor,
only a secondary input, closely influenced by a highly motivated political context. To suggest, as some people do, that this latter recognition
unfairly apportions too much blame upon the recipient, is often misplaced
sensitivity or, indeed, unrecognized patronizing. The African political
process (the management of multifarious social relationships) is after all
no less sophisticated or complex than elsewhere. This recognition does
not deny that donor motives, whether political, developmental or
commercial, can be counter-productive and can interfere in the
development process. It nevertheless renders this author's interpretation less sinister.

Another consideration that needs to be borne in mind, when considering the impact of ODA on development, is the evaluative nature of
the notions of success and failure. If aid as a resource has failed, then all
aid-related projects would be expected to have failed: this is obviously
not the case. If we think of the aid process as a 'system', then failure of
individual projects does not mean systemic failure. In this sense, then,
we have witnessed not the failure of aid but the limitations of the
resource. In terms of its inability to fulfil the expectations raised in the
1960s, aid might have failed, but then this is really a reflection upon the
expectations and *not* the aid resource itself. Drawing an analogy with

private sector investment is also instructive. Investment resource x always has a large proportion of risk and the possibility that it will give a low rate of return y for a good many years ahead is in the nature of the enterprise. ODA also has this risk, as well as an additional risk that most private investment could perhaps not shoulder, due to the high risk–low capital return ratio on much of ODA investment. Unfortunately, critics often point to the low rate of return over only a short period of time. Here we must explicitly recognize the fallibility of ODA: there is no automatic causal relationship between it and development. It is therefore necessary that these shortcomings are openly debated so that the whole system may be improved.

On the macro-level, then, ODA has made a significant contribution in many parts of Africa, particularly the LICs, to increasing real income and improving living standards. By the beginning of the 1980s infant mortality had been reduced by 30 per cent, life expectancy had risen by nearly one-fifth, primary schooling had been doubled, whilst the illiteracy rates had been significantly reduced. Per capita income levels had fallen by 1980, but this was largely as a result of population growth.

Furthermore, whilst it is true that ODA has often been mis-allocated, a large amount of infrastructure has been built, while manufacturing and agriculture have been promoted. The reach of many basic services has been extended in much of sub-Saharan Africa and the provision of skilled manpower certainly helped in these efforts. In turn ODA has helped to encourage the building of institutions that can help the 'modern' state exercise its responsibilities fully.

Whilst we should acknowledge these results, we must recognize that Africa has had specific problems, some of which have already been mentioned, and, therefore, ODA did not achieve the same degree of success as it did in many of those often quoted 'miracle countries' like South Korea, Taiwan, Brazil—the Newly Industralizing Countries—or even India.

The figures in Table 2.2 provide an illustration of the amounts of aid involved in the African development process over the last decade and the significance of this aid as a proportion of national income. It is clear, for example, that in some of the smaller states ODA is a major resource and covers a significant proportion of national income and that in most of sub-Saharan Africa this proportion has grown over the past decade.

Table 2.2   Net receipts of ODA for African nations from all sources 1979-85

Country Group	1979 Amount*	1979 %†	1981 Amount	1981 %	1983 Amount	1983 %	1985 Amount	1985 %
Angola	47.1	1.0	61.0	0.9	75.3	1.1	91.5	—
Benin	84.8	9.0	81.6	7.5	86.4	8.3	95.9	9.4
Botswana	99.7	17.2	96.9	12.1	103.6	12.6	96.8	13.1
Burkina Faso	198.4	15.6	216.8	16.3	183.5	17.6	197.4	19.2
Burundi	95.1	12.4	122.0	12.6	140.0	13.0	141.4	13.3
Cameroon	277.1	5.3	198.7	2.7	128.9	1.8	159.5	2.1
Cape Verde	33.4	41.8	50.3	50.3	59.9	59.9	69.7	69.7
Central A. Rep.	83.6	11.8	101.6	14.5	92.9	15.0	104.7	15.9
Chad	85.6	15.3	59.7	14.9	95.3	22.7	181.7	—
Comoros	17.5	19.4	46.6	42.2	38.2	27.3	47.6	43.3
Congo	90.9	8.3	81.0	4.3	108.4	5.6	71.2	4.0
Djibouti	23.2	8.9	64.5	19.0	65.6	19.9	81.4	—
Equatorial Guinea	2.7	—	10.2	—	11.1	—	17.3	—
Ethiopia	190.6	4.9	245.0	5.7	339.3	7.1	709.7	15.1
Gabon	36.7	1.4	43.5	1.3	63.7	2.1	61.1	1.9
Gambia	36.6	17.4	68.2	34.1	42.1	21.1	50.1	31.3
Ghana	169.3	4.2	147.7	3.4	110.0	2.6	204.4	3.5
Guinea	55.9	3.8	106.7	6.6	67.5	3.8	119.2	10.4
Guinea-Bissau	52.8	44.0	65.2	43.5	64.2	49.4	57.8	38.5
Ivory Coast	161.5	1.8	123.7	1.6	155.3	2.6	124.7	1.9
Kenya	350.9	6.0	449.4	6.9	400.5	7.1	438.7	7.6
Lesotho	66.3	12.5	104.2	14.3	107.7	12.8	94.4	16.6
Liberia	80.8	8.7	108.6	11.1	118.4	12.2	90.6	8.9
Madagascar	138.0	4.9	234.3	8.3	179.1	6.6	182.2	8.2
Malawi	141.7	14.5	137.6	12.6	116.8	10.6	113.0	10.7
Mali	193.2	15.7	230.3	20.6	214.5	21.7	379.9	35.5
Mauritania	167.1	27.9	233.7	32.5	175.6	23.7	204.5	31.5
Mauritius	32.3	2.7	58.4	5.3	40.7	3.8	28.8	3.1
Mayotte	18.2	—	14.9	—	14.6	—	20.8	—
Mozambique	145.8	3.9	143.6	3.2	210.8	4.2	300.1	—
Namibia	—	—	—	—	—	—	6.0	—
Niger	174.3	11.2	193.4	9.4	174.8	13.4	304.6	24.8
Nigeria	26.8	0.04	40.7	0.05	47.6	0.07	32.3	0.04
Reunion	392.9	21.7	643.4	33.7	410.7	22.8	383.5	—
Rwanda	148.3	14.3	153.7	12.2	149.4	9.5	181.4	10.8
St. Helena	8.4	—	8.3	—	9.9	—	12.2	—
São Tomé & P.	3.1	6.2	6.1	12.2	11.6	29.0	12.5	31.3
Senegal	306.7	11.6	396.7	16.8	322.2	13.2	294.8	12.2
Seychelles	25.2	21.0	17.0	11.3	15.6	10.4	22.2	—

Table 2.2 *cont.*

	1979		1981		1983		1985	
Country Group	Amount*	%†	Amount	%	Amount	%	Amount	%
Sierra Leone	53.5	5.6	60.1	5.3	66.0	6.3	65.9	8.8
Somalia	194.0	15.4	374.6	22.4	326.6	21.5	353.7	—
Sudan	686.6	10.0	631.9	7.4	956.9	13.0	1128.6	19.2
Swaziland	50.5	12.0	36.7	5.6	33.5	5.8	25.7	6.4
Tanzania	589.0	13.4	702.7	13.0	593.9	13.5	486.9	13.0
Togo	109.7	12.3	62.9	6.8	112.0	15.8	114.0	16.5
Uganda	46.5	1.7	135.8	4.8	136.7	2.9	183.8	—
Zaïre	416.4	6.7	393.6	7.7	314.5	7.1	324.2	11.6
Zambia	278.0	9.1	231.6	5.9	216.9	6.9	329.0	15.4
Zimbabwe	12.5	0.3	212.3	3.4	208.5	3.7	237.1	5.3

Source: Geographical distribution of financial flows to developing countries 1982/1985 (Paris, OECD, 1987).

* Millions of $US.
† % of GNP.

The limitations of ODA in Africa

Africa has been a particularly harsh environment for rapid economic development and ODA. There has been a considerable conflict between the various domestic and external inputs into the aid process, no less because of the recent colonial history and the indelible mark this left on the perceptions of a whole generation of African and Northern leaders alike. This often resulted in a mismatch of inputs, and a consequent diminishing of the possible impact of aid on development.

The incompatability of some domestic inputs also led to similar results. Having achieved political statehood at independence, the drive to achieve nationhood thereafter often resulted in a direct clash of these inputs—the expectations of material development often pulling against the expectations of political development.

Africa had other significant problems. Most of the newly independent African states, inherited only small proportions of literate or formally educated citizens. Throughout its early post-colonial history, and particularly since the onset of severe economic *malaise*, it suffered from a great deal of internally and externally induced political instability.

Furthermore in spite of a good deal of institution-building, the resources were often not available to provide a stable government machinery to execute government decisions. A scarcity of trained, managerial and administrative workers compounded this latter problem and presented the need for a good deal of technical assistance.

Juxtaposed with this, as we have seen, sub-Saharan Africa faced many acutely unfavourable external conditions. Dependence on primary commodities, exacerbated by a monocultural economic base facing unstable export markets, has led to prolonged periods of deteriorating terms of trade.

During the 1960s many African development strategies were conceptualized in terms of the experience of the Latin American economies, and in particular the work of the *dependencia* theorists was predicated on this latter experience.[39] The consequent heavy emphasis on using aid to promote industrialization led to heavy capital-intensive investment and uneconomic import substitution. The sums of money involved often encouraged the over-valuation of exchange rates, which in turn proved extremely disadvantageous to agricultural production for consumption—quite literally farmers were priced out of their own market by cheaper imports (often subsidized by the developed countries). The problem of overvalued recipient currencies is also often the result of an increased supply of foreign exchange, often in the form of ODA, which helps to discriminate against local exporters operating in the developing countries. In addition, capital as a factor of production becomes relatively cheaper due to the subsidized inflows from overseas, this has tended to increase the capital intensity of production (increasing human unemployment), which runs counter to the comparative advantage of most developing countries.

By the end of the 1970s the new understanding of the development process prompted a rethink of the contribution of aid to this process within the recipient countries and within the donor community. The divergence in the performance of so many developing countries suggested that universal prescriptions were unworkable. In particular the emphasis on import substitution seemed inappropriate in a policy environment which was emphasizing the importance of both the private and the public sectors, encouraging greater export orientation in the developing economies as well as new approaches to poverty alleviation and the harmonization of stabilization and growth policies.

This industrial development, which had been equated with modernization, was seen to have encouraged a bias away from agricultural production, which in turn has proved one of the single most important factors in limiting the impact of ODA on alleviating poverty and redressing the imbalances implied in the 'basic needs' approach.

Largely as a result of the colonial structure of agricultural production, particularly the emphasis on growing export crops for valuable foreign exchange purposes, production for consumption was generally ignored with the now familiar disastrous consequences of famine and food shortages, for example, in Ethiopia and the Sahel region. Moreover, when agricultural changes did occur, for example during the early stages of *Ujamaa* in Tanzania, it occurred in large-scale farming rather than in smallholder development. This latter development merely exacerbated the rural-urban divide, increased unemployment and furthered rural decay, all of which are trends that are more difficult to reverse than initiate.

At times the excessive intrusion of a donor's commercial and political motives, as well as the resulting poor project design, often meant that aid was not being used for the most appropriate purposes given the increasing importance placed on the strategy of 'basic needs'. The recipient policy environment, administrative deficiencies or even the unwillingness of recipient governments to implement certain projects also contributed to this inappropriate usage. It was often privately recognized, but not publicly acknowledged, that recipients also had commercial and political priorities which were at odds with development.[40] For example, a recipient's excessive attachment to prestige projects, sometimes with a low developmental priority, did nothing to enhance the reputation of ODA; it often meant that advanced and unsuitable technology was being used.[41]

Certainly the practice of 'switching' aid from one project to another (also known as the 'fungibility' of aid resources) has been poorly understood,[42] and it is possible, as Lipton has recently suggested, that early models like the Harrod–Domar model of investment and savings could actually provide an improved understanding of what the aid resource actually does.[43] For example, it is suggested that aid might 'crowd out' domestic savings and investment and increase consumption of imported goods. ODA may even reinforce distortions in the price structure, thus inevitably having an effect on production patterns in recipient countries.

A few figures will suffice to illustrate the static nature of the structure of production in sub-Saharan Africa over the past twenty years. From 1965 to 1984 the production patterns in the four main sectors of the

Table 2.3   The structure of production in sub-Saharan Africa in 1965 and 1984 as a percentage of GDP

	Agriculture	Industry	Manufacturing	Services
1965	43	16	9	41
1984	39	18	10	43

Source: *World Development Report 1986* (New York, OUP, 1986).

economy remained virtually the same, as the figures in Table 2.3 suggest: production has been, and continues to be, relatively neglected in the agricultural sector even though there have been changes in the use of aid. This takes us back to the problem of 'aid lag'; indeed, the results Africa is now experiencing are the results generated by programmes being implemented up to ten to fifteen years ago.

In a recent World Bank sustainability study it was reported that only one in thirteen ODA-funded projects in sub-Saharan Africa were performing adequately when revisited for impact studies up to five years later.[44] This is often the result of poor project management and the inability to service the project after ODA funding has ceased due to a lack of foreign exchange, and this naturally questions the long-term viability of projects. It is apparent that the recession reduced the recipient governments' capacity to provide the cash to meet their existing budget commitments in support of many aid projects, reducing the rate of return and leaving less breathing space for donor and recipient error.

In addition to these problems each donor to, and each ministry in, a recipient country may experience what Lipton has called a 'prisoners' dilemma'.[45] By pursuing self-interested policies the effectiveness of ODA in the recipient country is often impaired. However, the dilemma is that if each individual ministry or donor does not pursue the self-interested strategy then it will lose out to other ministries and donors. Although this is by no means a cut and dried argument, consideration of it highlights the importance of the political constraints being constantly imposed on the implementation of aid policies.

'Absorptive capacity' is another significant limitation on the most effective use of ODA. It is held that diminishing returns are experienced on any given unit of ODA, in some developing countries much earlier than would be expected in a developed economy, simply because the human and financial capital cannot be absorbed due to a shortage of technical ability, often manifesting itself in weak administrative back-up for adequate policy analysis. In other words the information acquired in order to distribute the available funds in the most appropriate fashion was inadequate.

A more general limitation is the flawed fundamental assumption of the 1960s and 1970s that aid would guarantee development, however conceived. Even if there is a correlation between growth and ODA, this does not necessarily signify causality. As early as 1968 Mikesell had written that:

Historically some countries have developed without significant capital imports and, in some cases, the achievement of sustained growth preceded a substantial capital inflow. On the other hand, large capital inflows have frequently made little contribution to development. As a general proposition external capital or aid is neither necessary nor a sufficient condition for development.[46]

Indeed, there are some scholars who have argued that the chief restriction is not capital, but a lack of cultural pre-conditions for growth and social structures that inhibit development coupled with an unfavourable domestic economic policy-setting.[47]

There have been, in sum, a number of serious limitations or constraints on the effective use of aid for development, even in achieving the modest strategy of re-orientation of aid towards the LICs. Therefore the emphasis in the mid-1970s of most governmental donor agencies (on increasing employment opportunities, helping the poorest countries as well as the poorest groups within these countries, largely for the reasons of the broader economic environment)[48] fell on large tracts of infertile ground in Africa. Clearly there were larger barriers to overcome. This does not point to the failure of ODA itself, rather the weakness of policy and political decision-making in donor and recipient agencies. It might take Bob Geldof to highlight the fact, but it has long been understood that serious civil instability and war in Africa cannot be conducive to economic development. Europeans have been masters of that art for centuries.

The prospects for ODA and African development

The aid debate in the 1980s has been characterized by 'aid fatigue' in donor countries, although this has to some extent been counterbalanced on the intellectual level by more confident and authoritative voices of African analysts themselves. It is not without value to observe that the further into history the colonial period passes, particularly in terms of individuals' experiences, the less pertinent will be the cleavages that are associated with the colonial order. The *Lagos Plan of Action*,[49] the Berg Report,[50] and the Please Report,[51] as well as the 1985 OECD Report on crisis and recovery in sub-Saharan Africa,[52] all display shifts away from a 'post-colonial mentality'. By establishing what issues are prominent in the current policy-making environment we can make some suggestions about the likely prospects for ODA and African development.

Several issues would appear to be at the centre of current debates on the role of ODA in the development process, particularly with reference to sub-Saharan Africa. Firstly, there is the question of the effectiveness or the quality of ODA. Secondly, given the 'aid fatigue' alluded to above, the support for ODA in donor countries remains critically important. Thirdly, there are those questions concerned with the overall volume of aid, that is how much aid is needed to meet the developmental needs of the African states, and indeed what those needs are.

Quality of ODA

ODA has not been the main factor in African stagnation. Even if we acknowledge this state of affairs, we should still recognize that ODA's limited or marginal effectiveness in promoting development in Africa over the last thirty years must raise questions over the manner in which the decision-making and policy-making processes have been operating. Two new emphases affecting these processes seem particularly important. The first revolves around the concept of 'policy dialogue', the second follows on from the first—improved 'coordination'.

If we accept that the current direction of developmental aid policies has a two-fold purpose, stuctural adjustment in the wake of a decade of recurrent crises and the continued emphasis on reaching the poorest groups, then the concepts mentioned above are brought into sharper relief.[53]

Policy dialogue is a significant manifestation of the willingness to shed a post-colonial mentality and its method is becoming increasingly popular, even though it has taken severe economic *malaise* in sub-Saharan Africa to force the issue on to the political agendas of the North and the South.[54] It is particularly aimed at removing the dilemma aid administrators had found themselves confronted with for a long period. Essentially this notion of 'policy dialogue' describes exchanges between donors and recipients about the domestic policy framework, in order to influence the outcome of the aid transfer, as well as the behaviour of the economy as a whole. Some observers have claimed that the major function to aid is to act as an inducement to policy reforms engendering efficient resource allocation and economic growth rather than to relieve scarcities of foreign exchange or domestic savings.[55] Others have suggested that aid is primarily a catalytic agent in the development process, helping to complement resources already available to recipient governments.[56] This latter view in fact tends to complement the former idea of ODA as an inducement.

In short, what policy dialogue seeks to achieve is the improved compatability or matching of aid policies with the economic and development policies of the recipient nations. The more frequent use of aid consortia to arrange packages of aid for a recipient from a number of sources point in this direction. Tanzania, Cameroun, Kenya and Côte d'Ivoire are just some of the states which have recently engaged in this form of policy dialogue. Furthermore, it attempts to match means with possibilities and implicitly to limit expectations.

Two types of approach to tackling developmental problems seem to be emerging out of this policy dialogue. One is to organize (within the framework of the aid consortia) a mixture of budget support, import-financing and technical assistance to a sectoral service, like research in the agricultural field. The second approach aims at improving the complex management of government.

The increasing emphasis on 'sectoral dialogue', to promote sector strategies of individual donors, has specific importance for the development of the agricultural sector. Although a belated discovery, it is now recognized that agriculture must become the 'engine of growth' in sub-Saharan Africa. It is recognized as particularly important that African governments redress the balance between the production of food for consumption and the export of crops in which they have a comparative advantage on an intra-African trade basis.[57] The emphasis on encouraging smallholding farmers has placed particular importance on more coherent policy-making and better administrative support than was hitherto available. Moreover, it stresses the problems, prevalent in many states within the sub-Saharan area, of sharp conflict between public and private sectors in the development process. It can be argued, however, that public and private sectors have mutually significant roles to make in the development process.[58]

This sectoral dialogue has great promise for promoting 'reciprocal conditionality'. Under these conditions programmes for specific actions are formulated and prepared by African governments, often with the help of technical advisers or World Bank officials, who provide assistance for policy analysis. Donors are then expected to provide programmes that will support and sustain these African efforts. The international institutions, whether the World Bank or the regional arm of the UN—the ECA—could then assist in the monitoring of this reciprocal conditionality.[59] The international institutions would seem to be particularly important in this process of policy dialogue: the International Monetary Fund, the World Bank and its affiliates, and the UN system. Many donors' aid programmes seem to take the lead from IMF reports, and their own financial programmes have a significant impact on the overall resources available to many recipient governments. Furthermore, the IMF has accumulated the most experience in negotiating conditional programmes.

Policy dialogue could therefore provide for better information gathering and feedback for both recipients and donors, helping to establish priorities and monitor as well as sustain projects once started. The power of the donors in the aid process has often lain in their access to information; the flow of information between recipients and donors will help to redress this imbalance and provide a more stable basis for a future partnership.

'Coordination' is the second important method that would appear to be important in the improvement of the effectiveness of aid. This coordination takes place on a number of levels, and it refers to consultation between the various agencies providing concepts as well as resources to any of the recipient country programmes. It aims to help all the agencies in question maximize the efforts being pursued on current priorities and ensure a consistency in approach, along with avoiding the duplication of efforts on the part of the donor community or indeed the repetition of another donor's mistakes.

It is important that on the multilateral level the UN and the European Development Fund (EDF), among others, improve the coordination of their projects within the context of the domestic policy-making environment. The introduction of UN resident coordinators at the national level has done much to improve the UN's coordinating structure. Coordination is also a significant way of minimizing the 'prisoners' dilemma' mentioned earlier. It is a way of encouraging cooperation on the basis of reciprocity among donor agencies, in particular the various ministries that compete for resources, and amongst individual donors. It also provides a basis for the coordination of policies between Africa and the developed countries.

The major responsibility for aid coordination must lie with the African governments. The African governments need to balance the priorities and make the political choices between greater regional cooperation, self-sustaining economic policies and external involvement in their development. A recent study on Togo,[60] however, illustrates the importance of ODA for African development, as well as emphasizing the importance of recipient coordination. It suggested that development aid has helped to sustain investment funding, estimating that approximately 80 per cent of total investment finance came from concessional foreign financing. It also suggested that a significant continuing problem in allocating resources lay with the lack of a coherent rural development strategy, which had produced 'a patchwork of scattered and disparate projects'.[61] The authors also emphasized the need for donors to consider how actual project preparation and implementation were often hindered by incompatible donor procedures, highlighting in particular the point that different donor procedures often lead to delays in project implementation and therefore the effectiveness of the results.

Achieving a balance between politics and economics should be a matter of aiming for compatibility between ideas and action, and in this sense policy dialogue and coordination are a way of exercising a *proactive* rather than a *reactive* approach to managing the aid process (aiming at coordinating aid and development more closely), a process that cannot be divorced from the broader political and economic environments.

Support in donor countries for ODA

Research has consistently shown that there is a high degree of general support for the concept of development assistance. Furthermore, these general attitudes do not seem to have changed significantly over the past two decades.[62] The findings of the Cassen report on this issue were consistent with the results of earlier research conducted in this field. 'Band Aid', 'Live Aid' and many other spontaneous efforts by communities in the developed world are evidence of this general concern.

However, it also suggests that people's concern is on a moral or humanitarian basis and not on the specific forms ODA should actually take, nor on the specific countries that might benefit from ODA, nor on the abstract level of the notion of development. Furthermore, in most donor countries support is poorly articulated and diffuse, whilst aid ranks low on the scale of public priorities when compared to domestic or apparently more immediate concerns, like unemployment or local issues of social inequality.

In this sense, political will permitting, those who feel aid could make a more significant contribution to African development need to reconcile this residue of support with action. In this regard public support would seem to be linked to the effectiveness of ODA and more needs to be done to improve the effectiveness in order to increase public support and sustain or even increase the resources made available through ODA. It also suggests that more needs to be done to give the general public access to information on ODA and maximize public 'education'.

How much aid is needed?

The third major issue is inextricably linked to the previous two. Given the earlier discussions it must almost be self-evident that the needs of African states for ODA are unlimited, although we need to bear in mind the fact that there is a problem of absorptive capacity in some sectors of a recipient's economy. However, this is probably the wrong way to approach this question of need. ODA is in fact supply-determined and bears little or no relation to any conceptualization of need.[63] This is most clearly demonstrated by the fact that recipient nations have tended to draw up development programmes with a view to what they are likely to *receive* rather than what they are likely to *need* in terms of ODA.

There are costs to be incurred by recipient governments which reduce relative demand. Tied aid, for example, will negatively limit the recipient's demand for aid, as there are a whole series of economic and political costs to be incurred as part of the relationship of exchange that tied aid involves between states.[64] However, in developmental terms, African governments, particularly in the LICs, *need* to alleviate poverty, *need* to make structural adjustments to their economies to overcome their monoculturally biased economies and promote diversification, *need* to sustain investment and growth and *need* to be able to respond to emergencies like drought, famine, war and the influx of refugees.

Given this needs/supply paradox it is clear that qualitative issues of need have been translated into quantitative terms of supply without having been resolved. Nevertheless, with this in mind it is important to improve the effectiveness of aid and effect a redistribution among recipient countries as well as a redistribution to poorer target groups. A combination of ODA and less concessional flows to the MICs would help to release funds for the poorest LICs. More co-financing between official aid agencies and non-governmental organizations (NGOs) would help to augment non-concessional finance to Africa and also prevent duplication of development efforts. The large proportion of aid from private sources in 1984, US$2.5 billion or 9 per cent of non-concessional finance to the developing world, was directed towards Africa.

Aid is a marginal resource and as such can be seen as a catalyst for change rather than change in itself. The change that is needed above all is that outlined by the *Lagos Plan of Action* (LPA) and the Please Report, the development of more self-reliant, but not autarkic, economies in sub-Saharan Africa. ODA needs cannot, however, depend on a universal notion of development. Needs must depend on situation x^1 at time x^2. Moreover, development itself should perhaps mean that there are a number of developmental choices available to a community x^3 at time x^4; it necessarily follows that for community x^3 sometimes these needs and choices will be more extensive than at others. It should be the object of the aid process to match these four variables as closely as possible.

Concluding remarks

The first observation to make is that a new generation of analysts are unencumbered by colonial anxieties and can make a significant contribution to the understanding of the aid process, and particularly the relationship between aid and development.

The period since the independence of the Ghana, 1957–87, has been a thirty-year learning experience for both donors and recipients. ODA is conditioned by the broader political and economic environments both on a national and international level, it appears, at least to this author, that it is excessively deterministic to suggest that we should forget ODA altogether and rely on the 'magic of the market' or a distant hope that a

New International Economic Order will be instituted. In the former case in particular, there appears to be no reason why this debate should be any less involved than the debate on the respective roles of the state and private sectors in the developed world. It would appear that much of the criticism pitched against aid in this guise is a direct translation of the role the critics feel the state should play in their own domestic economies. Those proponents of ODA are at liberty to disagree on both counts. Moreover, we should not ignore the fact that this market-place is not uni-cultural, precisely because the values that determine the nature of the political process affect the transfers in the economic market-place.

In particular, the 'free marketeers' tend to ignore the significant evidence which indicates that private capital tends to flow towards areas that have an established technological base, trained manpower and an established infrastructure.[65] In the absence of these elements, African states have had to assume a commercial role and encourage official sources of external finance.

Here it is also important to recognize that policy-making is not amoral; likewise foreign aid policy-making and the components of that process are not amoral. In this sense alone, it is undesirable to 'close our purse' to the Third World and particularly those poorer areas concentrated in sub-Saharan Africa.[66] In fact it is rarely doubted that the single most important objective of aid should be its own eradication: the question arises over the probable timescale.

The entire aid process for development should be one where the involved parties share the risk of failure. This requires a good deal of sensitive political judgement based on a firm understanding of the prevalent conditions. This judgement must be predicated on the assumption that the process is dynamic—that is, constantly evolving. Furthermore, in the words of strategic studies specialists, the aid process is in need of 'confidence building measures'. The methods offered by 'policy dialogue' and 'coordination' have the potential to fulfil these latter needs and promote a greater degree of trust between nations engaged in a series of aid relationships, as they inherently recognized the complexities of the relationships that exist between Africa and the developed countries. Without falling into the convenient deception that throwing money at a problem will resolve it, clearly more resources are needed by African states to overcome a period of severe economic *malaise*.

ODA might be seen to have failed to fulfil the over-optimistic expectations associated with it in the 1960s and 1970s: however, there appear to be no grounds for associating this with a general systemic failure, even though some of the structures within the system quite evidently need fundamental questioning. There need be no unquestionable loyalty to a system that has obvious failings, but what is needed is a greater understanding of these failings and possible remedies. While ODA may not be a sufficient condition for African development, it remains for the foreseeable future, a necessary external resource for the invigoration of the temporarily constrained African development process.

Notes

1. Foreign aid is fraught with the problems associated with defining a loosely termed concept. Generally the most commonly used definition, is that adopted by the Development Assistance Committee (DAC) of the OECD, when it adopted the Supplement of the 1965 Report on the Recommendations on Financial Terms and Conditions in 1969. In this definition ODA is: 'Those flows to developing countries and multilateral institutions provided by official agencies, including state and local governments or by their executive agencies, each transaction of which meets the following tests.' (a) It is administered with the promotion of development and welfare of developing countries as its main objective; and (b) it is concessional in character and contains a grant element of at least 25 per cent. ODA consists of two major elements: capital assistance (financial or materials) for projects and programmes; and technical assistance, which puts qualified manpower and expertise at the disposal of recipient governments as well as providing for training of local officials in donor countries.

2. In this chapter the author wishes to leave to one side the problems prevalent in a quantitative assessment of this impact, and concentrate rather on a qualitative assessment of ODA. However, it is acknowledged that the reader should bear in mind the constraints imposed on any assessment by questions raised by the 'criteria debate'. See for a recent example of this debate Mosley, P., 'Aid Effectiveness: The Macro-Micro Paradox', *IDS Bulletin* (**17**, no. 2, 1986), pp. 22-8.

3. Pearson, L.B., *Partners in Development: Report of the Commission on International Development* (New York, Praeger, 1969).

4. Brandt Commission Report, Independent Commission on International Development Issues, *North–South: A Programme for Survival* (London, Pan Books, 1980); Second Brandt Commission Report, Independent

Commission on International Development Issues, *Common Crisis—North–South: Cooperation for World Recovery* (London, Pan Books, 1983).

5. The World Bank, *Accelerated Development in Sub-Saharan Africa* (World Bank, Washington, DC, 1981).

6. Brandt, W., and Manley, M., *Global Challenge—From Crisis to Cooperation: Breaking the North–South Stalemate* (London, Pan Books, 1985).

7. Report for the Task Force on Concessional Flows set up by the Development Committees of the World Bank and the IMF, led by Robert Cassen—Cassen, R., *Does Aid Work?* (Oxford, Clarendon Press, 1986). For a summary of the principal conclusions of this report see Burki, S.J., and Ayres, R.L., 'A Fresh Look at Development Aid', *Finance and Development* (**23**, no. 1, 1986), pp. 6-10.

8. The proportion is naturally open to varying considerations but this is a matter well catered for in political debate. This view is often referred to slightingly as an international welfarist attitude. It can be seen as an adoption of normative (and not normalizing) standards for fundamental human interactions.

9. This is not an insignificant use of language. To date there have been few authoritative analyses of the causal relationship in question, and certainly none on the global level. It is therefore critical that readers bear in mind that even their own interpretations might be partially correct. This chapter in this respect is an interpretive example adding to the body of knowledge that seeks eventually to establish an overall picture.

10. See Amin, S., *Impérialisme et Sous-Développement en Afrique* (Paris, Anthropos, 1976); Frank, A.G., *Capitalism and Underdevelopment in Latin America: Historical Studies of Chile and Brazil*; Galtung, J., 'A Structural Theory of Imperialism', *Journal of Peace Research* (**13**, no. 2, 1971), p.81; Hayter, T., *Aid as Imperialism* (Harmondsworth, Penguin, 1971); Mende, T., *De l'Aide à la Recolonisation: Les Leçons d'un Echec* (Paris, Editions du Seuil, 1972); Myrdal, G., *An International Economy: Problems and Prospects* (New York, Harper and Row, 1957); Myrdal, G., *Asian Drama: An Inquiry in to the Poverty of Nations* (Allen Lane, Penguin Press, 1968); Prebisch, R., *The Economic Development of Latin America and its Principal Problems* (New York, United Nations, 1950). Contrast these works with the more recent literature on cooperation in international relations: Virally, M., 'Le Principe de Réciprocité dans le Droit International Contemporain', *Recuil des Cours de l'Academie de Droit International* (no. 3, 1967) p. 1; Keohane, R.O., 'Reciprocity in International Relations',*International Organization*, (**40**, no. 1, 1986), pp. 1-27; Keohane, R.O., *Beyond Hegemony: Cooperation and Discord in the World Political Economy* (Princeton, NJ: Princeton

University Press, 1984); Phillips, A., 'The Concept of Development', *Review of African Political Economy* (8, January-April 1977), pp. 7-20.

11. Nyerere, J.K., *The Arusha Declaration*, Address by the President to the National Assembly, 6 July 1970 (Dar es Salaam).

12. Bauer, P.T., *Dissent on Development: Studies and Debates on Development Economics* (London, Weidenfield and Nicholson, 1971). See for a brief comparison of views, Bauer, P.T., and Ward, R., *Two Views on Aid to Developing Countries*, Occasional Paper 9, Institute of Economic Affairs, London, 1966. Also, Heimenz, U., 'Aid Has Not Lived up to Expectations', and Nuscheler, F., 'A Qualified Plea for Development Aid' (two articles under the heading of 'Is Development Aid Superfluous?'), *Intereconomics* July/August, 1986), pp. 176–85.

13. Brandt, W., and Manley, M., op.cit.; Cassen, R., op.cit.; White, J., *The Politics of Foreign Aid* (London, Bodley Head, 1974).

14. This categorization is according to World Bank criteria. According to these criteria the Low Income Countries (LICs) are those with a GNP per capita of less than US$400. Middle Income Countries (MICs) are those with an income between US$400 and US$7,000. The MICs are subdivided into lower and upper echelons. Here we need to bear in mind that twenty-two of the categorized LICs lie within the territorial boundaries of the African continent.

15. Note the following interesting contradiction: the suggestion that ODA is non-developmental is self-contradictory, as ODA by definition is developmental. Even the suggestion that foreign aid (that is, as a broader definition than ODA) is non-developmental suffers from the same internal contradictions, as one of the most fundamental criteria used for defining foreign aid, has been whether or not public concessional finance has indeed promoted development. See for a further discussion of this point the 'Introduction' to White, J., op. cit.

16. This author intrinsically recognizes the limitations to this discussion and recognizes that donors and recipients have a mixture of motives for disbursing ODA. This chapter will, however, concentrate on the developmental consequences of foreign aid.

17. See Ohlin, G., *Foreign Aid Policies Reconsidered* (Paris, OECD, 1966); Walters, R.S., *American and Soviet Aid: A Comparative Analysis* (Pittsburgh, University of Pittsburgh Press, 1970); Poats, R.M., *Twenty Five Years of Development Cooperation: A Review* (Paris, OECD, 1985).

18. See for example Rostow, W.W., *The Stages of Economic Growth* (London, Cambridge University Press, 1961). See also the Harrod–Domar savings model showing a linear progression: starting with the basic resource of foreign aid, investment funds are then generated, a growth in income results with a resulting incremental capital output (the so-called ICOR equation). This emphasis on savings can be traced back to two

important articles: Harrod, R.F., 'An Essay in Dynamic Theory', *Economic Journal* (**49**, no. 193, 1939), pp. 14-33; Domar, E.D., 'Rate of Growth and Employment' *Econometrica* (**14**, no. 2, 1946), pp. 137-47.

19. For example, in the United Kingdom the Labour government set up a Ministry for Overseas Development (1964); the French set up the *Ministère de la Coopération* (1961); the US administration established USAID (1961); Belgium set up its *Bureau de Coopération pour le Développement* (1962); NORAD, the Norwegian Agency for International Development, was instituted in 1962. In addition a number of donor governments conducted major reviews of their foreign aid policies. France commissioned the Rapport Jeanneney—Jeanneney, J.M., *Rapport sur la Coopération avec les Pays en Voie de Développement* (Paris, La Documentation Française, 1964). The newly instituted ODM in the United Kingdom published a White paper, *Overseas Development: The Work of the New Ministry* (London, HMSO, Cmnd. 2736, 1965).

20. For an overview of the operations of the DAC as well as a 'well-educated' assessment of the efforts of the donor community over the period in question see Poats, R.M., op. cit.

21. Economic development model building had tended to assume that, or at least portray, the various relationships in the development process as static, taking little or no account, for example, of the changing balance in a whole series of political relationships.

22. For example, the 1967 Arusha declaration and the subsequent drive for Ujamaa in Tanzania, op. cit.

23. See Leys, C., 'African Economic Development: Theory and Practice' *Daedalus* (**3**, no. 2, 1982), pp. 99-123; Roemer, M., 'Economic Development in Africa: Performance Since Independence, and a Strategy for the Future', *Daedalus* (**3**, no. 2, 1982), pp. 124–47.

24. This author accepts the evaluative nature of the notion of efficiency, but a simple equation to give the reader a general perspective might be, the level of return y of a resource input x, measured in terms of an established set of criteria. Naturally the criteria used to set the level of return which is deemed to be effective is a political decision. See White, J., op. cit.; Singer, H.W., 'External Aid: For Plans and Projects', *Economic Journal* (**26**, no. 299, 1965), pp. 539–45.

25. Although the 1963 Clay Report, *The Scope and Distribution of Military and Economic Assistance Programmes*, did recommend limiting economic assistance programmes directed towards Africa, which significantly curtailed any large growth in US aid to Africa.

26. See Shearman, P., 'Soviet Foreign Policy in Africa and Latin America: A Comparative Case-Study', *Millennium: Journal of International Studies* (**15**, no. 3, 1986), pp. 339–66.

27. The International Finance Corporation was also set up in 1956 as an

equity financing affiliate of the World Bank, with the purpose 'to further economic development by encouraging the growth of productive private enterprise in member countries, particularly in the less developed areas'. This particular body, however, did not offer non-concessional finance and therefore does not come within the scope of this paper.

28. For example, UNDP, UNFPA, UNICEF, UNEP.
29. For example, FAO, ILO, WHO, UNESCO, UNIDO, UNCTAD.
30. See Etim, E.U., chapter 4 in this book.
31. Jackson, R.G.A., *The Study of the Capacity of the United Nations' Development System* (Geneva, United Nations, 1969).
32. See McNamara, R.S., Presidential speech to the Annual Meeting of the World Bank and IMF in Nairobi, 1973. This approach was adopted by the UN General Assembly when declaring its approved strategy for the Second UN Development Decade in 1970. This approach sought to combine economic growth with greater satisfaction of 'basic human needs', especially amongst the very poor sections of the community. At about the same time the International Labour Organization launched its World Employment Programme, to increase productive employment and in particular reduce underemployment in the Developing World. See Centre for Development Planning, 'Foreign Aid and Development Needs', *Journal of Development Planning* (**10**, 1976), pp. 1-22.
33. See Spero, J.E., *The Politics of International Economic Relations* (London, George Allen & Unwin, 1985).
34. See World Bank, *World Development Report 1986* (New York, World Bank, 1986).
35. See Martin, M., Chapter 10 in this book. See also Statistical appendices.
36. See Stevens, C., ed., *Hunger for the World* (London, Hodder & Stoughton, 1982).
37. See Eisen, H., and White, J., 'What Can a Country Do to Get More Aid?', *IDS Bulletin* (**6**, no. 4, 1975), pp. 65-84.
38. Mosley, P., op. cit.
39. See for example, Ikonocoff, M., 'Projet de Développement: Acteurs et Modèle de References', *Revue Tiers Monde* (**26**, no. 104, 1985), pp. 781–93; Phillips, A., op. cit.; Léca, J. 'Idéologies de la Coopération', *Etudes Internationales (Quebec)* (**5**, no. 2, 1974), pp. 226–43.
40. This was cited by John White as a form of the 'aid administrators' dilemma'. The dilemma being that in the early post colonial period, donors were reluctant to interfere overtly in a recipient's domestic policy-making process, lest they be accused of neo-colonialism, in spite of the fact that they were often aware that the resources they were providing could be more profitably utilized; see White, J., op. cit.
41. See Simpson, M., Chapter 9 in this book for a discussion of 'tropicalized technology' as an alternative, pp. 206-11.

42.   Singer, H.W., op. cit.
43.   Lipton, M., 'Introduction: Aid-effectiveness, Prisoners' Dilemmas, and Country Allocation', *IDS Bulletin* (**17**, no. 2, 1986), pp. 1-7.
44.   Operations Evaluation Department (Report no. 5718), *Sustainability of Projects: First review of Experience* (Washington, DC, World Bank, 1985).
45.   Lipton, M., op. cit.
46.   Mikesell, R.F., *The Economics of Foreign Aid* (Chicago, Aldine, 1968).
47.   Bauer, P., op. cit.
48.   See for example the following official reports; Abelin, R., *Rapport sur la politique française de Coopération* (Paris, La Documentation Française, 1975); ODM, *Overseas Development: The Changing Emphasis in British Aid Policies. More Help for the Poorest* (London, Cmnd 6270, 1975); Martin, B.M., *Development Cooperation: Efforts and Policies of the members of the DAC. A Review* (Paris, OECD, 1972).
49.   *Lagos Plan of Action*, op. cit.
50.   The Berg report was requested by the African governors of the World Bank, op.cit. See also the World Bank, *Recovery in the Developing World: The London Symposium of the World Bank's Role* (Washington, DC, World Bank, 1986).
51.   World Bank, *Towards Sustained Development in Sub-Saharan Africa* (World Bank, Washington, DC, 1984).
52.   Rose, T., ed., *Crisis and Recovery in Sub-Saharan Africa* (Paris, OECD Development Centre, 1985).
53.   A particularly important piece of work which suggests that redistribution to the poorer groups is not incompatible with economic growth is Chenery, H.B., *et al.*, *Redistribution with Growth* (New York, Oxford University Press, 1974).
54.   For 'white' and 'black' men to be relieved of their respective burdens.
55.   Kreuger, A.O., and Ruttan, V.W., *The Development Impact of Economic Assistance to LLDCs* (University of Minnesota for USAID, 1983).
56.   Sir Crispin Tickell, Permanent Secretary at the Overseas Development Administration (UK), made a clear expression of this view in 'Aid as a catalyst for change', *New Scientist*, 14 August 1986, p. 47.
57.   In the *Lagos Plan of Action*, African leaders recognized that the root cause of the food problem, which directly affects the general economic *malaise*, had been the failure to give priority to agricultural development. This was also the general thrust of African argument during the UN General Assembly's special session on recovery in sub-Saharan Africa from 27 May to 1 June 1986, see 'Anger over lack of fresh African aid commitments', *Financial Times*, 3 June 1986, p. 1. See also Please Report, op. cit.; Green, R.H., 'Agricultural Crises in Sub-Saharan Africa: Capitalism and Transitions to Socialism', *IDS Bulletin* (**13**, no. 4, 1982). For a view of

future prospects see Green, R.H., 'Consolidation and Accelerated Development in Africa: What Agendas for Action?', *African Studies Review* (**27**, no. 4, 1984), pp. 17-34. It is worth noting that it was the coordination of food production policies that was one of the major driving forces behind the establishment of the EEC. Although the analogy might appear to be tenuous, the point is that many African leaders now recognize that the security of food supplies, is a necessary condition for the construction of a 'modern' nation, whereas previously it had been construed as anathema to such an objective.

58. Note the current initiatives of UNIDO, which is launching a Multilateral Investment Guarantee Agency (MIGA). In addition the International Finance Corporation (IFC) is currently trying to encourage an expansion of its capital base by encouraging investors to put money with them, through an initiative called the Guaranteed Recovery of Investment Principle (GRIP). See the article in the *Financial Times*, 'Learning to live with capitalism', 13 February 1987, p. 18.

59. This was the thrust of the conclusions arising out of the General Assembly special session on sub-Saharan Africa in June 1986, which endorsed the US\$128 billion five-year recovery plan drawn up by the African states. See *Financial Times*, 3 June 1986, op. cit.

60. Kiellstrom, S.B., and d'Almeida, A-F., 'Aid Coordination: A Recipient's Perspective', *Finance and Development* (**23**, no. 1, 1986), pp. 37-40.

61. Ibid., p. 38.

62. See for example, Institut Français d'Opinion Publique, *Attitudes des Français vis à vis des Problèmes de Coopération* (Paris, La Documentation Française, 1964); Rauta, I., *Aid and Overseas Development: A Survey of Public Attitudes, Opinions and Knowledge* (London, OPCS, 1971); ODM, *A Survey of Attitudes Towards Overseas Development* (London, HMSO, 1978); Cassen Report, op. cit.

63. For a good introduction to this debate see Wall, D., 'How Much Aid is Needed' in *The Charity of Nations: The Political Economy of Foreign Aid* (New York, Basic Books, 1973), chapter 5.

64. Ibid.; Bhagwati, J., 'The Tying of Aid' in Bhagwati, J., and Eckaus, R.S., (eds), *Foreign Aid* (Harmondsworth, Penguin Modern Economic Readings, 1970); Clifford, J., 'The Trying of Aid and the Problem of Local Costs', *Journal of Development Studies* (**2**, no. 2, 1966) pp. 153-73.

65. See for an excellent discussion of these ideas, Brett, E.A., *The World Economy Since the War: The Politics of Uneven Development* (London, Macmillan, 1985).

66. See article by Bauer, P.T. and Yamey, B., 'Why we should close our purse to the third world', *The Times*, 11 April 1983 and reply May 10 1983. See also response by Clausen, T., interviewed by Watt, D., in an article 'Third World aid must not be cut', *The Times*, 22 April 1983.

3 Development through integration: the politics and problems of ECOWAS

S.A. Olanrewaju and Toyin Falola

[ECOWAS] was both a political and socio-economic coup in a region renowned for its differences and divisions and more frequently associated, until 1975, with disintegration . . . Our aim was a new political and economic order in the region that would one day usher in an era of political, social and economic justice for all our peoples and that would be an example for the other regions in Africa and for developing countries elsewhere in the world.[1]

This meeting [the 1975 ECOWAS summit in Lagos] is a symbol of an enterprising, imaginative and wise Africa, anxious to find the best solutions to the problems posed on the development of its economy and the changes of its social structure . . . We find solace in our determination to rely, above all, on ourselves and no longer satisfied with these convenient substitutes of international egoistic tendencies characterised by sympathy and charity of the rich.[2]

West Africans have not genuinely accepted it [ECOWAS] as the only viable weapon for fighting poverty and economic dependence.[3]

Introduction

The harsh realities of the gloomy economic development prospects of African countries have provoked suggestions and reappraisal of ideas and thoughts about the development process. As early as 1961, the United Nations Economic Commission for Africa (ECA) mooted the idea of regional cooperation in the continent when it divided Africa into sub-regions for the purpose of economic cooperation.[4]

Furthermore, the debate on the New International Economic Order (NIEO) has also demonstrated to the African leaders the need to create and consolidate 'power bases' in the South at sub-regional levels if the developed North is to be compelled to make some concessions. Additionally, the increasing crisis and contradictions within the world capitalist system, in which the African countries operate at the periphery, and the reproduction of these contradictions within the various economies make the need for a form of collective self-reliance important or desirable. These considerations in part led to the *Lagos Plan of Action* for the rapid development of Africa.[5]

These ideas and thoughts about the development process in Africa found practical expression in the formation of the Economic Community of West African States (ECOWAS). ECOWAS demonstrates a prevailing sense of realism that many of the problems facing Africa cannot be solved by individual nations acting on their own. Attempts by individual nations to maximize their gains or minimize their losses in isolation may reduce the welfare of all.

Of the West African states Nigeria is probably the exception that might be able to develop alone along the capitalist line by expanding its domestic market through policies of agricultural self-sufficiency, export diversification and aggressive marketing policy at home and abroad. Nevertheless, it is difficult to see how Nigeria alone could circumvent the tariff and other barriers that were incrementally being established within the region and elsewhere in the world economy. It is indeed doubtful whether the Nigerian market is itself sufficiently large and prosperous to sustain an important and eventually competitive manufacturing base. Despite its large and rapidly growing population, its oil and agriculture, Nigeria has more in common with its smaller neighbours than with either the advanced industrial nations or the wealthy and small oil states of the Middle East. Because of its population and its underdevelopment Nigeria remains vulnerable to price fluctuations for its major export commodity and to sudden climatic variations where food production is concerned.

General Gowon, one time Nigerian Head of State and one of the founding 'fathers of ECOWAS, has argued that regional economic integration did seem to provide a more reliable and rational basis for re-ordering economic priorities, and a more effective means of promoting economic and social development throughout the region.[6] Thus, the concept of regional economic integration is predicated on the philosophy of collective survival and group welfare maximization. The purpose of this chapter is to address the issue of development through regional economic integration with particular reference to ECOWAS. The first part of the chapter is on the theoretical considerations of the impact of integration on development, and the second is on ECOWAS as a case study.

Development through integration: conceptual and theoretical issues

Integration has in general been employed to denote the bringing together of hitherto autonomous regions or countries into a whole. According to John Renninger, regional economic integration involves the progressive elimination of discriminations between national borders normally accompanied by the creation of new institutions with the power to make certain decisions on behalf of the integral parts.[7] Ernst Haas, in a similar vein, conceives integration as the process whereby political actors in distinct national settings are persuaded to shift their loyalties, expectations and political activities towards a new and large centre whose institutions possess and demand jurisdiction over the pre-existing national states.[8]

Economic integration may take slightly different forms depending on the extent of surrender of national sovereignty by member countries. The principal forms are free trade area, customs union, common market, economic union and total economic unification. Both econo-mists and political scientists appear to agree on the above rank ordering of economic integration experiments.

A free trade area eliminates import tariffs and other restrictive measures on imports from member states. Individual member countries are, however, free to maintain their restrictive measures on imports from non-member countries. The customs union, in addition to elimin-ation of tariffs and other barriers on imports from member countries, provides for a common structure of tariff rates, otherwise known as a common external tariff wall, on imports from non-member countries. In addition to these characteristics of a customs union, a common market provides for free mobility of factors of production among union member countries. An economic union, in addition, provides for some form of policy harmonization among member countries. Total economic unifi-cation is the highest level of economic integration among nations: it involves the unification of monetary, fiscal, social and counter-cyclical policies under the supervision of a supranational organization.

Development is also variously defined and in a narrow sense has usually been used to suggest economic development. This may be due to the fact that national development (which has various dimensions: political, social, cultural and economic) is often meaningless without a certain degree of either economic self-reliance or autonomy of decision-making.

The conventional definition of economic development focuses on three inter-related indicators: real gross national product, real per capita income and economic welfare. Using real gross national product (that is, national income after adjusting for fluctuations in the price level) development is measured in terms of an increase in a country's physical output over a long period of time. If a rise in the gross national product is, however, accompanied by a faster growth in population, real per capita income (that is real income per head of population) will decline and the result cannot logically be termed development. Thus development is often measured in terms of per capita income, to take care of the population factor. Using these factors, Meier defined economic development as 'the process whereby the real per capita income of a country increases over a long period of time'.[9] This means defining economic development in terms of economic growth and the two concepts are therefore often used interchangeably. As such, it is possible, as Aboyade has demonstrated, for a geographical area like Liberia to attain growth without achieving development.[10] Structural change permits viable growth to occur, while growth provides the materials for subsequent structural change—a development process thereby evolves. To achieve economic development, per capita income should not only increase over a long period of time, there should also be structural changes in the economy. Such structural changes involve improvements in the technology and organization of production, which raise the productive capacity of an economy.

If development is to be meaningful to the masses of the people, it has to lead to improvements in their welfare. Thus the level of economic welfare is an important indicator of development. This indicator takes into consideration questions of distributive justice, what Mabogunje refers to as interest in 'development as social justice'.[11] This perspective of development, according to Mabogunje, gives sharp relief to three major issues, namely, the nature of goods and services provided by governments for their people (that is, public goods), the question of the accessibility of the different social classes to these goods, and the problem of how the burden of development (defined as externalities) is to be shared among these social classes. If development is to enhance the economic welfare of the people, it must ensure an increasing flow of goods and services to the poor segment of the society. Thus measuring development in terms of economic welfare lays emphasis on the reduction of mass poverty, both in its absolute and relative dimensions.

This concern for distributive justice and reduction in the level of poverty has led some countries to adopt the basic needs approach to development. According to the International Labour Organization (ILO) which initiated this strategy:

Basic needs are the minimum standard of living which a society should set for the poorest groups of its people. The satisfaction of basic needs means meeting the minimum requirements of a family for personal consumption: food, shelter and clothing; it implies access to essential services such as safe drinking water, sanitation, transport, health and education; it implies that such person available for and willing to work should have an adequate remunerated job. It should further imply the satisfaction of needs of a more qualitative nature: a healthy, human and satisfying environment, and popular participation in the making of decisions that affect the livelihood of the people and individual freedom.[12]

Development has also been defined in such other terms as 'modernization'[13] and 'socio-economic transformation'.[14] However, for our purpose in this chapter, the definition which lays emphasis on improvements in the welfare of the masses is adequate. If mass participation in the development process is to be ensured, the question of distributive justice cannot safely be ignored. Having offered a definition of 'integration' and 'development' we will now attempt to relate the two concepts.

Before the pioneering study on the theory of customs unions by Jacob Viner,[15] integration had been viewed favourably. Since regional economic integration aims at free trade, and free trade in turn maximizes welfare the reasoning was that integration will increase welfare though this may not necessarily be maximized. By implication, if improvement in welfare is the main thrust of development as earlier argued, it follows that integration will promote development. The appearance of Viner's work initiated vigorous theoretical analysis on this topic. Viner showed that the traditional notion that integration (customs union) necessarily increases welfare was incorrect.

Viner introduced two key concepts into the theory of customs unions, namely, trade creation and trade diversion. Trade creation is a consequential expanded opportunity for trade and exchange within the region which forms the union. If integration permits a union member least-cost producer of a given commodity to secure the entire regional market for the commodity, such trade creation will lead to the growth of the region and improved welfare of the citizens. If, however, a non-member country is the least-cost producer and the formation of the customs union switched imports from the low-cost supplier outside the union to a high-cost (inefficient) supplier inside the union, trade diversion will result. Hence, trade diversion is a movement away from competitive trade and thus will lead to a reduction of trade and hence a lowering of welfare. Since this also entails a less efficient allocation of resources, trade diversion will impede growth and development. Thus, the theory predicts that countries which integrate would benefit collectively when trade creation occurs, but would lose when there is trade diversion.

Subsequent writers have, however, criticized the underlying assumptions of the Vinerian theory and disagreed with his conclusions. For instance, it has been mentioned that the analysis is of a neo-classical type in which case full employment is assumed both before and after the formation of customs union. The analysis is, therefore, concerned primarily with the effects of integration on resource allocation and the welfare implications of these effects. Viner further assumes that there are no possibilities of substitution in consumption—that is, all price elasticities of demand are equal to zero. He also assumed that supply elasticities are infinitely large, so that all products are produced at constant costs. Thus if goods are consumed in constant proportion irrespective of prices and if costs are constant, then the only interesting thing left to study is the shifts in production between countries as given by trade creation and trade diversion.[16] Viner's assumption of no substitution in consumption is quite unrealistic.[17] Integration will normally lead to a change in relative prices, which will definitely induce substitution in consumption. If this happens, contrary to Viner's views, the effect of trade diversion on welfare is then no longer given— consumers' welfare may remain constant or may even improve. Thus integration can still lead to an improvement in welfare even if it is of a trade-diverting nature.[18]

The orthodox theory of customs unions also discusses the preconditions for successful integration. It is argued that integration will have detrimental effects if the union members are complementary in the list of goods they produce. One might, for instance, suggest that an agricultural country ought to form a union with an industrial country. However, contrary to this, the theory stipulates that agricultural countries should form customs unions with each other, while industrial countries should act likewise. Thus integration is more likely to lead to an increase in welfare if the union partners are actually competitive but potentially complementary. This makes the scope of trade creation larger. It is also argued that the larger the cost differentials between the countries of the union in goods they both produce the larger is the scope for gains.[19]

Another set of preconditions is built around the price elasticities of demand and supply of traded goods that enter international trade. The higher the price elasticities of supply and demand of traded goods between union members before integration, the greater will be trade creation and hence the scope for increase in welfare. Also, the lower the price elasticity of supply of goods imported by the union and the lower the price elasticity of demand in the union for such goods, the lower will be trade diversion and hence the lower will be loss in welfare. In other words, the degree of substitutability of goods traded between the union members and the outside world should be low to avoid reduction of such trade after integration. Also, the lower the tariffs to the outside world, the smaller are the losses on trade diversion.

The magnitude of trade between union partners in the pre-union period is also important. The larger the part of trade originally covered by trade between the union partners, the greater is the scope for gains from integration. Also, if integration leads to a realization of dynamic impact such as the reaping of economies of scale and enforced competition, it would be important, and these will have to be added to the effects of a comparative-static nature.

The conclusion that seems to emerge from an examination of the orthodox theory of customs unions is that integration would not benefit developing countries, due to the structure of their economies and their heavy dependence on markets in developed industrial economies. Such consideration had impeded regional economic integration efforts in developing countries for a long time. However, such received theory and its preconditions bear little relevance to situations in developing countries with different economic conditions and structures. For example, much of equilibrium analysis and the many conclusions of the orthodox theory do not seem relevant to what is in fact a situation of profound disequilibrium in the developing economies.

H.W. Singer has developed a set of preconditions which seem relevant to ECOWAS and economic integration in the developing world generally.[20] He proposes that the chances of success of economic integration would be higher if member countries are of equal economic importance and there are no extreme disparities in their geographical size. This will remove the fear of domination by the larger nations and no country will be large enough to contemplate a national industrial policy as an alternative to regional coordination. For example, in ECOWAS, the size and economic importance of Nigeria, relative to other member countries, has been a constant source of fear to other members. He proposes further that the chances of success of integration would be higher if countries in the union have an exceedingly small industrial base consisting almost entirely of processing of natural resources products and small-scale industries. Hence there will be no vested interest and the distribution of new industries created will be easier to handle. Singer suggested that there should be a possibility of a regional or foreign source of aid, channelled through special institutions whose objective is to support the integration idea. Such a fund would be used to compensate a number of countries which suffer losses due to declining industries and forgone tariffs as a result of integration. Consequently, fiscal compensation has been an important consideration in ECOWAS.

The concept and process of integration cannot be divorced from the process of development, especially in developing countries. Confronted by intractable economic problems and foreign economic dependence, developing countries must consider regional economic integration as one of the main pillars of development strategy. Through integration schemes, these countries must hope to increase the bargaining base of their economies through a pooling of economic sovereignty to transform their economies and improve the living standards of their peoples. Integration should also be perceived as a potent weapon of economic decolonization. By forming viable economic blocks in the South, integration efforts among developing countries can form an integral part of a wider desire of the poor nations of the world to achieve a new international economic order. By strengthening their bargaining power, integration could thus be an important weapon for reducing international inequalities in income and welfare. Thus, the process of economic integration in the Third World should be seen as an instrument of regional economic policy capable of accelerating development and expanding both the economic and political opportunities of the poor nations.

The rationale, aims and objectives of ECOWAS

After a series of meetings and negotiations, the hope of economic integration in the West African subregion was partially realized when on 28 May 1975, Heads of State and Government of fifteen independent states, later joined by a sixteenth, cutting across linguistic, political and cultural orientations and background, signed the Treaty of Lagos establishing the Economic Community of West African States.[21] Thus about 150 million people in the sub-region became bound together to share a common destiny in the largest sub-regional economic grouping on the African continent.

The creation of ECOWAS has been seen by a number of analysts as one of the boldest political initiatives ever taken within the second decade of the post-African independence era. The rationale behind the formation of ECOWAS is predicated on three important goals of public policy.[22]

(1) Ensuring success in the struggle against economic domination and subjugation by external forces. To ensure success in the struggle, small states need to co-operate as much as possible to enable them to effectively resist external domination. A strong regional economic base will no doubt be an effective weapon in making such resistance effective.

(2) Alleviation and eventual elimination of poverty, the achievement of which also depends on a strong and buoyant economy.

(3) National economic development limitations. The failure of economies of most West African States to develop during the two United Nations Decades was due, among other things, to the fact that the pattern of development in the sub-region was isolationist, based as it were on small national markets in several cases. It is hoped that a large community market comprising 150 million consumers should be a big boost to production. It should encourage the expansion of the existing industries and the creation of new ones. This should make possible the reaping of economies of scale.

Given this rationale, the general aim of ECOWAS as specified in Article 2(1) of the 1975 Treaty of Lagos is:

To promote cooperation and development in all fields of industry, transport, telecommunications, energy, agriculture, natural resources, commerce, monetary and financial questions and in social and cultural matters for the purpose of raising the standard of living of its people, of fostering closer relations among its members and of contributing to the progress and development of the African Continent.[23]

The Treaty makes provisions for the creation of a common market among the member countries. It aims at trade liberalization by eliminating customs duties and other quantitative and administrative restrictions on trade in the sub-region, the creation of a common external tariff wall and a common commercial policy towards countries outside the union. ECOWAS aims at the elimination of obstacles to the free mobility of persons, services and capital within the sub-region as well as the harmonization of agricultural and industrial policies and the promotion of development projects in several sectors. The Treaty also aims at the evolution of a common policy in the area of industrial incentives, the elimination of regional disparities in whatever form and the establishment of a fund for cooperation, compensation and the financing of development projects in the sub-region. Given these ambitious aims, the objective of forming ECOWAS can be summarized as 'fostering rapid and balanced development of the West African sub-region'.

To ensure effective implementation of its aims and objectives, ECOWAS has set up major institutions with clearly defined spheres of authority and functions.[24]

The Assembly of Heads of State and Government is the supreme body of the Community. It is responsible for the general direction and control of the performance of the executive functions of the Community. Its decisions are binding on all institutions of the Community and it is required to meet at least once in a year. The Chairmanship rotates among member states.

Subordinate to the Assembly is the Council of Ministers which comprises two representatives of each member state. The Council has responsibility for policy-making, ensuring the functioning and development of the Community in accordance with the Treaty and giving direction to all subordinate institutions. It thus acts as an intermediary between the Assembly and other institutions of the Community. The Council meets twice a year and one of these meetings is held immediately before the annual meeting of the Assembly.

The Secretariat, made up of eight departments,[25] is headed by an Executive Secretary who is the Principal Officer of the Community. He is assisted by two Deputy Secretaries and a Financial Controller in the day-to-day administration of the Secretariat, the issuance of annual reports and the conduct of studies required for the operations of the Community. The officials of the Secretariat are regarded as international civil servants and accorded the privilege and immunities of foreign diplomats. The temporary headquarters of the Secretariat is located in Lagos, Nigeria.

Another important organ of ECOWAS is the Fund for Cooperation, Compensation and Development, simply called the 'Fund'. The 'Fund', which has its headquarters in Lomé, Togo is headed by a Managing Director and assisted by a Deputy Managing Director. The Fund was set up to pursue the following objectives:

(1)   to provide compensation to member states which may suffer losses as a result of the operation of community enterprises and trade liberalization within the community;
(2)   to finance development projects in member states;
(3)   to guarantee foreign investments made in member states; and
(4)   to promote development projects in less developed member states of the community.

The Fund is governed by a Board of Directors, made up of one minister from each member state. The Fund has six departments: Administration, Operations, Legal Affairs, Finance, Studies and Office of the Secretary.

Another major institution of ECOWAS is the Tribunal, which has responsibility for settling disputes among member states as well as for ensuring the observance of law and justice in the interpretation of treaty provisions.

There are four special commissions, namely,

(1)   the Trade, Customs, Immigration, Monetary and Payments Commission;
(2)   the Industry, Agriculture and Natural Resources Commission;
(3)   the Transport, Telecommunications and Energy Commission; and
(4)   the Social and Cultural Affairs Commission.

The membership of the commissions is made up of technocrats from member states. It is the duty of the commissions to draw up programmes in their relevant fields of competence and to assess the implementation of such programmes. In addition, there is a Committee of the West African Central Bank and a Capital Issues Commission in the Community.

Problems and politics of ECOWAS

The institutions of ECOWAS appear very adequate in scope and delineation of authority to ensure efficiency and effectiveness. However, this is not exactly the case. In the first place, the organization gives too much power to the Assembly of Heads of State instead of the Executive Secretariat, which is more equipped to handle the complexities and problems of an integration arrangement. The weaknesses of many leaders in the sub-region and the lack of regime continuity due to frequent *coups d'état* contribute to lack of efficiency and effectiveness in the sub-region.

Another point worthy of note is that 'beautiful' institutions with clearly defined spheres of authority do not necessarily make a community. The crucial point relates to how the member countries perceive and relate to the institutions and the Community as a whole. It is noteworthy that few countries in the Community have any national organization for coordinating and promoting its policies. There is also an absence of, or weak, national links with the Secretariat. This has made it difficult for the Secretariat to know what is happening in member states about their development strategies. In the circumstances, it is hardly surprising that the organization still has very little to show since its establishment. However, problems with institutional arrangements are only part of the problem afflicting ECOWAS.

The organization ECOWAS has been bedevilled by many problems within its eleven years of existence. These problems, which partly emanate from the politics of the sub-region and the structure of the economies in the respective member states, have raised doubts as to the worth of the whole concept of ECOWAS.[26] The average assessment is that ECOWAS has not lived up to the great expectations of its founding fathers and the 150 million community citizens. Some have even written-off its first decade as an entirely wasted period.

ECOWAS started running into crucial problems right from its inception. Though its Treaty was signed in May 1975, the Executive Secretariat and the Fund began work only in March 1977 with a task force. So for two years after the signing of the Treaty, the Community was dormant. Even worse, the task force was not replaced by a permanent staff until 1981.

No sooner had the two principal organs of the Community, the Secretariat and the Fund, come into operation in 1977 than problems and differences between the Executive Secretary and the Managing

Director of the Fund virtually paralysed the Community as there was no means of communication between the two offices. It was fundamentally a power struggle between them. Without communications between the Fund and the Secretariat, the specialized commissions could not function and projects could not be coordinated. The personality conflict reached a crisis dimension which necessitated the intervention of the Council of Ministers and the Assembly of the Community to resolve it.[27] This was an unfortunate development since there was no doubt what-soever in the minds of the founding fathers of the Community that the Executive Secretary was the principal officer of the Community.

ECOWAS has also been faced with the problem of recruiting permanent staff. The problem apparently stems from two causes. One is the allegation constantly circulating along the West African corridors of power that the former Director of the Fund, Mr Romeo Horton had filled several posts with Liberians without using the proper bureaucratic procedures for recruiting. The normal procedure is that recruitment should be on a quota basis. The second cause of the problem is that West African leaders have been playing some kind of 'politics' with staffing. The leaders have been unable to identify ECOWAS staff as 'community citizens' but as nationals of their respective countries. This politicization of staffing had led to considerable strains and competition within the Community. This is what prompted a former Nigerian President, Alhaji Shehu Shagari, to comment that 'One requirement for progress in ECOWAS was that its institutions should be manned by competent and dedicated staff whose term of office depended on performance rather than political sentiments'.[28]

Commenting in 1980 on why ECOWAS was short staffed, Roy Stephens explained that the staffing complications were so severe that the Council of Ministers had to decide that:

... because of the current difficulties all current staff should be laid off, pending the appointment of permanent staff. This in effect meant that after the three months notice period given to the staff as it then existed, ECOWAS ceased functioning as an effective entity. The only people left on permanent employment were Dr Quattarra, Mr Horton, their Deputies and the minor secretarial staff.[29]

A decision like this was bound to erode the confidence of qualified staff to work for the organization. The subsequent dismissal of the Managing Director of the Fund accused of filling positions with

Liberians, mismanagement and excessive spending, further cast a shadow of doubt on the amount of freedom officials have to take decisions and act on them. The question of shortage of qualified staff has also affected project execution in the Community.

The awareness of lack of progress in the Community prompted its leaders to request the United Nations Economic Commission for Africa (ECA) to conduct a study on ways of strengthening economic integration in West Africa. The ECA report was presented to the ninth summit meeting in Lomé in November 1984.

The report attributed poor progress to factors such as lack of commitment by member states, the multiplicity of other groupings in the sub-region, and faulty perception of the reason for integration.[30]

The lack of commitment manifests itself in several ways. Foremost is the failure of member states to implement decisions commonly reached for advancing integration. For example, several protocols signed since 1978 are still to be ratified by up to seven of the sixteen member states, the number required to bring them into form. A number of other decisions have also been ignored by members.[31] Other problems include the failure of the intergovernmental organizations either to meet, or to meet regularly, the absence in most countries of national organizations for coordinating the Community's programmes and policies, and the tendency of member states, even when not pressed, to choose autark and nationalistic objectives in preference to the Community's objectives.

A second major obstacle that the study identifies is the multiplicity of intergovernmental economic groupings in the sub-region. Currently there are some thirty-two, involving sixteen members of ECOWAS in various combinations with some countries belonging to more than twenty, while some belong to as few as two. The objectives and integration strategies of these organizations vary widely, sometimes tending to highlight the historical differences between groups of countries. In the absence of any effort they represent a considerable dissipation of energy.[32]

One of the critical questions for ECA's grand design has been the role of groupings within groupings, smaller units that have been set up to meet one or other political need, but which are sometimes seen as detracting from the larger groupings. This is the case of the CEAO and Mano River Union, which exist within ECOWAS.[33] The CEAO has in particular been seen as being competitive with ECOWAS. This point has been well made by Renninger thus:

Since it does duplicate ECOWAS and since the membership overlaps, CEAO does present a serious potential future problem for ECOWAS. One cannot expect the CEAO countries to disband the organisation or even change their areas of emphasis to be more accommodating to ECOWAS until ECOWAS has proven itself. Until, in other words, they are certain the benefits to be derived from membership in ECOWAS equal, if not excel, those to be derived from membership in CEAO. This would involve a drastic change in the present CEAO mode of operations. The CEAO members are not yet prepared to give up their historical ties to each other and to France for ties to their West African neighbours.[34]

This point is further strengthened when he notes that the

UNDP has given assistance to CEAO and may in future assist ECOWAS and since CEAO is a miniature ECOWAS, difficult policy measures arise, to support CEAO and hence strengthen it may make its absorption into ECOWAS more difficult and thus be dysfunctional in the long run and to support ECOWAS alone is equally risky as it is still uncertain.[35]

The current competitive spirit within CEAO has been largely responsible for the feeble loyalty of some Francophone states to ECOWAS. Moreover, competition between the two would put aid donors in a fix either in distributing the aid and duplicating projects or aiding one organization and antagonizing the other. Even for the ECOWAS member states themselves, there are some contradictions in the hybrid integration schemes. The existence of these several organizations also have implications for financial contributions and concessions among the member states.

The role of foreign powers like France in this problem cannot be overlooked. France is the chief sponsor of CEAO and it is quite unwilling to tolerate an expansion of Anglophone influence into Francophone states. The success of ECOWAS would no doubt substantially reduce France's influence in West Africa. There have been various moves at past ECOWAS meetings to try and phase out these other intergovernmental organizations, especially since it is derogations for them which have impeded the effective implementation of the trade liberalization programme.

A third problem noted by the ECA report is faulty perception of the reason for integration. The main thrust of the effort in all the intergovernmental organizations in West Africa, including ECOWAS, has been in integration of markets rather than of production. This emphasis is underscored by lack of progress in the areas of harmonization of agricultural and industrial programmes and policies. This emphasis is likely to accentuate uneven development and accounts for the fears of the poorer members that integration would be at their expense. In the event several countries are unenthusiastic about integration.

The fear of possible domination by Nigeria because of her size and resources, is not completely dead, irrespective of calls for 'dynamism', 'action' and 'unity' by West African leaders. Ex-President Senghor of Senegal sees 'ECOWAS as yet another channel through which Nigeria seeks to expand her wings over Africa South of the Sahara in her role as "Big Brother" '.[36] Yakubu Gowon has tried to defend Nigeria in a most assuring manner:

. . . international agencies and our future partners themselves recognized that, without Nigeria, there could be no effective West African Community. By reason of its size, population and oil resources, Nigeria constitutes a core-state, with no interest in territorial aggrandisement but concerned, understandably with its own security and, therefore, with the stability of the region. These objectives are best served by policies of political cooperation, economic integration and adoption of a form of collective self-reliance. Here Nigeria's perception of its development and security needs has coincided increasingly with those of the other states within the region.[37]

Nevertheless, Senghor's view reflects generally the Francophone position though a few of them have had cause to modify their views. Côte d'Ivoire, for instance, now sees Nigeria as a market. Other member countries even now see the slip in commitment to ECOWAS ideas by Nigeria as a major problem of the Community. This is partly why Presidents Diouf and Eyadema pressed for Nigeria's Chairmanship of ECOWAS at the Lomé Summit in 1985. There was also another collective move in the 1986 summit, once again proposed by President Diouf of Senegal, to put Nigeria in the ECOWAS Chair for another year.

President Babangida, as if to underline Nigeria's renewed commitment, mentioned the provision and renovation of accommodation in Lagos for ECOWAS staff, the provision of land in Abuja for a new Secretariat Headquarters, as well as a 5 million naira donation towards the total cost of the project estimated at some US$15 million. He also cited the case of the reopening of Nigeria's land border (on 28 February 1986), despite the persistence of 'destabilizing activities' such as smuggling (on which he made special plea for more ECOWAS cooperation), currency and drug trafficking.[38]

The closure of Nigeria's borders since April 1984 has been interpreted in many quarters as an anti-ECOWAS policy. Such border closure is not in the best interest of ECOWAS trade liberalization policy in the sub-region.[39] Trade links are crucial for continued ECOWAS development, yet over the first decade of its existence the pattern of trade links in the Community has followed the historical links with the developed market economies of Europe and North America. In fact, for critics of ECOWAS, the organization's principal failure has been in the area of trade promotion. It is pointed out that in the eleven years of the organization's existence, trade between member countries has remained stagnant at a low level. Before 1985 such trade between the sub-regions amounted to only 2.9 per cent of the countries' total external trade. By 1985 intra-ECOWAS trade is estimated still to account for less than 4 per cent.[40] The situation has not improved substantially since then.

Several reasons have been proffered for the slow progress in trade in the sub-region. Ojo, for instance, identified both non-monetary and monetary obstacles to intra-ECOWAS trade.[41] These include the non-complementary production structures of the economies of the sub-region, under-development of locally-controlled trade and finance institutions, generally poor (and cost inefficient) local and intra-regional network of transportation and communication facilities, the different colonial experience and trade ties of member countries, detrimental effects of exchange arrangements, absence of credit facilities for intra-ECOWAS trade and problems of dependent currencies.

Strong as these reasons are it cannot be overlooked that ECOWAS was set up to overcome them: its failure may therefore be one of the main reasons for lack of progress. Indeed, the articles of the ECOWAS Treaty dealing with the promotion of trade seem to be the least implemented so far.

The Treaty had envisaged the establishment of a customs union within a period of ten years. This implied that all customs duties and other charges on imports from member countries should be eliminated within ten years and the maintenance of a common tariff wall against third countries from the eleventh to the fifteenth year. So far negotiations about the dismantling of tariffs within the Community have been slow and unproductive, partly for economic reasons, such as the loss of revenues from import duties, but also for political reasons that have to do with various countries' desire to protect their sovereignty. The result is that, since the signing of the ECOWAS Treaty, trade regulations within the Community have remained virtually unchanged from what they were before 1975. Therefore the existence of the organization has not provided a significant impetus to trade promotion.

In the face of official reluctance, much of the trade between countries has gone underground, taking the form of smuggling. This trade is unrecorded and no precise figures are available, but most estimates agree that it is substantial and may be several times bigger than the official trade.[42] It has also expanded in recent times, helped in no small way by the ECOWAS protocol on free movement of persons as well as by the wide disparities in import and exchange rate policies in the sub-region.

Article 27 of the Treaty confers on citizens of member countries the right to be regarded as 'Community citizens'. Member states are also expected to undertake to abolish all obstacles to freedom of movement and residence within the Community. Article 27(2) further stipulates that following the conclusion of any bilateral agreements, community citizens will be exempted from holding visitors' visas and residence permits. Community citizens will also have the legal right to work and undertake commercial activities within the territories of member states.

Instead of the bilateral approach to free movement of persons provided for in the Treaty, the Assembly decided to adopt a common programme which would not only ensure easy movement of all Community citizens throughout the sub-region but would also provide the basis for equal treatment of peoples' right of residence and establishment in any part of the Community. A Protocol on Free Movement of Persons was, therefore, signed with three distinct phases: abolition of tourist visa requirements, right of residence and right of establishment. The reason for this protocol is simply that a community spirit cannot be built up when the nationals do not know themselves.

However, over the years the Community has witnessed ugly incidents arising from failure of member countries to adhere to agreements relating to the free movement of persons. Member states like Côte d'Ivoire, Ghana and Togo which have ratified the Treaty and protocols have been unable to uphold them. West African travellers at several airports in the sub-region have to contend with embarrassments and the risk of being turned back, because they have no entry visas, even though by virtue of being Community citizens, they are not expected to obtain visas. This underscores the fact that ratification of protocol does not guarantee its implementation.

Nigeria has also had cause to expel illegal aliens twice since 1983, although it has ratified the free movement protocol. The 1983 expulsion involved more than two million persons, while the recent one affected an estimated 700,000 people. Although the expulsion did not contravene ECOWAS protocol on free movement of persons, in the sense that illegal aliens are visitors who over-stay the ninety days limit without residence permits, it created 'bad blood' in the Community. It provided in fact a big dent in Nigeria's image as a leader and reliable 'core-country'. Ghana, whose nationals were mostly affected by the expulsion orders, was particularly unhappy with Nigeria's actions.

There is a general feeling in the Community that the protocol on free mobility could be a threat to national security. For example, in Nigeria the expulsion of aliens was motivated by the feeling that they engage in criminal acts that endanger national security such as armed robbery, currency trafficking and smuggling. In Sierra Leone, a recent 'strangers' drive' which ended in chaos arose as a result of the need for purging aliens from large towns and the capital city.[43]

The effectiveness of the institutions of the Community in carrying out their work largely depends on resources made available to them. Unfortunately, the resources have always fallen short of the requirement.[44] One major problem of ECOWAS is that monetary contributions do not flow regularly as scheduled. They show a random pattern of payment. By 30 April 1981 only one country had paid any of its contributions to the operational budget of the Executive Secretariat for 1981, while only seven countries had contributed to the 1980 budget, four fully and three in part. Seven countries had not settled their 1979 contributions, three to the 1978 budget and one country has still not paid its contribution to the 1977 budget. This meant an arrears total of US$12,133,160.[45] The problem of delays by member countries in paying their contributions was also highlighted during the ECOWAS summit held in Abuja from 30 June to 2 July 1986. President Babangida, the current Chairman of ECOWAS, in his welcome address described this problem as having virtually crippled the operations of the Secretariat. The summit directed that the Secretariat should agree with each member state in arrears on a timetable to enable them to pay up to 1983 by 31 October 1986 and the outstanding balance by 31 March 1987.[46]

One question that arises is why there is a problem with funding. Is it due to lack of confidence in ECOWAS on the part of member states or due to lack of commitment? Is it due to general poverty or that competing obligations make excessive demands on state revenue? It is difficult to come to a single answer. If the member states are suspicious of one another or lack the necessary commitment to the Community, then they are likely to be reluctant to put their money into the Community. It could also be that their perceived benefits from ECOWAS are not high enough to generate enough enthusiasm to fulfil their financial obligations. One also cannot ignore the membership of the countries in several regional organizations all within the West African sub-region, all of which are older than ECOWAS. All these multiple intergovernmental organizations compete for the same scarce state resources. In a region where the countries are underdeveloped and poor, dependence on aid is extensive. Thus to a large extent financial contributions to an intergovernmental organization could be inhibited by poverty. It is also quite difficult to justify external expenditure on external projects which has no direct visible impact on the livelihood of the citizens domestically.

Constant conflicts among member states have also not been in the best interest of the integration arrangements. Conflicts among leaders have tended to weaken the Community. For instance, the late Sekou Touré of Guinea accused Houphouët Boigny of 'political wickedness' and plotting to overthrow his government. Rumblings were heard from Guinea about the presence of Israeli and French soldiers in Côte d'Ivoire joining Guinean exiles for another invasion of Conakry to overthrow President Sekou Touré's government.[47] Benin and Cameroon accused Nigeria of draining oil from under their countries, and there were border clashes between Nigeria and Cameroon. Togo accused Ghana of conspiracy in attempts to overthrow her government, while Ghana and Nigeria came to blows over athletics on sports fields in Accra and Lagos. Such constant conflicts detract from unity and good neighbourliness essential for the success of integration.

Conclusion

The discussion so far tends to suggest that ECOWAS has failed in its integration arrangement. This represents a justified complaint in view of the obvious lack of progress in the past eleven years, and given the great expectations of its founding fathers.

However, contrary to this general impression it is not true that nothing has been achieved so far. Since 1978, eleven protocols have been signed and two—the protocol of Free Movement of Persons and the Third Party Vehicle Assurance Scheme (Brown Card)—have come into force. Several projects have also been started, including raising the funds for financing the trans-West African highway, for agriculture and for a telecommunications project to link the various capitals of member countries.[48]

The Fund for Cooperation, Compensation and Development is growing and playing an important role in financing projects within the Community. The Fund is helping to finance the first phase of the telecommunication project. Loan agreements totalling US$12.5 million have been concluded with different member countries.[49]

Other loan agreements for project financing approved by the Fund so far include also US$3.8 million with Benin for co-financing two bridges over the Mano and Sazue Rivers. Apart from loans, the Fund has also approved a number of grants for project financing. These include approximately US$990,000 in the fields of transportation, tele-communications and power, about US$54,000 in the fields of immigration and monetary matters, about US$215,000 in the field of agriculture and natural resources and US$365,000 to Liberia for engineering studies on the Tappita Toblin Blay Customs Highway.[50] Thus, ECOWAS failure is less in the area of project implementation, but more in the implementation of its protocols.

The principal failure in the area of protocols concerns the one dealing with trade, which perhaps is the main objective of establishing the economic community. Evidence of progress in implementing other protocols is also small. This slow progress is attributable to a general lack of commitment, reflecting a lack of political will among the member states. In the words of a contributor writing in *West Africa*: 'it is an expression of fears, some genuine and some not clearly so, about going into an agreement, in which all members will have to give up some part of their sovereignty in pursuit of a group objective.'[51]

In spite of these failures, it seems that a foundation has been laid to enable ECOWAS to generate some impetus for moving towards the justification of its existence as a viable tool for development in the sub-region. Leaders and their representatives continue to make public pronouncements of their commitment. Nigeria, which hosted the 1986 summit, tried hard to create the impression of a renewed interest while the members of the CEAO and the Mano River Union have accepted the dismantling of their existing arrangements, only requesting that since they were ahead of ECOWAS in the trade liberalization area, they be given more time for alignment, in order to surmount difficulties that may arise.[52] Rhetoric and pronouncements, however, will not bring success: the Community will need more of the political support it did not adequately receive in the first decade of its existence. Members will also have to continue with the struggle to create a new international economic order, one in which the North will lose its ability to control, exploit and dominate the South.

The ECA study has suggested some measures to overcome some of the obstacles impeding ECOWAS success. The study proposes fundamental changes in the existing framework for cooperation in the subregion. It recommends centralization of decision-making and advisory organs, decentralization of policy implementation for the time being coupled with a pragmatic and gradual approach to task implementation and merger, elimination of some existing intergovernmental organizations and the build-up of others, creation of focal points at the national level to coordinate and advance Community policies, and a radical change in the existing strategy of integration.[53]

The study also suggests the establishment of the Economic Integration Planning Commission and the Sectoral Commissions. The Economic Integration Planning Commission's function will be to draw up broad plans for economic development of the sub-region. It will try to synthesize the sectoral plans drawn up by the Sectoral Commissions. The Sectoral Commissions are to discuss the various sectors of the West African economy and fashion work programmes for the executing intergovernmental organization and member states. It also proposes setting up in each member state a National Commission of Economic Cooperation, under the Chairmanship of the President or the Prime Minister.

The proposed cooperation arrangement is to enable ECOWAS to focus on integration of production, rather than mere integration of markets. This will enable the Community to utilize ECOWAS as a viable tool of economic development and planning at a sub-regional level. The development of projects in the various member states in the sub-region will alleviate the fears of the smaller states regarding domination by the bigger states, and it is to be hoped that it will further strengthen their faith in the Community.

There is no running away from the fact: ECOWAS must be made to succeed at all costs. The present international economic environment does not give any hope for any development strategy based on a national isolationist approach and individual national efforts. The development of strong and viable groupings in the South to counter the negative responses from the North will be in the best interest of all and it is a task that must be accomplished.

Notes

1. Gowon, Y., 'The Economic Community of West African States: A study in political and economic integration' (Warwick University, doctoral thesis, 1984), pp. i-ii.
2. Statement by Houghouit Boigny, the Ivorian President, *Nigerian Trade Journal* (**22**, no.2, April-June, 1978), p. 6.
3. *West Africa*, 19 November 1984, p. 2303.
4. This is discussed in Ekei U. Etim, 'ECA: Towards a Sub-regional Economic Cooperation', Chapter 4 of this book.
5. The objectives of the plan were to achieve a more self-reliant and more economically integrated Africa by the year 2000. OAU, 'The Lagos Plan of Action for the implementation of the Monrovia Strategy for the Economic development of Africa', adopted by the second extraordinary assembly of the OAU Heads of State and Government devoted to economic matters (Lagos, 28-9 April 1980).
6. Gowon, Y., op. cit., p. 579.
7. Renninger, J.P., *Multinational Cooperation for Development in West Africa* (Toronto, Pergamon Press, 1979).
8. Haas, E.B., *Beyond the Nation State* (Stanford, Calif., Stanford University Press, 1964), p. 29.
9. Meier, G.M., *Leading Issues in Economic Development* (London, OUP, 1970), p. 7.
10. Aboyade, O., *Issues in the Development of Tropical Africa* (Ibadan, University of Ibadan Press, 1976), p. 52.
11. Mabogunje, A.L., *The Development Process: A Spatial Perspective* (London, Hutchinson University Library for Africa, 1980), p. 40.
12. International Labour Office, *Employment, Growth and Basic Needs: A One World Problem* (Geneva, ILO, 1976), p. 7.
13. Lerner, D., 'Social Aspects of Modernisation', in D.L. Jills, ed., *International Encyclopedia of the Social Sciences* (Vol. 10, 1968), p. 387.
14. Development as socio-economic transformation is defined in terms of the transformation of a society's mode of production. The mode of production determines the nature of the social structure and is maintained through political, legal and other means.
15. Viner, J., *The Customs Union Issue* (New York, Carnegie Endowment For International Peace, 1953).
16. Soderston, B., *International Economics* (London, Macmillan, 1971), p. 434.

17.   Ibid.
18.   Ibid., p. 436.
19.   Makower, H., and Morton, G., 'A Contribution Towards a Theory of Customs Union', *Economic Journal* (63, no. 249, 1953).
20.   Singer, H.W., 'Preconditions for Regional Economic Integration', *International Development Review* (9, September 1967).
21.   The literature on the history of the formation of ECOWAS is now extensive. Important works include: Gowon, Y., op. cit.; Adedeji, A., 'The Evolution of a West African Economic Community', speech delivered to the Conference of Ministers representing various West African countries, held in Lomé, 10-15 December 1973; Onwuka, R.I., *Development and Integration in West Africa* (Ife-Ife, University of Ife Press, 1982); Yansane, A.Y., 'The State of Economic Integration in West Africa, South of the Sahara: The Emergence of the Economic Community of West African States (ECOWAS)', *African Studies Review* (20, no. 2, 1977).
22.   'A Decade of ECOWAS', *West Africa*, 27 May 1985, p. 1055. See also 'Independence within ECOWAS', *West Africa*, 17 October 1977; 'Cementing ECOWAS together', *West Africa*, 7 November 1977; 'ECOWAS underway', *West Africa*, 15 May 1978.
23.   *The Treaty of ECOWAS* (1975). As amended, ECOWAS, Lagos, Article 2.
24.   These institutions include: (1) The Assembly of Heads of State and Government; (2) The Council of Minsiters; (3) The Executive of the Secretariat; (4) The Fund; (5) The Tribunal of the Community; (6) The Financial Controller; (7) External Auditor; (8) Specialised and Technical Commissions.
25.   These departments, each with its own head, are: (1) Trade, Customs, Immigration, Monetary and Payments; (2) Industry, Agriculture and Natural Resources; (3) Transport, Telecommunications and Energy; (4) Economic Research and Statistics; (5) Administration; (6) Finance; (7) Social and Cultural Affairs; (8) Legal department.
26.   Ihonvbere, J., and Falola, T., 'Contradictions and Crisis in the Origin, Structure, Operations and the Future of ECOWAS', in Falola, T., and Ihonvbere, J., *Critical Perspectives on Third World Integration* (Oguta, Zim Pan, forthcoming 1987), Chapter 8.
27.   'ECOWAS Hierarchy Clash', *New Africa*, December 1978, p. 26; 'Why ECOWAS is short of staff', *West Africa*, 26 February 1979.
28.   'ECOWAS', *African Research Bulletin*, May-June 1980.
29.   *West Africa*, op. cit., 26 February 1979.
30.   *West Africa*, 19 November 1984.
31.   Ibid.
32.   See Olofin, S., 'ECOWAS and the Lomé Convention: An experiment in

Complementary or Conflicting Customs Union arrangements', *Journal of Common Market Studies* (**16**, no. 7, 1977-8); Ramamutai, G., 'The Dynamics of Regional Integration in West Africa', *India Quarterly* (**26**, no. 3, 1970), p. 7; Robinson, P.T., 'The Political Content of Regional Development in the West African Sahel', *Journal of Modern African Studies* (**16**, no. 4, 1978).

33.   See *West Africa*, 28 August and 16 October 1978, 15 September and 27 October 1980, 22 June and 9 October 1981, and *The Courier* (no. 44, July-August 1977).

34.   Renninger, J., 'ECOWAS and Other West African Regional Organizations', paper at US Department of State Conference on ECOWAS, Washington, June 1980, pp. 4-5.

35.   Renninger, J., op. cit., p. 98.

36.   *West Africa*, 26 February 1979.

37.   Gowon, Y., op. cit., 'Abstract'.

38.   'Phase two begins', *West Africa*, 7 July 1986, p. 1412.

39.   *West Africa*, 25 February 1976, 4 August 1980; Jetes, S.V., and Uboukou, A., 'ECOWAS: A Regional Approach to Business and Investment in West Africa', *African Business and Economic Review* (Washington DC, 1981); Onwuka, R., 'The ECOWAS Protocol on the Free Movement of Persons', *African Affairs* (**81**, no. 323, 1982).

40.   'The underground trade', *West Africa*, 27 May 1985.

41.   Ojo, O.O., 'Monetary and Other Financial Obstacles to Intra-African Trade: A Case Study of the Economic Community of West African States (ECOWAS)', A report prepared for the African Development Bank, 1986, p. 1.

42.   *West Africa*, op. cit., 27 May 1985.

43.   'Mind the diamonds', *West Africa*, 21 May 1985, p. 63.

44.   *West Africa*, 7 November 1977, 19 March 1979, 25 February 1980.

45.   'Plenty of Words but little action', West Africa, 19 November 1984, p. 2324.

46.   *West Africa*, op. cit., 7 July 1986.

47.   'ECOWAS: Progress on Protocols', *Africa* (**61**, September 1976).

48.   *West Africa*, 29 May 1985, p. 1031.

49.   The loans arranged, to quote approximate figures of the loans ($US millions) with repayment interest rates of 7.5 per cent (Except for Burkina Faso and Niger at 6.5 per cent), are as follows: (a) Mali, 3.4; (b) Ghana, 0.663; (c) Niger, 0.412; (d) Benin, 0.515; (e) Burkina Faso, 4.1; (f) Côte d'Ivoire, 0.345; (g) Nigeria is also expected to benefit from the loans agreement in the first phase of the telecommunications project.

50.   *West Africa*, 19 November 1984, p. 2334.

51.   *West Africa*, 27 May 1985, p. 2334.

52.   Ibid.

53.   'Strengthening ECOWAS', *West Africa*, 19 November 1984, p. 2323.

4   ECA: towards a sub-regional economic cooperation

Ekei U. Etim

This chapter is concerned with the role of the ECA with regard to its promotion and facilitation of economic cooperation in Africa. We will examine the ECA's efforts to become Africa's regional and sub-regional mechanism. That is, its efforts to set out an extension of itself that would allow it to play a more immediate role in African regional cooperation and integration. It will involve the examination of the ECA's sub-regional structures and intergovernmental machinery for the period 1960-85. This essay is in two main parts. The first part is basically an overview of the role of the ECA in Africa, with the second part relating to the sub-regional structures and intergovernmental machinery.

The United Nations Economic and Social Council (ECOSOC), through its resolution of 29 April 1958, established the Economic Commission for Africa (ECA). Like other United Nations Regional Commissions, such as the Economic Commission for Europe (ECE) and the Economic Commission for Latin America (ECLA), the ECA operates under the supervision of the Economic and Social Council and the General Assembly. The terms of reference of the ECA require that the Commission initiates and participates in measures to relieve the economic and technological problems of Africa; that it makes or sponsors investigations into economic, technological and statistical information; that it performs such advisory services as countries of the region may desire, provided that these do not overlap with those provided by other bodies of the United Nations or its specialized agencies; that it assists the Economic and Social Council, at its request, in discharging its functions within the region in connection with any economic problems including those in the field of technical assistance; that it assists in the development of coordinated policies for promoting economic and technological development in the region; and that it deals, where appropriate, with the social aspects of economic development and with the relationship between economic and social factors.[1] The terms of reference of the ECA and other regional Commissions give wider scope to their activities and allows each to develop its own special character in line with the political processes in the regions.

The ECA operates within the framework of the policies of the United Nations and is subject to overall supervision of ECOSOC. ECA's programmes and priorities too are subject to review by ECOSOC. The core of ECA's operations and institution maintenance is funded from the regular United Nations' budget, though this is augmented through bilateral and other multilateral funding. Nevertheless, apart from budgetary links and the United Nations personnel structure, most of ECA's day-to-day operations, its policies and priorities are largely governed by ECA itself, with the approval of its membership through the Council of Ministers and more informal consultation with African governments and institutions. The membership of ECA is open to all independent black-majority-ruled African states.

The principal Legislative Organs of the ECA include: (1) Conference of Ministers, advised by the Technical Preparatory Committee of the whole; (2) Sectoral Ministerial Conferences, advised by appropriate Committee of Officials; and (3) Ministerial Council of each of the Multilateral Programming and Operational Centres (MULPOCs). Its subsidiary bodies include: (a) Joint Conference of African Planners, Statisticians and Demographers; (b) Intergovernmental Committee of Experts for Science and Technology Development; and (c) the Joint Intergovernmental Regional Committee on Human Settlements and Environment.[2]

ECA: an overview

The ECA began as an instrument of the developing countries' offensive to increase the size and scope of the aid package. The Commission's position in Africa was paradoxical—while economic conditions compelled African states towards formal cooperative arrangements, the profound political implications of such arrangements made them shy away from putting them into operation. Therefore, the ECA became an institution of 'marginal concern to the poor countries'.[3] In the search for a role in Africa, the ECA encountered administrative, financial and political problems. Magee referred to the ECA's peculiar status as part of the United Nations' system. Its budget forms part of the overall UN's budget and its Secretariat is part of the staff of the UN's Department of Economic and Social Affairs.

Some of the achievements of the ECA included: carrying out various studies; training African economists and statistians in preparing long-term statistical programmes and various surveys of resources in collaboration with the UNESCO and the regular publication of the Survey of Economic Conditions in Africa; helping to establish the African Institute for Economic Development and Planning (IDEP) in Dakar. Its major service to African countries to date has been its insistence on the need for multinational cooperation to overcome the handicap of economic smallness which besets so many African states. 'To this end it has been the main brain behind all the moves towards economic cooperation in the continent'[4] Furthermore, as Adedeji has pointed out, it assisted in the training of African nationals to acquire skills and experience in order to speed up the Africanization of public services which most newly-independent states had made a matter of the highest priority.[5] The Commission spearheaded the establishment of the African Development Bank (ADB), the West African Clearing Banks and the Economic Community of West African States (ECOWAS). By these, the ECA was a 'builder of African inter-state regional and sub-regional institutions',[6] although this author argued that the ECA failed to develop any identifiable profile at all. It failed to offer its members an ideology with which to generate increased resources for economic cooperation. Finally, the ECA was the first genuine pan-African organization, ante-dating the OAU by five years. By the late 1970s the ECA had become a high-powered think-tank through its efforts to initiate and formulate the *Lagos Plan of Action* as the strategy or blueprint for development in Africa.[7]

Various authors have argued that the ECA failed in its attempt to promote economic cooperation in Africa due to administrative, financial, economic and political factors. Such factors included: the sovereignty issue; the Anglophone and Francophone split; the ECA–OAU clash; the duplication of ECA's activities by other specialized agencies of the United Nations' system such as the UNDP, UNIDO and UNCTAD. In addition, the few studies on ECA since 1958 have been confined principally to questions and issues relating to the pre-1975 period, when the Commission was generally bedevilled by a serious crisis of confidence and therefore had a very limited impact on African development, the re-organization of its secretariat and the need for strengthening the Commission. The discussion on the ECA's structure has so far been confined to the work of the Commission at its Secretariat. None of these studies attempted to show an in-depth analysis of the ECA as a prime motivator or catalyst to development in Africa through its operational capacity at the grassroots (that is, in the sub-regions). This would have entailed an examination of the sub-regional structures and inter-governmental machinery established by the ECA to date. The key to understanding the role of the ECA in development in Africa, primarily, lies in its operational capacity, projects, programmes, priorities, resources at its disposal and its relationship with its members in the sub-regions. The Commission's relationship with its members is very important because the ECA's programmes and priorities have to reflect the specific needs in each sub-region.

Regionalism has been given a new lease of life in both the inter-national arena and the African region. Regionalism must be understood in a broad sense as the strengthening of ties between countries sharing not only a geographical location but also common problems, common economic positions and development strategies. In the case of Africa, the states have nominal political sovereignty over their population, but not economic and financial control. Their monetary resources and economic surpluses are by and large transferred abroad rather than being retained at home to promote their own development. Their governments are debtors to the industrial nations, the IMF, the World Bank and other intergovernmental institutions. The size of the national market in most African countries is too small and their individual resources too limited to permit the development of industrial specializ-ation and the achievement of economies of scale. Individual nations and governments are unable by themselves to break out of this system. If they try they face economic, financial, political and military sanctions. Each state cannot 'go it alone' because it lacks self-sufficiency in resources. Thus, African states have recognized and realised the importance of economic cooperation as a strategic element in economic development in the *Lagos Plan of Action* (LPA), which was adopted by the heads of state of the members of the Organization of African Unity (OAU) in April 1980. Regionalism constitutes an integral condition for the implementation of the LPA. In this respect, Economic Cooperation between African states is seen as a

necessity, not just as a framework for their demands, but also, as a means of cultivating a development mentality based on collective self-dependence in order to change the living conditions of millions of men and women whose poverty is the cause of their increasing marginal existence.[8]

The contemporary African belief as regards development is that the approach to regional economic cooperation and integration must be a pragmatic and gradual process; that consolidation must have its roots at the sub-regional level, or in some specific sector and build on such sub-regional or sectoral cooperation to geographically wider or multipurpose forms of cooperation arrangements.

In the international arena, the Bertrand Report of 1985 reconsidered the role of the United Nations in development the world over and recommended a more regional approach. The report stressed that any action in respect of development at world level means ignoring regional or national peculiarities and makes for a superficial view of the problems and generalities. According to the report, the only possible structural response to development lies in the organization of integrated systems of cooperation at a regional level.

What is needed is a comprehensive view and a precise programme on a reasonable geographic scale, and the handling of problems must be done on the spot, in close collaboration with the peoples concerned. This is why the solution can only be regional or subregional and integrated, which means that all those having to do with development must be sent into the field, in other words the headquarters of the bodies concerned must be located in the regional or subregional capitals, and all the organizations decentralized today by sectors must be centralized and transferred to each region, as part of a single, interdisciplinary development agency or enterprise responsible for health, agriculture, industry and education . . .[9]

At the level of the United Nations system, this can only mean a total reconversion of all the operational structures, that is, the structures of all the main programmes such as UNDP, WFP, UNICEF and most of the technical cooperation services of the main agencies such as the regional Economic Commissions of the United Nations (with the exception of the ECE) with a view to constituting, by region or sub-region 'regional development agencies or enterprises'.[10]

Sub-regional offices and intergovernmental machinery 1960-85

The 1960s: sub-regional offices

In the 1960s, there was a shift in the thinking on sub-regional economic cooperation in Africa. Before this decade, the ECA had adopted an all-embracing approach to sub-regional cooperation. This was a manifestation of the demands of its member states. African states favoured Pan-Africanism and an all-embracing regional organization. They talked about the need to create an African council for economic cooperation, the establishment of a Joint African Development Bank and an African Commercial Bank. These states also called for the formation of an African Common Market, an African Payments Union and an African Bank for Economic Development. The attainment of economic cooperation based on this approach met with little success due to inadequate transportation links, differential needs of the sub-regions, the complexity of socio-economic problems following independence, the vastness of the continent and differences in political ideologies among African states. These factors forced the ECA to reconsider its programmes and priorities in the continent. At its Third Session, the Commission adopted resolution 23(III) which stated that the best immediate practical approach to overcoming obstacles to regional economic cooperation was to make provision for dealing with 'economic problems peculiar to subregions'.[11] Thereafter, integration at the sub-regional levels became the key element of ECA's development strategy; and the designation of sub-regions was accepted as a pragmatic approach and the most practical formula for promoting cooperation among African countries.

Based on geographical considerations and economic and political conditions which existed in the late 1950s and early 1960s, the ECA decided that its work could be made easier by dividing the African region into four sub-regions: Eastern and Southern, Central, West and North Africa. Four sub-regional offices were established in Niamey (1963), Tangier (1963), Lusaka (1964) and Kinshasa (1965).[12] These offices were financed from the regular budget of the United Nations and they were recognized as part of the organizational structure of ECA. Their objectives were to provide liaison between the ECA headquarters and the governments of the sub-regions; provide the Secretariat with direct information on the needs and problems of the sub-regions through the collection of statistical and other information and the carrying out of research of interest to governments in the area; provide advisory services requested by governments; the organization of training courses and seminars; coordinating development and trade policies; and providing a centre for consultation with, and briefing of, government officials visiting missions, regional advisers and technical assistance experts.[13]

With reference to their respective activities, the Tangier sub-regional office worked closely with the Maghreb Standing Consultative Committee, preparing various studies and assembling data of sub-regional interest, at the request of the Committee. The following studies were undertaken:

(1) the pattern and institutional framework of economic integration in the Maghreb;

(2) proposals for economic cooperation in the North African sub-region;

(3) historical data on the macro-economic structure and development of the North African sub-region.[14]

The Lusaka sub-regional office drew up measures for the liberalization of trade in the East African sub-region and assisted in preparing documentation for the first meeting of the Interim Committee of the proposed Economic Community of Eastern Africa, held in November 1967.[15]

The Kinshasa office, in collaboration with the Institut de Recherches Economiques et Sociales (IRES), completed the Economic Survey of Central Africa.[16]

The Niamey sub-regional office relayed information to the ECA's Secretariat on the special needs for technical assistance in the countries of the sub-region and continued to develop closer contact with established sub-regional intergovernmental organizations, such as the commissions on river basin development. It also rendered assistance to member governments and the Conseil de l'Entente in the negotiations for trial shipments of meat exchanged between Niger, Upper Volta (now Burkina Faso) and Ghana.[17]

On the whole, the ECA's record on establishment of sub-regional structures for the promotion of economic cooperation in the continent was dismal. When they were established it was hoped that the ECA sub-regional offices would be focal instruments for the creation of sub-regional economic cooperation arrangements; each of which would be supervised by its own intergovernmental Policy Organ or machinery.[18]

In Eastern and Southern Africa, the launching of ECA's programme for the creation of a sub-regional economic cooperation arrangement coincided with the signing in 1967 of the Treaty for East African Cooperation establishing the East African Economic Community, comprising Kenya, Tanzania and Uganda. The groundwork for the Community was laid during the colonial period.

Endeavours to establish multinational economic cooperation arrangements in Central Africa began during the colonial period. The process led to the creation of UDEAC in 1966. However, UDEAC did not embrace all countries of the Central African sub-region as defined by ECA.

In the West African sub-region, as in the other two regions, the multinational integration process started before political independence. It was the ECA, however, which assisted in the earlier preparations for the creation of ECOWAS when, in May 1967, the Articles of Association for setting up an Economic Community of West Africa were adopted at a sub-regional meeting on economic cooperation convened by the ECA and signed by twelve countries.

In the case of North Africa, the first sub-regional meeting was held in June 1966, but no firm decision was taken on the creation of sub-regional economic machinery.

For several reasons, the sub-regional offices never operated effectively. At its Seventh Session, in 1965, the Commission advised all member states to set up intergovernmental machinery at the sub-regional level for the harmonization of economic and social development; and suggested that in the creation of this machinery, account should be taken of existing institutional arrangements inside and outside Africa. It further recommended that intergovernmental consultation on the setting up of appropriate machinery be undertaken at an early date.[19] Sub-regional meetings were held to consider ways of implementing the Commission's resolutions. Progress was slow as no country had built up a strong technical arm to work out policies and projects by 1968.[20] The obstacles to progress in the sub-regions were highlighted by both the ECA's Secretariat and the member states. The Executive Secretary of the ECA pointed out that on the part of the Secretariat, 'the problem was that of foresight without the necessary resources'.[21] (At its Thirteenth Session in 1970, the Commission proposed that individual states should make constitutions to complement ECA's regular resources, which were subject to the slow growth rate as those of all United Nations' agencies.)

The representative of Nigeria to the Annual Conference of the Commission in 1970 said that his government was concerned about the low returns of the efforts expended by the ECA Secretariat and its resignation to the achievement of nothing but the recording of recommendations, decisions and resolutions. It was also dismayed at the slow pace of cooperation arrangements. He pointed out that Africa needed a whole new physical and organizational infrastructure to survive in the main stream of the world economy.[22] The representative of Senegal recommended that the ECA should go beyond its purely consultative role, relying on United Nations Interdisciplinary Development Advisory Teams (UNDATs) which would be transformed into viable centres for implementing projects.[23] The representative of Upper Volta said that the ECA's efforts to bring about real economic integration of African states would not be complete without some recognition of the effects of the disparity between the most advanced developing countries and the most underprivileged ones, especially those which were landlocked.[24] Furthermore, the representative of Zambia stressed the need for ECA to assume a more active rather than consultative role.[25]

The central issue of the Ninth Session of the ECA held in Addis Ababa, 3–14 February 1969, was sub-regional economic cooperation. The Commission adopted several important resolutions, which *inter alia* emphasized the need for self-reliance, multinational and sub-regional cooperation and it recommended the restructuring of ECA to make it more effective during the Second Development Decade.[26]

At the Second Meeting of the ECA's Executive Committee, held in October 1969, the Secretariat supported the plan for reorganization of the sub-regional offices in view of the policy of decentralization of the United Nations' system. The trend of debate on the subject generally showed that the member states were themselves worried about the workings 'of the sub-regional offices and the sub-regional groupings. Acting on a decision arrived at during the Ninth Session of the ECA, that the structure of the four existing sub-regions be re-examined with a view to making them effective and operational, the Committee adopted proposals for action towards reorganization of the sub-regional groupings.[27] At the Second Meeting of the Executive Committee, October 1969, the Secretariat of the ECA was also requested to undertake consultations with the member states and intergovernmental organizations in order to determine: (a) the criteria for economic cooperation in the sub-regions, and (b) the ways in which the existing intergovernmental organizations could be expanded and strengthened to foster economic development in the sub-regions. Following these recommendations, the Executive Secretary sent an ECA mission on Economic Cooperation to West Africa in April 1970, led by the Deputy Executive Secretary, Prosper Rajaobelina, and a similar mission to Central Africa in June 1970. The objectives of these missions were in general to provide a new impetus to economic cooperation in these sub-regions, and in particular to determine: (a) the assistance which the ECA Secretariat could give to individual countries wishing to set up economic cooperation groupings designed to enable them to carry out a consistent programme of economic development;[28] (b) the reactions of the member states to the proposals adopted by the Second Meeting of the Executive Committee for the creation of new sub-regions in West and Central Africa; and (c) the reaction of the member governments to the proposal for the establishment of UNDATs to assist in the realization of sub-regional development programmes.[29]

The Report of the West African Mission (doc.E/CN.14/478) high-lighted two findings: (1) that the countries of the West African sub-region were not keen to create a new sub-region but rather felt that the establishment of a second sub-regional office would serve the purpose; (2) the idea of a larger West African grouping still influenced the thinking and planning for development in the area.

The Central African Mission Report (doc.E/CN.14/487) revealed that there were no immediate prospects for the creation of a larger economic grouping in the Central African sub-region, but rather that if the political situation turned more favourable there was a likelihood of strong economic links between the Democratic Republic of the Congo, Rwanda and Burundi. There was no enthusiasm towards the creation of the second sub-region. The countries welcomed the proposals for the establishment of UNDATs in the sub-region as this would enable adequate attention to be given to the problems of economic development in the area. The two missions succeeded in obtaining the information which provided the basis for further action in the field of economic cooperation as well as the determination of these countries to overcome their political, social and economic problems through concerted action. The reports also revealed that the problems of sub-regional cooperation should be approached with great realism. Within the existing sub-regions, the bonds of cooperation were established not with all the members of the sub-region but in accordance with the special relations already existing between certain countries.

At the Fourth Meeting of the Executive Committee held in Addis

Ababa, 9-13 November 1970, the Committee was of the opinion that the existing four sub-regions be maintained and that the Secretariat should render more aid to sub-regional groupings of states in order to strengthen economic cooperation and integration in the region.[30]

In summary, the ECA's effort to set out an extension of itself to allow it to play a more immediate role in African regional cooperation and integration in the 1960s was minimal. The sub-regional offices were treated as an extension of the Secretariat since no mechanism was established to ensure involvement of the governments in each sub-region in their activities and work programme. The centres were hampered by manpower and financial shortages and did not contribute much to the slow and complex process of sub-regional cooperation and integration. The 1968 Joint Inspection Unit report on the ECA urged the re-assessment of the need for the offices since the four sub-regional offices combined had only nine professional staff.

The 1970s: the United Nations Interdisciplinary Development Advisory Teams (UNDATs)

The response of member states to the ineffectiveness of the sub-regional offices was the demand for a restructuring of the organs of the ECA Secretariat. Within the General Assembly of the United Nations, Third World countries were demanding a decentralization of the United Nations system. They also argued that the United Nations should play a more positive role in the development process in each region. The result of these demands was the creation of UNDATs. The UNDATs programme was initiated in response to General Assembly resolution 2563(XXIV) of 13 December 1969 in which the Assembly requested the Secretary General and the heads of the regional Commissions to intensify their efforts to meet more satisfactorily the requirements of member states in development planning, plan implementation, public administration and management, especially by organizing, wherever possible and appropriate, continuing advisory services in these fields. The Economic and Social Council, in resolution 1552(XLIV) of 30 July 1970, considered that the provision of such technical assistance in the form of advisory services through sub-regional interdisciplinary teams might be a particularly useful way of assisting some of the developing countries to build up their own services in those fields.

The UNDATs were conceptualized as flexible task forces serving multinational interests. They were supposed to concentrate on fostering cooperation in areas such as transport, trade and industry. Structurally, the teams were instruments of UN headquarters, although they were supposed to work in conjunction with the ECA. Of the seven UNDATs established at the time, three were located in Africa: the Naimey-based UNDAT for seven West African countries; the Yaoundé-based UNDAT for six Central African countries; and the Lusaka-based UNDAT which was an integral part of the ECA sub-regional office for Eastern and Southern Africa. No UNDATs were established for North Africa and for the three Central African countries of Burundi, Rwanda and Zaïre, primarily because of lack of financial resources. The West African and Central African UNDATs existed side by side with the ECA sub-regional offices. Except in the case of Lusaka however, their activities were never integrated with those of the ECA sub-regional offices.

The choices of team leaders for the African UNDATs were made jointly by the UN Department of Economic and Social Affairs in New York and the ECA. Team members were chosen by a similar procedure. The team leader had the responsibility for the day-to-day workings of the team; his position was one of potentially great authority and creativity. He was to coordinate the activities of the UN agencies and bilateral donors, and to consult with the local resident representatives of the countries in his region. UNDAT reports were to be sent to the Department of Economic and Social Affairs, the UNDP Resident Representative and the governments concerned.

The UN financed the UNDATs partly through its regular budget and partly out of funds-in-trust deposited under bilateral arrangements with interested governments. The UN supplied experts and equipment for the teams.

The Yaoundé-based UNDAT has provision for seven experts and three junior experts. A total of about sixteen national and multinational projects were carried out by this UNDAT. Among the multinational projects were: a cereal project covering Chad, Cameroon and the Central African Republic; a livestock and meat marketing project for UDEAC and Chad; and transport and industrial activities in collaboration with UDEAC.

The Niamey-based UNDAT had provision for eight experts and three junior ones. The resources of this UNDAT were at the disposal of the permanent inter-state Committee for the fight against the drought in the Sahel, to assist in finding short-term and long-term remedies for the ravages resulting from the cycle of drought.

The Lusaka-based UNDAT had twelve staff while provision was made for twenty-six senior experts and seven juniors. The shortage was due to financial constraints. This UNDAT carried out studies on transport in the region, rural development and sub-regional trade. Its activities proceeded rather slower than planned.

The significance of the UNDATs was that the ECA's largely inoperative sub-regional offices gradually went out of business, becoming absorbed by the UNDATs. It also indicated that there was an element of duplication of activities in the sub-region. The fact-finding mission organized to carry out a survey of technical assistance in the seven countries to be served by a proposed Dakar-based UNDAT, concluded that it was clear from the outset that the proposed UNDAT should make a qualitative rather than quantitative contribution, since almost 500 experts from the UN system were available in the area. A smaller group of high-level advisers was necessary.[31] The ECA policy organs sought to re-orient the UNDATs toward a policy and operational role more relevant to pragmatic Member State needs for development and economic integration.[32] At its Twelfth Meeting in 1975, the Executive Committee discussed the possibility of consolidation and sub-regional offices with the UNDATs to ensure that greater resources and staff were made available. The Chairman of the Committee pointed out that regrettably the UNDATs had never had enough resources at their disposal and that they had been very thinly spread over the continent.

In order to ensure effective operation and representation at country level, a Joint UNDP/ECA Evaluation Mission on UNDATs and ECA sub-regional structures was organized in 1975. One of the key recommendations of that mission was that the UNDATs should be transformed from being mere advisory bodies to more positive operational instruments for development. It recommended the integration of UNDATs work programme with that of the ECA so that the UNDATs would become the operational arms of ECA and that ECA sub-regional offices should be phased out. The mission further recommended that three more UNDATs be created in North, Central and West Africa respectively, to give Africa a better coverage. For each UNDAT, policy organs at the ministerial and official levels should be established to supervise the administration and substantive activities of the UNDATs. The joint ECA/UNDP mission cited inadequate personnel and financial resources as the most serious constraint on UNDAT operations.

In the light of these difficulties, the ECA Conference of Ministers decided in 1977 to replace the sub-regional offices and UNDATs with

ECA Multinational Programming and Operational Centres
(MULPOCs), with work programmes to be integrated with the ECA
work programme, and with their own policy organs to develop and
supervise the activities of each centre. In adopting the resolution for
the establishment of the MULPOCs, the Conference took account of
the experience gained during the 1960s and the early 1970s especially in
the context of the ECA sub-regional offices and the UNDATs, which
had shown that follow-up action on the implementation of resolutions on
economic cooperation is a difficult and slow process, and that the
operational effectiveness of sub-regional institutions created by ECA
for the purpose would depend on their integration into the decision-
making machinery of the governments concerned; their cooperation
with existing intergovernmental organizations and appropriate national
agencies; their capacity to be flexible and pragmatic in their approach in
the light of the socio-economic circumstances prevailing in each sub-
region; and the financial resources and professional skills available
to them.

Accordingly, the ministers resolved that in order to ensure that the
MULPOCs would be fully integrated into the decision-making
machinery of governments and would therefore reflect the priorities of
governments, individually and collectively, it should be supervised by
intergovernmental policy organs at ministerial and official levels. The
ministerial organ would be a council consisting of ministers responsible
for development planning from all member states served by a
MULPOC. It would act on behalf of the regional ECA Conference of
Ministers, and would be the supreme policy organ of a MULPOC. The
Council of Ministers would be assisted by a subsidiary body which
would be a committee consisting of officials who are permanent or
principal secretaries responsible for development planning in their
respective countries. The functions of the Committee of Officials would
include identification of projects and preparation of a detailed work
programme for the approval of the Council of Ministers, monitoring and
evaluating of implementation of approved projects, advising on personnel and administrative structure of the MULPOC and assisting in
mobilization of resources.[33]

In accordance with Conference of Ministers resolution 311(XIII),
1977, each MULPOC, with the exception of the North African
MULPOC, whose structure differs slightly, now comprises a Council of
Ministers advised by a Committee of Officials. The Lusaka and Yaoundé
MULPOCs also have supervisory committees. For North Africa, the

inaugural meeting of experts, held in March 1978, recommended that the highest policy organ should be a Conference of Plenipotentiaries.

The Council of Ministers of each MULPOC is responsible for: (a) ensuring the effective integration of the MULPOCs into the decision-making machinery of governments, so that the work programmes of the MULPOCs can reflect the priorities of African governments individually and collectively; (b) formulating the necessary policies and strategies for the MULPOC work programmes in their respective areas of operation; (c) taking appropriate decisions relating to programme and project priorities, their formulation and implementation; (d) undertaking periodic reviews of the structure and activities of the MULPOCs; (e) assisting in the mobilization of the human and financial resources necessary for the efficient and effective execution of the work programmes of the MULPOCs; (f) bringing to the attention of the Conference of Ministers of ECA, for its consideration, through the appropriate channels, reports and recommendations affecting the economic and social development activities in the areas of operation covered by the respective MULPOCs.[34] The Council of Ministers and its subsidiary body—the Committee of Officials—would meet once a year. Structurally and constitutionally, these organs were delegated full responsibility to approve the MULPOC work programmes and to supervise as well as monitor their implementation on behalf of the ECA Conference of Ministers. The sectoral projects of each MULPOC are an integral part of the work programmes of the appropriate ECA substantive divisions and implemented as part of the whole ECA work programme.

The orientation of the MULPOCs is thus different from that of the ECA sub-regional offices and UNDATs from the point of view of both their structure and their basic objectives. While the ECA sub-regional offices were primarily administrative outposts of the ECA and the UNDATs primarily advisory bodies, the MULPOCs are a substantive and operational arm of the ECA and their basic principles emphasize that the process of optimum national development in Africa can be fully achieved only through a multinational process and that this is the foundation and objective of sub-regional economic cooperation arrangements.

As their terms of reference indicate, the MULPOCs are concerned with identification of activities/projects of multinational and multi-sectoral character (plus national activities which have a multinational potential), which countries of the specific sub-region wish to pursue; they provide assistance to the governments of their sub-regions in pursuing these activities by undertaking feasibility studies and in the process of implementing the projects. Finally, they are to provide such assistance on the basis of the identification, by the countries of the sub-regions themselves, of the core development issues of the sub-region to which the governments wish to address themselves as a matter of priority.[35] The determination and the implementation of multinational projects at the sub-regional level are thus a joint responsibility.

The priority sectors of the MULPOC work programmes are agriculture, industry, transport and communications, trade promotion, natural resources including energy and human resources. It will be noted that these are identical with the priorities contained in the *Lagos Plan of Action*.

Since the adoption of Conference of Ministers resolution 311(XIII) and 296(XIII), five MULPOCs have been established consisting of the Lusaka-based MULPOC serving eighteen countries of Eastern and Southern Africa, the Gisenyi-based MULPOC for the three countries which constitute the Economic Community of the Great Lakes Countries (CEPGL), the Yaoundé-based MULPOC for seven countries of Central Africa, the Niamey-based MULPOC for the sixteen countries that are members of ECOWAS and the Tangier-based MULPOC for six countries of North Africa.

The 1980s: the Multinational Programming and Operational Centres (MULPOCs)

The period beginning in 1973 marked a new and important phase in the development of ideas and programmes of action on sub-regional economic cooperation. There was a revived commitment to African economic development through collective action as revealed in the resolutions and declaration adopted by the ECA and OAU at the time, as well as in the development strategy formulated by the ECA Secretariat following the Sixth and Seventh Special Sessions of the General Assembly of the United Nations held in 1974 and 1975, and in the recommendations of the ECA/OAU Monrovia Seminar on Alternative Patterns of Development. For most of Africa, the decade of the 1960s was that of high hopes and expectations. The decade of the 1970s failed even to see growth maintained in Africa. For the 1980s the World Development Report 1981 gloomily forecast no measurable growth in per capita income for Africa. It was precisely this economic stagnation which nourished the birth of two documents—*Accelerated Development in Sub-Saharan Africa* (Berg Report) and the *Lagos Plan of Action* (LPA).

The concept of the LPA was nurtured by the ECA and OAU through a prolonged series of meetings and consultations among African development experts and including technicians and ministers from planning and other ministeries. In July 1979, there emerged the Monrovia Declaration, a call by the African Heads of State for the African nations to rally around a programme of mutual support and development, self-reliance and economic integration. To provide some guidelines for implementation of this declaration, the ECA together with the OAU prepared the document, which suggested steps to be taken towards the achievement of the objectives which had been identified in the Monrovia Declaration. This document was adopted at an extraordinary session of the Heads of State and Government of the OAU in April 1980 and has come to be known as the *Lagos Plan of Action*. The Plan is the instrument which African countries through their Heads of State and Government have designed to assist in the creation of a New International Economic Order.

The basic proposition of ECA is that an increasing measure of self-reliant and self-sustaining development and economic growth is a most important accompaniment of political independence since it would lead to the economic decolonization of Africa. Self-reliance is defined by ECA in terms of: (a) the internalization of the forces of demand which determine the direction of development and economic growth processes and patterns of output; (b) increasing substitution of factor inputs derived from within the system for those derived from outside; and (c) increasing participation of the mass of the people in the production and consumption of the social product.[36] Increasing self-sustainment is taken to mean the deliberate installation of patterns and processes of development and economic growth in which different components mutually support and reinforce each other so that when related to the internalization of the forces determining demand and supply, the whole system develops its own internal dynamics.[37] Self-reliance implies the capability and capacity of a national or of a group of nations acting collectively to initiate and implement autonomous decisions in various walks of life: the capacity and capability to provide over time a greater part of the needs of their peoples whether in terms of factors of production and/or of final goods and services.[38] Self-sustainment implies also the capacity and capability of a nation or groups of nations also acting collectively to sustain whatever values and standards of living that they have established as being desirable and reasonable for their peoples through the use of the resources both human and material with which nature has endowed them.[39]

In the context of the LPA, the MULPOCs have both proximate and ultimate objectives. The ultimate objective is the promotion of multi-national economic cooperation at the sub-regional levels with a view to the creation of some form of sub-regional common market or customs union as a step towards regional economic integration. The proximate objective is that the MULPOCs are to mobilize groups of African countries for collective action in the identification and implementation of a limited number of projects/programmes which are critical for the progressive promotion of the multinational process at sub-regional levels, taking into account the unique socio-economic characteristics and constraints of each sub-region. As part of this objective, the MULPOC machinery will promote the creation of national develop-ment agencies which will ensure that national programmes are pro-gressively related to multinational programmes.

An 1978 ECA Progress Report on MULPOCs described their est-ablishment as 'an important step towards the transformation of ECA into an operational institution'. The MULPOCs are considered as the principal ECA mechanisms for fostering economic and technical cooperation at the sub-regional and regional levels in Africa. They are intended as the focal points of activities of all specialized agencies and intergovernmental organizations and are expected to play a catalytic role in the economic development of their respective sub-regions. The MULPOC structure places particular emphasis on 'grassroots' programming.

The ECA/UNDP Inspection Unit Report on the ECA in 1981 stated that in the three to four years since the MULPOCs began operation, this programming approach has been generally institutionalized and has made some considerable progress, perhaps most notably in the actions taken to establish a Preferential Trade Area for Eastern and Southern Africa through the Lusaka MULPOC and in the very active and par-ticipative women's programmes centred at the sub-regional level. How-ever, the report pointed out that the North African MULPOC was still largely dormant because of political fragmentation. The report high-lighted some of the programming problems, such as numerous needs, limited resources, many multilateral and bilateral factors (thirty-three sub-regional intergovernmental organizations in the West African

MULPOC area alone), and competition between national and sub-regional priorities inhibit cohesive programming. The MULPOCs' most effective programming linkages thus far, have been with Member States, either through the policy organs' expert groups or through key sub-regional organizations. Finally, Member State and United Nations System agency officials expressed considerable concern that the MULPOCs are presently spread too thinly in their desire to encompass all ECA headquarters' activities. They felt that the MULPOCs needed more technical specialists with practical competence, who can become involved in fewer but better planned activities which address the critical development problems in the sub-regions in more depth. While the MULPOCs have already filled an important political role in encouraging greater sub-regional cooperation, it was felt they now needed to move to a stronger programming and monitoring role for the implementation of key projects.

Conclusion

For more than twenty years the ECA has been attempting to establish an effective network of sub-regional offices. The latest effort, the MULPOCs, holds out significant promise that this objective might be realized, given the emphasis on sub-regional work programming and sub-regional policy organs, and the new overall operational role involving the ECA and the substantial progress ECA itself has made in decentralizing authority and activities to the MULPOCs. The MULPOCs could greatly aid African development and ECA operations as a decentralized network to facilitate the self-reliant sub-regional cooperation which is essential to fulfilling the Lagos Plan. But the ECA's resources for its sub-regional structures are inadequate. The centres are hampered by manpower and financial shortages. These have hindered its contribution to the slow and complex process of sub-regional cooperation and integration.

With the creation of the MULPOCs, the ECA has provided the mechanism to ensure the involvement of the governments in each sub-region in their activities and work programme. In the 1960s and early 1970s, African states were disinterested in the ECA, hence the poor link with the sub-regional offices. The MULPOCs have made it attractive for African governments to participate in the decision-making process in each sub-region. The MULPOCs are an 'outreach' which brings ECA programmes closer and makes them more relevant to member state needs. This paper shows the dynamism of the political process in the sub-regions through the organs of the ECA and the response by the Secretariat. ECA's decisions were shaped by the requests and needs in each sub-region. On the whole, the ECA has given intellectual and administrative support to regional economic cooperation in Africa through the creation of the MULPOCs and the *Lagos Plan of Action*—a step in the right direction for the organization and future development prospects in sub-Saharan Africa.

Notes

1. Terms of reference and Rules of procedure of the ECA, E/CN.14/111/Rev.8. These were amended by Resolution 974D.1(XXXVI) of 5 July 1963, Resolution 1343(XLV) of 18 July 1968, and Resolution 1979/68 of 4 August 1978.
2. *United Nations Handbook*, New Zealand, Ministry of Foreign Affairs, p. 60.
3. Magee, J.S., 'ECA and the Paradox of African Cooperation', *International Conciliation* (no. 580, November 1970).
4. Akintan, S.A., *The Law of International Economic Institution in Africa* (Leyden, 1977), Chapter 2.
5. ECA, '*21 years of Service to Africa, 1958-1979*', *African Target/Objectifs Africains* (3, no. 1, April 1979), p. 6.
6. Gruhn, I.V., *Regionalism Reconsidered: The Economic Commission for Africa* (Westview Special Studies on Africa, Westview Press, Boulder, Co: 1979).
7. Interview with Adebayo Adedeji, 'Adedeji Interview', *West Africa*, 25 April 1983, p. 991.
8. *Final Report on the Future Development Prospects of Africa Towards the Year 2000*, COL.MO.790AU/ECA/RP/AT held in Monrovia, 12-16 February 1979, p. 8.
9. 'Some reflections on reform of the United Nations', prepared by Maurice Bertrand, Joint Inspection Unit Report: JIU/REP/185/9, Geneva (United Nations, New York 1985).
10. Ibid.
11. *25 Years of Service to African Development and Integration*. Silver Jubilee Anniversary 1958-1983 (Economic Commission for Africa, Addis Ababa, 1983), p. 83.

12. Member States of four sub-regions:
    (a) *Eastern and Southern Africa* consisted of fourteen countries: Botswana, Ethiopia, Kenya, Lesotho, Madagascar, Malawi, Mauritius, Somalia, Swaziland, Tanzania, Uganda, Zambia—Burundi and Rwanda were included in the Eastern and Southern sub-regions. The two countries also belong to the Central African sub-region.
    (b) *Central Africa* consisted of nine countries: Burundi, Cameroon, Central African Republic, Congo (now Zaïre), Congo Democratic Republic, Chad, Equatorial Guinea, Gabon and Rwanda.
    (c) *West Africa* consisted of fourteen countries: Dahomey (now Benin), Gambia, Guinea (Conakry), Côte d'Ivoire, Liberia, Mali, Mauritania, Nigeria, Niger, Sierra Leone, Togo, Senegal and Upper Volta (now Burkina Faso).
    (d) *North Africa* consisted of six countries: Algeria, Libya (Libyan Arab Jamahiriya), Morocco, Sudan, Tunisia and United Arab Republic (Egypt).
13. ECA, Annual Report, E/CN.14/290/Rev.1, 3 March 1963–2 March 1964 (United Nations, New York 1964), p. 3.
14. ECA, Annual Report, E/CN.14/413, 26 February 1967–29 February 1968 (United Nations, New York, 1968), p. 7.
15. Ibid.
16. Ibid., p. 8.
17. Ibid., p. 9.
18. Adebayo Adedeji, *Regional Options—The Case of the African Region* (Economic Commission for Africa, Addis Ababa 1983), p. 7.
19. ECA, A Venture in Self-Reliance, Ten Years of ECA 1958-1968, E/CN.14/424, (Economic Commission for Africa, Addis Ababa, 1969) p. 29.
20. ECA *African Target/Objectifs Africains* (Vol. 1, no. 3, December 1968), p. 6.
21. ECA *African Target/Objectifs Africains* (Vol. 3, no. 4, December 1969), p. 8.
22. ECA, Annual Report, E/CN.14/683, 1 March 1976–3 March 1977, Vol. 1, para. 186 (United Nations, New York, 1977) p. 35.
23. Ibid., para. 190, p. 36.
24. Ibid., para. 191, p. 37.
25. Ibid.
26. 'Report of the Economic and Social Council, 3 August 1968–8 August 1969', United Nations, New York, p. 26.
27. It was agreed that seven sub-regions might be created instead of four existing ones. Suggested re-groupings were as follows:
    (a) The first sub-region was to consist of: Algeria, Libya, Morocco, the Sudan, Tunisia and the United Arab Republic. There would be no

change from the existing sub-region.

(b) The second sub-region could consist of: Gambia, Guinea, Liberia, Mali, Muaritania, Senegal and Sierra Leone.

(c) The third sub-region could consist of: Dahomey, Ghana, Côte d'Ivoire, Niger, Nigeria, Togo and Upper Volta (now Burkina Faso).

(d) The fourth sub-region could consist of: Cameroon, Central African Republic, Chad, Congo, Equatorial Guinea, Gabon.

(e) The fifth sub-region could consist of: Burundi, Democratic Republic of the Congo and Rwanda.

(f) The sixth sub-region could consist of: Ethiopia, Kenya, Somalia, Tanzania, Uganda and Zambia.

(g) The seventh sub-region could consist of: Botswana, Lesotho, Madagascar, Malawi, Mauritius, Mozambique and Swaziland.

28. *African Target/Objectifs Africains* (3, no. 6, September 1970).

29. Ibid.

30. *African Target/Objectifs Africains* (3, no. 7, December 1970).

31. ECA, Annual Report, E/CN.14/619, 24 February 1973–23 February 1974, (United Nations, New York) p. 5.

32. The UNDATs were advisory in their orientation and therefore could not be operational instruments for promoting economic cooperation. In 1973 the ECA Conference of Ministers recommended in Resolution 241(XL) that the terms of reference of the UNDATs should be re-orientated in such a way that they would become operational institutions for the promotion of economic cooperation.

33. ECA, MULPOCs—A Progress Report, ECA/MULPOC/LUSAKA/129, 24 October 1978. (Economic Commission for Africa, Addis Ababa).

34. *25 Years of Service to African Development and Integration.* Silver Jubilee Anniversary 1958-1983, p. 15.(Economic Commission for Africa, Addis Ababa, 1983).

35. ECA/MULPOC/TANGIER/E.VI/18, ECA, Meeting of the Committee of Experts, Morocco, 17-19 March 1986. Economic Commission for Africa, Addis Ababa.

36. Adebayo Adedeji, *The Evolution of the Monrovia Strategy and the Lagos Plan of Action: A Regional Approach to Economic Decolonization.* (Economic Commission for Africa, Addis Ababa, 1983).

37. Ibid.

38. J.O. Aiyegbusi, 'The Genesis and Goals of the Lagos Plan of Action' in David Fashole Luke and T.M. Shaw (eds), *Continental Crisis: The Lagos Plan of Action and Africa's Future*, (Centre for African Studies, Dalhousie University, 1984).

39. Ibid.

5 Dying separately or living together: regional security and economic cooperation in Southern Africa

Scott Thomas

We could have used moralists less joyfully resigned to their country's misfortune and patriots less ready to allow torturers to claim that they were acting in the name of France. It seems as if metropolitan France was unable to think of any policies other than those that consisted of saying to the French in Algeria: 'Go ahead and die; that's what you deserve', or else, 'Kill them, that's what they deserve'. That makes two different policies and a single abdication. For the question is not how to die separately, but how to live together.

Camus, on the Algerian revolution[1]

Regional security and economic development in Southern Africa are more closely linked than ever before. This link is not new since the interdependence of the states in the region has been recognized since the late 1960s, even if there was no agreement on the geographical extent and nature of the state system in the region.[2] What is new, is the extent to which South Africa's influence over the existing political and economic order in Southern Africa is being challenged as the forces of popular resistance within South Africa are challenging the state. The re-emergence of the oldest nationalist movement in the country, the African National Congress (ANC), from which mass organizations and community groups have effectively lifted the ban, represents the most significant factor in South Africa, and in the relationship between the states in the region. The Front Line States have adopted a variety of security and economic arrangements to alleviate their dependence and vulnerability on South Africa, which the ANC has supported. These states have also supported the ANC's 'diplomacy of liberation', calling for the political and economic isolation of South Africa, and recognition

of the political legitimacy of the ANC at the OAU, the UN and other
international organizations.

This chapter will examine the relationship between South Africa's
domestic policies and regional policies as they relate to political reform
in South Africa and economic cooperation in Southern Africa. South
Africa no longer effectively has a separate foreign policy; domestic change
and the country's foreign relations are now so inextricably linked that only
political accommodation with the black majority can restore the
Republic's international position. Regional security and economic
development throughout Southern Africa now depends on the resolution of the crisis in South Africa.

South Africa's search for security and economic cooperation: the total national strategy and the constellation of states

Although it was articulated in different places and under different
guises, P.W. Botha's 'Total National Strategy' was broadly conceived as
a national strategy for security, prosperity, and peaceful progress for the
entire region of Southern Africa.[3] Botha's conception of a constellation
of Southern African states was not new since Vorster first mentioned the
idea during his *détente* initiative in 1974–5.[4] P.W. Botha, however,
gave the constellation of states idea a new role to play in regional
security and economic cooperation because of its relationship to the
Total National Strategy.

The constellation idea emerged out of South Africa's deteriorating
regional security situation with the collapse of the Portuguese colonies
and the independence of Zimbabwe.[5] The concept includes, in addition
to security issues, economic cooperation among the states of the region,
and the re-integration of the homelands into South Africa's regional
security and economic relations. For this reason South Africa's conception of regional security cannot be separated from its policies of
economic cooperation and domestic reform.

The constellation of states was meant to provide the functional
structure for the government (now private sector's) regional economic
cooperation and development plans. The constellation included the
Republic, the four 'independent' homelands of the Transkei, Bophu-

thatswana, Venda and the Ciskei (called the 'TBVC states' or 'national states'), and the six non-independent homelands or Gazankulu, Kwa-Ngwane, KwaNdebele, KwaZulu, Lebowa and QuaQua (called 'self-governing states'). Two new development institutions, the Development Bank of Southern Africa (DBSA) and the Small Business Development Corporation (SBDC) were formed to help finance this strategy.[6] Because of the changes in the constitution at the national level, the changes in local government, and at the level of regional development promoted by the DBSA and SBDC.

An important assumption of the constellation idea was that 'moderate' African states in the region are confronted with a Communist 'onslaught' as is the Republic and that the region's security is largely determined by East–West relations.[7] The 1984 Defence White Paper states that as part of the USSR's 'pursuit of world domination', that country instigates and exploits conflicts throughout strategically important parts of the world. The paper holds that South Africa is 'one of the destabilization targets of the USSR', and is destabilized in two ways.[8] The first of these ways is through continuing regional arms build up: by supplying increasingly sophisticated conventional and other arms to the Front Line States, the USSR 'creates a protective umbrella which allows the ANC and SWAPO to enjoy greater freedom of movement in these states'.[9] Second, the Republic is 'destabilized' by the Front Line States which 'are increasingly prepared to allow the ANC, in a clandestine way' under the protection of refugee status, to work 'through and from their territories'.[10]

A regional accommodation with the states in Southern Africa is an essential component of Botha's constitutional reform process. The government believes this can occur either by re-establishing South Africa's *cordon sanitaire*, which collapsed with the independence of the Portuguese colonies and Rhodesia (this, arguably, was the purpose of Botha's Constellation of Southern African States)[11]; or, less ambitiously, South Africa can establish peaceful co-existence with its neighbouring states through jointly agreed principles of regional inter-state relations. These principles would include, first, a non-ideological approach to regional relations based on cooperation in areas of mutual interest; second, non-interference in another state's domestic affairs; third, states should not allow their territories to be used by groups interested in interfering in the internal affairs of neighbouring countries; and, fourth, states have the right to defend themselves against any form of aggression. If the Front Line States agreed to these principles they would effectively be accepting Pretoria's 'hegemonic presumption' in the region, if not re-establishing the Republic's *cordon sanitaire*.[12]

Although the proposed constellation is still a part of Botha's regional vision, the government would like this minimalist programme for regional security to be formalized through non-aggression pacts and joint regional security monitoring commissions.[13]

In January 1986, Botha proposed the establishment of a permanent joint mechanism for dealing with matters of security, particularly threats to the peace and prosperity of the subcontinent.[14] The Minister of Defence, Magnus Malan, reiterated this offer in April 1986.[15] Botha's recent appeal at the Orange Free State National Party Congress in September 1986 for peaceful co-existence and development indicated where he thought the threats to regional security came from. 'The socialism of the Soviet Bloc', he said, not only threatened the region's security, but also its potential economic development.[16]

Botha's constellation was supposed to meet both of these threats, but, since the Front Line States rejected the offer, the South African government has resorted to military and economic coercion to establish this minimal programme of regional order. South Africa does not possess the same degree of hegemony in Southern Africa as the Soviet Union does in Eastern Europe. The Republic cannot 'do a Czechoslovakia' by surrounding itself with a string of client regimes in the sense of applying a Southern African version of the 'Brezhnev doctrine'.[17] This is true except in the case of Botswana, Lesotho and Swaziland, the more vulnerable so-called 'BLS' states. In January 1986 South Africa wanted Chief Jonathan's Lesotho government to hand over refugees and discuss a non-aggression pact. South Africa blamed Lesotho for the bomb at Amanzimtoti on 23 December 1985. The Lesotho government refused the request and South Africa applied its own form of economic sanctions, which led to a military coup in Lesotho within twenty days. The new Lesotho government agreed that neither state would allow its territory to be used to attack the other,[18] and South African refugees were flown to Zambia where they were met by representatives from the United Nations High Commissioner for Refugees (UNHCR). The military regime in Lesotho agreed to create a joint security committee, and as an example of economic cooperation, South Africa agreed to proceed with the Highlands water project, delayed because of this disagreement over security.[19]

The government's perception of external threat (externally-based subversion) means it does not consider the goal of forming a constellation of states to be inconsistent with regional destabilization. The purpose of both, it believes, is to establish the regional conditions favourable for domestic reform. Once the proposed constellation fell through, the government found it necessary to establish (through economic and military destabilization) the minimal requirements of regional security that would allow the reform process to continue. South African policy has been, in Grundy's words, 'destabilization with a purpose'.[20]

The SADF (South African Defence Forces) can shield the Republic from the threat of conventional and guerrilla warfare, but the real challenge to the government does not come from a regional military threat, but from popular political and economic resistance by the black majority.

Economic development and domestic reform

The current reform programme of the Botha government is the domestic response to what it considers to be a 'revolutionary onslaught', engendered, in part, by the reforms the government has introduced since Botha became Prime Minister in September 1978.[21] Since 1982 the resistance in the townships to changes in black local government, the growing crisis in black education since the 1976 Soweto riots, the opposition of squatter communities to forced removals, the growing force of the trade-union movement, the rejection of the new constitution and the inevitable power struggles in the black community, have become part of wider and more integrated struggles. This has occurred through the proliferation of community groups, and the organizational efforts of mass groups (like the UDF).[22] Black politics has come of age in South Africa at time of economic recession and growing black unemployment. Consequently, Botha's current reform programme goes farther than 'adapting the policy of separate development to new realities'[23] as part of the Total National Strategy. Although these changes are publically presented as the natural evolution of government policy, black resistance and, to some extent, foreign pressure have played no small part in contributing to these changes by the government.

The politics of reform has led to a new government reform strategy. Economic prosperity created by a free enterprise economy is meant to support the government's entire reform process by creating a stable black middle class with a vested interest in gradual political reform. The government states that

if the system of private enterprise is to survive in South Africa, all the people should be given an opportunity of sharing in its benefits. Obviously, the best way to neutralize the appeal of Marxist promises would be to allow private initiative free play to help establish a substantial core of contented business-men, property owners and well-paid workers in all communities. The 'economic cake' must be seen to be available to all with the ability to claim their share on merit.[24]

For this reason the private sector's support for the government's domestic reform policies is as crucial as its support for the government's regional policies. Regional security, economic growth and domestic reform, therefore, are integrally related to each other.

Regional security and regional development

The proposals for regional development at the Good Hope Congress in November 1981 were in part a tacit admission by the government that its previous industrial decentralization programme had failed.[25] This policy began in 1960 and resulted from the government's 1956 White Paper on the report of the Thomlinson Commission. South Africa's programme of industrial decentralization was meant to establish industries on the borders of, or within, the homelands in order to stop the migration of Africans from the rural areas of the homelands to the white cities and towns. A year before the Good Hope Congress, an influential semi-official research institute, whose research functions have now been absorbed by the Development Bank of Southern Africa reported that the homelands could not develop viable economies and hence become independent national states.[26] The South African govern-ment was implicitly acknowledging that economically the apartheid policy of creating separate national states had failed.[27] These develop-ments, and more recent political events discussed below, suggest the constellation idea could be an intermediary stage towards a confeder-ation or federal political system for the country.[28] If this is true, it 'is an instrument to join together what apartheid has put asunder'.[29]

South Africa's constellation was initially supposed to include the states of Southern Africa south of the Cunene and Zambezi rivers, a region encompassing about forty million people. It was hoped Zambia, an independent Zimbabwe (then under internal settlement rule) and Namibia (presumably under the Democratic Turnhalle Alliance) would later join the constellation. The inclusion of Marxist states—regarded as a clear reference to Mozambique—was left open. About three months after the government launched its constellation proposals, in July 1979, the Front Line States formed a 'counter-constellation' called the Southern African Development Coordination Conference (SADCC). By this time, Zimbabwe, a key state in South Africa's proposed constellation, became independent under a government far more hostile to Pretoria than if Muzorewa had won the April 1980 Lancaster House elections. Even South Africa's most immediate (and hence vulnerable) neighbours, Botswana, Lesotho and Swaziland rejected Pretoria's offer of further cooperation. These states were already linked to South Africa through the Southern African Customs Union (SACU), and Lesotho and Swaziland were even more closely tied to South Africa by using the South African currency as part of the Rand Monetary Area (RMA). The BLS states also have other political and economic links on the continent as members of the Organization of African Unity (OAU), the UN and relations with other Third World countries in the Non-Aligned Movement (NAM).[30]

This explicit rejection of freely joining with South Africa in regional economic cooperation should not have surprised the government. Nevertheless P.W. Botha, in his address to the Natal National Party Congress in 1985, recalled the way 'the idea was belittled and prejudice [was] created against it [in spite of] the best intentions on my part'.[31] Botha may still be particularly stung by this rebuff (that is, by making explicit a regional vision only to have it rejected) since it was one of the reasons he gave for not making a detailed 'statement of intent' regarding his domestic reform plans.[32]

The constellation has now been scaled down to include only the Republic and an inner constellation of the TBVC states. The 'outer constellation' comprising the rest of the states of Southern Africa has been indefinitely postponed, but is still government policy as P.W. Botha indicated at the signing of the Nkomati Accord in March 1984. A part of his personal vision once regional security and stability are guaranteed is 'the nations of Southern Africa cooperating with each other in every field of human endeavour: a veritable constellation of states working together for the benefit of all.'[33]

The effective collapse of the 'wider constellation' has meant that South Africa has sought stronger relations with the 'inner constellation' through what it calls 'multilateral cooperation', functional economic cooperation with the other states in Southern Africa, and a minimalist programme of regional order through peaceful co-existence, preferably guaranteed by non-aggression pacts with the states in the region or by functional cooperation on security issues.

After the signing of the Nkomati Accord the Development Bank of Southern Africa (DBSA) contacted Mozambique to assess its development needs and capital requirements. The Bank decided Mozambique's reconstruction programme involved short-term needs, but as the DBSA was involved with long-term finance, it could help Mozambique 'later'.[34] The South African government has invested R200,000 in a feasibility study for the rehabilitation of and extension of the harbour facilities in Maputo. More recently, it appointed a short-term 'labour representative' to Mozambique to discuss labour relations issues. In fact, these discussions may have been a prelude (that is, a 'threat') to South Africa's decision to repatriate Mozambican workers working in the Republic.[36]

In South African parlance, therefore, 'regional cooperation' and 'multilateral cooperation' have come to refer to the Republic's relations with the TBVC states. Since 1980 functional economic and political cooperation has become more closely institutionalized, reinforcing the view that the constellation idea could eventually bring together what apartheid has divided. In June 1979 the then Minister of Cooperation and Development, P.G.J. Koornhof, stated 'Our intent is to reform South Africa on the basis of a commonwealth or even a confederation in which all its components would play a meaningful role, in which there would be full rights for all South Africans'.[37] P.W. Botha told parliament in 1982 that the constellation could take the form of a confederation linked by a council of states.[38] He stated that the homelands are 'being treated more and more as integral parts of the region or regions of which they were a part,' and the development regions established by the Good Hope proposals are 'becoming the organizational basis not only for industrial decentralization but also for a variety of features of political, economic and social life (in spheres such as economic planning, influx control and second-tier government.' In the face of the failure of the government's past decentralization policies it is just conceivable that these regions, presumably drawn up on the basis of economic criteria, could form part of the further functional re-integration of the homelands into the Republic on grounds other than their current boundaries. They could be the first provinces of a future federal Republic.[40] This seems to be the current direction of government policy in spite of P.W. Botha's claim that the existence of the TBVC states and the self-governing states should be accepted as a reality of the South African situation. He has also said South Africa forms one state. The government now recognizes the national states it has created are not viable economically and are increasingly politically untenable as independent units.[41] This interpretation of government policy is strengthened by the government's current plans, released in December 1985, to form a confederation including the Republic and the TBVC states, and a federation including the self-governing states and the larger black townships which could become 'city states' or 'cantons'.[42] This point was reiterated by Botha in his address to the Federal Congress of the National Party in August 1986.

South Africa's System of regional economic cooperation: the rand monetary area and the South African Customs Union

South Africa's domestic regional policy, and foreign economic policy in Southern Africa are closely related. Security and economic development are complementary foreign policy objectives of any state. The constellation of states was meant to provide the organizational framework for South Africa's policy of regional security and economic cooperation. The government believes it promotes regional cooperation through trade, the employment of legal contract workers and illegal immigrants, development capital, finance, transport, and monetary and fiscal cooperation through the Southern African Customs Union (SACU) and the Rand Monetary Area.[43] Although it has not been possible to involve most of the majority ruled states in a regional system of cooperation, the geographical and economic positions of Botswana, Lesotho and Swaziland rendered them economic hostages of the Republic, and they cooperate with it in both the Customs Union and the Monetary Area.

The rand monetary area

Because of the political crisis in South Africa and its effect on the value of the rand, the Rand Monetary Area (RMA) is in disarray. Botswana, Lesotho, and Swaziland (the British High Commission Territories during the colonial period) were all integrated into the economic and monetary system of South Africa. At the time of independence in the 1960s they were members of a customs union and *de facto* members of a currency area with South Africa. This area was formalized as the RMA in 1974; Botswana withdrew a year later.[44] The collapse of the rand since P.W. Botha's 'Rubicon I' speech in August 1985 finally led Swaziland to withdraw from the RMA in April 1986.[45] When the RMA was operating fully, the BLS states all used a common currency (the South African rand) and their own currencies (the Maloti of Lesotho and the Emalangeni of Swaziland), which were interchangeable with the rand. The South African Reserve Bank acted as a central bank for all three states. The bank paid compensation to Swaziland and Lesotho for the rand notes and coinage in circulation in their countries, and most of their foreign reserves in the form of rand balances were invested in the South African money market.

Throughout the area there were uniform exchange control regulations. Funds could be freely transferred from any of the three states, but Lesotho and Swaziland had the right to unilaterally impose restrictions on the flow of funds to South Africa. They also had free access to the South African capital markets through which they raised substantial foreign loans. One of the factors that contributed to the success that these floating loans achieved in the past was the international confidence in the rand.

The RMA effectively meant Lesotho and Swaziland left the control over their monetary and balance of payments policies to the South African authorities. At the time of independence, the RMA offered these countries a consistent exchange rate in their financial dealings with their major trading partners, and reduced their responsibility for an independent monetary policy for which they did not have the necessary expertise. As Gargano (1986) states, 'this reliance on South Africa probably resulted in much sounder monetary policy', and 'the absence of exchange control kept banking administration to a minimum thereby reducing expenses'.[46] Lesotho, and to some extent Swaziland, do not have the same economic base as Botswana, and so in the past there has been some merit in tying their currency to the larger South African economy.[47] It was these advantages which led Lesotho and Swaziland to formalize the monetary agreement in 1974 with some marginal adjustments.[48] The duties and responsibilities of each state was reviewed at regular sessions of the Rand Monetary Area Commission.

Because the economies of Lesotho and Swaziland were tied to the rand, South Africa's future and the future of these states were linked together, The precipitous decline in the exchange rate of the rand, and hence the decline in the exchange rate of the currencies of these countries as well, has been a mixed blessing. The foreign loans of these countries have become more expensive so they need more foreign exchange to pay back these loans. The rand crisis increased the value of Swaziland's external debt, raising the debt service ratio from 4.1 per cent in 1982 to 7.6 per cent in March 1985.[49]

This increase in the value of the external debt should normally be offset by an improvement in the balance of payments since the depreciation of the rand has made the imports of these countries more expensive and their exports outside the RMA cheaper and more competitive, yielding higher export earnings. The value of Swaziland's major export, sugar, nearly doubled in the first half of 1985, and other major exports (wood pulp and canned fruits) also improved.[50] Except for the exports listed Swaziland was faced by a generally depressed world market, and so was unable to realize greater export earnings in spite of the rand's depreciation. Small land-locked countries like Swaziland and Lesotho, however, have a high propensity to import and so were particularly hard hit by the imported inflation from South Africa (the origin of most of their imports) as a result of the rand's depreciation.

Depreciation, however, also erodes the value of their foreign reserves held in rands, the value of which has been cut in half in less than two years.[51] The collapse of the rand also meant Lesotho and Swaziland have had to follow South Africa's interest rate structure which has deterred industrial development and economic growth in both these countries.[52]

Swaziland withdrew from the RMA in April, and by July 1986, the RMA was superseded by a new Tripartite Monetary Area (TMA).[53] The TMA consists of the same RMA countries—South Africa, Lesotho, and Swaziland—but the rand will no longer be interchangeable with the other currencies. This allows these countries greater control over their monetary policies. Apart from the monetary area, fiscal cooperation is also achieved through the Southern African Customs Union (SACU).

A customs union between the various sections of Southern Africa gradually emerged for the first time after 1889, but the present arrangement between Lesotho, Swaziland, Botswana, and South Africa dates back to the founding of the Union of South Africa in 1910.[54] SACU includes the same countries involved in the RMA except for the addition of Botswana. In 1969 this agreement was revised on more favourable terms for the BLS states. Botswana is the only Front Line State involved with South Africa in a major Southern African organization of economic cooperation, although South Africa is involved in technical and scientific cooperation with other Front Line States in a variety of veterinary, agricultural and medical areas.[55]

In order for South Africa to promote its conception of regional economic cooperation, the government would like the TBVC states, potentially able to introduce their own currencies, to join SACU. Since a national currency is one of the 'badges' of international sovereignty, it is noteworthy that the national states have not sought this degree of independence from Pretoria. Indeed, if monetary matters became part of the multilateral cooperation between South Africa and the TBVC states, relations would become even more complicated than they are already. The BLS states, however, are loathe to have these homelands admitted to the SACU as separate national states since this implies tacit recognition of the 'independence' these homelands have received from Pretoria.

The SACU agreement provides for a common external tariff and uniform trade regulations regarding goods imported from outside the customs area. The BLS states have easy access to the larger South African market so what is available in South Africa is available in these countries. Because South Africa is the dominant partner in the union, trade policy is decided according to South African interests. South Africa largely decides the tariff structure which is primarily aimed at protecting South African industries.[56] Since 1946 South Africa's industrialization has been based on a restrictive trade regime using a system of import licences allocated by the government.[57] The duty-free flow of domestic goods between SACU countries and of goods imported from outside the customs area is guaranteed. Other than South Africa, the members of SACU are land-locked states, and all the major ports of entry are in South Africa. South Africa collects the customs duties in a common revenue pool including sales and excise duties. The pool is distributed according to a self-adjusting formula which compensates the BLS states from the customs pool at a greater amount than would normally be the case on a strictly pro rata basis.

This compensation is for the imposition of a tariff which is aimed mainly at the protection of South African industries. It is also supposed to be for the protection of the manufacturing industries in these countries although most new industries tend to gravitate toward South Africa because of its well-developed infrastructure and markets and access to these other countries through SACU. This compensatory provision, however, may be undercut by South Africa's new regional development plan that began in 1982. The nine development regions created by this decentralization strategy are competing with the BLS states (all SACU members) for capital. These regions appear to be attracting industrialists from within the BLS states. Even though these states have their own decentralization incentives, they are not effectively competing with those offered by South Africa. Various manufacturers have relocated their industries from the BLS states to South Africa's homelands, and the situation could get worse if homelands such as the Transkei formally join the SACU.[58]

The current political instability in South Africa could contribute to a shift in the regional pattern of manufacturing investment from a concentration on the Republic and the homelands to economic development in the BLS states. Foreign firms are now even more unlikely than before to invest in South Africa's homelands in spite of their generous investment incentives, yet they would have access to the wider South African market through SACU. This appears to be happening in Swaziland where manufacturers in South Africa have considered moving to or investing in Swaziland to avoid the domestic political hassle of South African investments as well as the unrest and labour-related conflicts in South Africa.[59] Swaziland has just reorganized and privatized its industrial development agency in order to attract such potential investors now hesitant to invest in South Africa.[60]

SACU also affects the BLS states' foreign economic relations with non-SACU states. This problem is particularly important since SACU membership prevents the BLS states (which are also members of SADCC and the Preferential Trade Area) from granting other states tariff preferences. SACU effectively hinders the ability of these states to diversify their trade links away from South Africa, one of the declared purposes of SADCC. It would be possible for the BLS states to grant tariff preferences if they formed a free trade area rather than a customs union. If the BLS states withdrew from SACU, and formed a free trade area instead, their customs revenue (arguably the main advantage of a customs union) would decrease considerably. In terms of the customs union agreement, the following amounts were distributed in 1982–3 to the BLS states: Botswana, R116 million; Lesotho, R71 million; and Swaziland, R117 million. Since the economies of the BLS states are small compared to the South African economy—their combined GNP is about 3 per cent of the Republic's— this share of the revenue from the SACU comprises a significant share of the total revenue: Botswana, 32

per cent; Lesotho, 37 per cent; and Swaziland, 61 per cent.[61] This is one
of the main reasons why these states stay in the customs union, even
though it contributes to their dependence on South Africa.

South Africa, however, also benefits from SACU. Politically, the
government argues SACU is a successful example of regional economic
cooperation. It also provides the Republic with a wider market for its
products in Southern Africa, and potentially, in Europe. Goods from the
BLS states enter the EEC duty free because of their membership in the
Lomé Convention. This is an incentive for South African industries to
establish subsidiaries in these states as it also contributes to their
development.[62] The revenue these states receive from the SACU
increases in proportion to South Africa's economic growth. This means
the greater the flow of imports into the region through South Africa the
higher the customs revenue to the BLS states will be. Since the growth
of the South African economy is export-led growth, a decline in exports,
and especially imports, because of sanctions could diminish this
important source of income for the BLS states.

The BLS states' dependence on SACU for such a large share of
government income, gives South Africa, the dominant economic
partner in the union, important leverage over these other countries.
After the Nkomati Accord, Botswana authorities have alleged in August
1984 that South Africa delayed disbursements from SACU owed to the
country because the Botswana government refused to sign a non-
aggression pact, similar to the one Mozambique signed.[63]

The front line states' search for security and development

Pitched directly against South Africa in the Southern African region, are
the Front Line States of Zambia, Mozambique, Angola, Zimbabwe,
Tanzania and the BLS states. The Front Line States believe regional
security and economic development are only possible after the liberation of South Africa.[64] The differing degrees of geographical proximity to
the Republic and dependence on South Africa's transportation network
and economy, means each of the states in the region will approach its
relations with South Africa in accordance with the extent of its own
vulnerability and national interest. In the absence of a Western commitment to the Front Line States' defence against South African aggression,
these states have been forced into adopting a variety of security

arrangements including the involvement of foreign troops to ensure the country's defence (for example, the Cubans in Angola), signing non-aggression pacts with South Africa (Mozambique, Swaziland, and Lesotho), *ad hoc* security agreements (joint Zimbabwe–Mozambique military operations against the MNR), and an alternative to confront-ation, *détente* (Malawi).[65] The black-ruled states of Southern Africa have also formed three regional groupings, the Front Line States, SADCC and the PTA, in order to improve their freedom of manoeuvre in their political and economic relations with the Republic. Although these states are united in their belief that economic liberation from South Africa is the prelude to genuine economic cooperation, there is no unanimity regarding the importance of each of these regional groupings in promoting the objectives of economic development in Southern Africa and political liberation in South Africa.

The diplomacy of regional security: the front line states

The rise of the Front Line States as a regional security grouping in Southern Africa occurred because of the decline in effectiveness, if not failure, at the international level (through the UN), and at the contin-ental level (through the OAU) to secure a satisfactory settlement of the Rhodesian and Namibian disputes. The failure of these organizations to resolve regional conflicts is not unique to Southern Africa, however, and regional security groupings have developed in many parts of the Third World where the security of the states surrounding a conflict area is threatened[66] (other examples include the ECOWAS defence pact, the security concerns of ASEAN, the Contadora group in Central America and the Gulf Co-operation Council).

Although various states in East, Central and Southern Africa (Botswana, Tanzania, Uganda, Zambia, Zaïre) have regularly met since the mid-1960s, it was not until the Rhodesian conflict began to spill over into the surrounding states in the mid-1970s, that a more regular regional grouping including Botswana, Tanzania and Zambia began to meet in order to coordinate their diplomatic response both to Western peace initiatives (through the Contact Group) and to South Africa's own regional *détente* policy.[67]

These states found two areas where their interests converged. First, it became clear that without regional stability, economic growth and trade could not continue. Stability not only provided the context for greater interregional trade, investment and economic growth, but the absence of stability created domestic pressures in the form of greater military spending, and greater spending on aid for the flood of Southern African refugees which exacerbated the existing economic and political problem of these countries. Second, keeping the interlocking Southern African transportation network working was imperative for the economic survival of the Front Line States since most of them are landlocked and depend on South African ports and railways for the transport of their exports and imports.

The diplomacy of the Front Line States on the Namibian and Rhodesian disputes was hindered by the fact these two interests differentially affected the states in the region. The war in Namibia affected mainly Angola and Zambia, while the Rhodesian conflict affected Botswana, Zambia and Mozambique.[68] In contrast South Africa's military and economic dominance in the region means that the interests of the Front Line States converge on a wider variety of issues, which makes political cooperation and economic cooperation more feasible than on the Namibian and Rhodesian disputes. Although the Front Line States seek to act as a regional power in Southern Africa, their capability to do so is constrained by three factors. All the Front Line States, with the possible exception of Zimbabwe, have weak economies that could hardly hold up to the economic and military strains of a real regional war. Many of the states have weak political centres because of domestic political/ethnic cleavages.[69] South Africa is not adverse to using these cleavages to its own advantage.[70] South Africa's dominant economic and military position deters any aggressive action by the Front Line States against the Republic. Because of these constraints on the Front Line States' ability to act as an effective regional security grouping, SADCC can be seen as a long-term attempt to help make the Front Line States' capability to act as a regional power more commensurate with its intentions.

Southern Africa's 'diplomacy of liberation' since the mid-1970s has come full circle, back to where it was in the early 1960s. The Front Line States' diplomacy in support of the diplomatic isolation of South Africa, and economic sanctions (the 1960s agenda) can help make the economic development of the region coordinated by SADCC more effective in diminishing their dependence on the Republic. In the short term, the militant rhetoric of Mugabe and Kaunda not withstanding, the Front

Line States have stepped back from the brink in their unilateral advocacy of economic sanctions.[71]

The Front Line States have realized that effective sanctions depend on the support of the Western powers, and have decided not to unilaterally impose sanctions themselves against Pretoria. At the same time they have declared that the vulnerability of some states in the region is no excuse for the Western powers not to impose economic sanctions against South Africa.

The Front Line States have reinvigorated continental diplomacy regarding sanctions (at the OAU) and international diplomacy on the sanctions issue (in the Commonwealth and at the UN). They have developed a coordinated diplomatic strategy for the OAU, the UN and the Non-Aligned Movement. This strategy calls for the Security Council to make the sanctions package they have agreed upon to be made mandatory for all UN-member states, under Chapter Seven of the UN Charter. This sanctions package is broadly similar to the one worked out by the Commonwealth, but would be extended world-wide to all UN-member states and would be mandatory.[72]

The ANC's diplomacy of liberation

The re-emergence of the ANC as the main nationalist or liberation movement in South Africa with external links has made cooperation with the Front Line States easier. The ANC's relations with the Front Line States, especially with the two dominant states in the grouping, Zambia and Tanzania, merely formalizes for the ANC the loose and *ad hoc* cooperation which these states have given the movement since the early 1960s. The historical and personal ties which the ANC has had with the leaders of Zambia and Tanzania has been an important element in the ANC's role in the Front Line States' diplomacy. In 1969 the President of the ANC, Oliver Tambo, met delegates from Tanzania, the OAU, and the two liberation movements, FRELIMO and the MPLA in Tanzania where they pledged full support for the ANC's struggle for freedom. The 'unholy alliance' of Vorster, Smith and Portugal's Caetano was to be met with an alliance between the liberation movements.[73] Zambia and Tanzania, and now Angola and Mozambique, have given the ANC institutional and diplomatic support, which has afforded the ANC links at the inter-state level that are ordinarily more difficult for a liberation movement to pursue.

These personal ties and the firm commitment of both Kaunda and Nyerere to African liberation have given the ANC a constituency in the Front Line States with which to advocate ANC positions and influence the policy of the Front Line States. Prior to the independence of Mozambique, Angola, Tanzania and Zambia (along with the OAU) sponsored conferences at which only the MPLA, FRELIMO, SWAPO and ANC were recognized as the legitimate liberation movements.[74] The ANC, along with SWAPO, have also participated in various Front Line State Summit meetings. This diplomacy is a crucial part of the ANC's international relations. These states support the ANC in inter-African diplomacy at the OAU and at the UN, two vital forums for consolidating the ANC's legitimacy in diplomatic circles as the 'natural alternative' to the current government.

The politics of regional economic relations: SADCC

Because of the economic dominance of South Africa, politics has always influenced the economic relations among the states of Southern Africa. This was even true before the existence of the apartheid state, and will probably be true of the region after the post-apartheid South African state is created. After the Transvaal obtained self-government in 1906, the Boer government wanted to leave the customs union established in 1889 in order to escape British imperial hegemony. This threat was only withdrawn, after the Union was formed in 1910. The first attempts to develop an independent rail network in the region dates to 1894 when the Boer Republic of the Transvaal began a direct link to Lourenço Marques in Mozambique in order to escape British imperial domination. In 1955 Southern Rhodesia, then a self-governing colony, opened a direct rail line to Lourenço Marques in order to escape Afrikaner domination. After black majority rule came to Mozambique in 1975, however, white-ruled Rhodesia hastily completed its direct rail link to the Republic in order to defy international sanctions, a delay of almost fifty years in completing Rhodesia's rail link with South Africa.

Now that the Afrikaners, the descendants of the Boers, are in power, other parts of Southern Africa have questioned their relations with South Africa. Thus, SADCC's attempts to redirect the region's economic relations is not new. It does not represent the primacy of politics over economics since the economic history of the region shows that political factors have always influenced the region's economic development. What makes SADCC's plans particularly difficult, however, is the organization's attempt to reverse a century-old pattern of regional development.

Any natural regional development scheme would want to include the country with the most developed infrastructure and greatest number of ports and harbours, that is, South Africa. South Africans, such as Dr Simon Brand, Chief Executive of the DBSA, believe SADCC 'cannot succeed' because it does not take into account 'the reality of economic interdependence' between the states in the region. Development should build on the links that already exist, rather than waste resources through misallocation. Almost as a warning, Dr Brand suggests SADCC 'can reinforce the building up of tension in the region'.[75] South Africa correctly sees SADCC as an alternative to its own programme of regional economic cooperation through a Constellation of Southern African States, and as the economic counterpart to the diplomatic cooperation through the Front Line States.

The Lusaka Declaration of April 1980 stating SADCC's principles declared the organization sought to reduce economic dependence particularly, but not only, on South Africa. SADCC in fact has no other purpose. The organization was formed as a result of P.W. Botha's new regional policy.[76] The Front Line States knew their confrontational foreign policy toward the Republic would be constrained by their economic relations with the Republic.

This does not mean SADCC cannot usefully promote regional economic integration. The sad history of economic integration in Africa (for example, the apparent failure of ECOWAS to promote trade barrier reduction)[77] does not offer much hope for SADCC countries to redirect their trade away from South Africa. As in Western Europe, however, the fear of an external power could be what is necessary to promote the kind of economic integration that can bring about benefits of its own.

The current level of resistance in South Africa, and the success of the international sanctions campaign has caught the SADCC countries unprepared for South Africa's regional 'survival' policies of economic retaliation for economic sanctions. In the end this may turn out for the best since it has increased the level of foreign aid to these countries, especially from the European Economic Community (as all SADCC countries have signed the Lomé III Convention).[78] Economic liberation from South Africa, however, is a long way off. The Front Line States could lose as much as US$6.5 billion over the next three years if and when international sanctions are applied.[79] Most economists argue South Africa could withstand full sanctions for at least this long.[80] In the end, it will be domestic black resistance, not only in the form of popular struggles in the rural areas and black townships, but the power of black trade unions and the power of black consumers which will lead the state toward an accommodation with the black majority.

The preferential trade area (PTA area)

The SACU is currently the only union of its kind in Africa, although in December 1981 a number of Eastern and Southern African countries established a preferential trade area (called the PTA area) with the objective of eventually creating a customs union and economic community. It was the culmination of a long process associated with the UN's Economic Commission for Africa. At about this time (October 1981) South Africa agreed to a further revision of the revenue-sharing formula of SACU as the BLS states decided not to join the new PTA. South Africa, however, backed out of the new agreement in 1982 before it had come into operation. Apparently the South African cabinet would only revise the revenue provisions of SACU if the Botswana, Lesotho and Swaziland governments recognized the independence of the TBVC states.[81] By this time, two of the BLS states (Lesotho and Swaziland) had joined the PTA. It is possible South Africa was using a revision of the SACU as an incentive for these states not to join the PTA. The PTA would have diminish their links with the Republic by integrating their economies with black Africa. It could also be that the South Africans were running out of money.[82]

Since the PTA area includes those states which also are members of SADCC, the creation of a PTA area can be seen as a long-term strategy by these states to diminish their trade links with South Africa and promote greater inter-African trade, economic cooperation, and eventual integration. The PTA began operations in July 1984 by announcing tariff reductions. Although PTA's broader membership means it is not directly related to the South Africa issue, the significant 'pull' of the PTA towards the issues confronting Southern African states has been institutionalized. The headquarters for the Secretariat of the PTA is in Lusaka, and the Reserve bank of Zimbabwe acts as the clearing house for the transactions of goods and services within the PTA.

The PTA has just created a development bank based in Bujumbura, Burundi with initial capital of US$400 million.[83]

A number of states that take part in the PTA have conflicting political and economic loyalties. It includes the three states of the now defunct East African Community (Kenya, Tanzania and Uganda), two states with a long history of mutual political strife (Ethiopia and Somalia), and two states (Lesotho and Swaziland) that are also members of the SACU. PTA, however, recognizes this 'unique situation', and has granted these states 'temporary exemptions' from applying certain PTA provisions 'while the BLS states remain parties' to SACU.[84]

There are also ideological divisions. Those states that are 'believers' in PTA include Malawi, Lesotho, Swaziland and Zambia. The 'sceptics' include five Front Line States: Mozambique, Zimbabwe, Angola, Tanzania and Botswana. All of these states, except Botswana, have managed on socialist-oriented economies and are cautious about the kinds of economic cooperation which could disrupt their plans for socialist transformation.[85]

The PTA is not necessary to promote trade where it already exists, such as in East Africa, and it is unlikely to promote trade where it does not exist. Because the membership is so broad it lacks the urgency and political will which accompanies SADCC. The overlap in the functional areas of cooperation is apparent by comparing the PTA and SADCC action programmes. There is some concern that Zimbabwean influence in SADCC could become as great as when the country dominated the Central African Federation. This suspicion does not bode well for the future of SADCC once political change comes to South Africa.[86]

Conclusion

Just before the Boer War Lord Milner stated, 'There is only one way out of the troubles in South Africa: reform or war. And of the two war is more likely.'[87] Since the passage of the sanctions legislation in the US Congress, a regional war in Southern Africa has become more likely than ever before. The new economic warfare between South Africa and the Front Line States could easily turn into military conflict. The differing strategies for security and economic development which the states of Southern Africa have followed were based on trying to build on the past or on trying to escape from it. South Africa, seeking to build on the economic relations with its neighbours established during the colonial era, has cited the SACU and the RMA as successful examples of regional economic cooperation which P.W. Botha's government wanted to formalize and extend through a Constellation of Southern African States.[88] At a time of deteriorating regional security, the extension of these economic links were one way in which South Africa sought to guarantee a regional order, to 'shield' the Republic while the government continued with its domestic reform programme. As these efforts were quickly rebuffed by the country's neighbouring states, South Africa sought another way of ensuring a regional order favourable to its security: economic and military destabilization.[89] This policy had the added propaganda advantage of portraying South Africa as a country of peace and prosperity, amid a region of instability and economic failure due to 'Marxist' development policies.

The Front Line States believe regional security and economic development are only possible after the liberation of South Africa.[90] As stated by Polhemus (1985) 'The problem of liberation in adjacent territories is a problem in international relations and foreign policy.'[91] The primary thrust of the Front Line States' foreign policy, and to some extent that of the OAU and the diplomacy of the African states at the UN, has been to get the Western powers to acknowledge that liberation is a legitimate foreign policy objective in African international relations. This they have not been able to do. As the crisis in South Africa continues unabated, the most these states have accomplished is to get the Western powers to acknowledge that something, finally, must be done about South Africa if Western interests and influence in the region are to be preserved.

The crisis in South Africa has pre-empted any further serious effort by the Republic towards a regional foreign policy based on economic cooperation. Foreign policy has now fully given way to national security policy, which may eventually lead to war. Yet the link between South Africa's domestic policy and regional policy remains the basis for any peaceful accommodation in the region. For as long as South Africa has a government unacceptable to the majority of its people, so too will it be unacceptable to the Front Line States, and regional insecurity will remain the fundamental obstacle to further economic development in South Africa and the entire region.

This point, which is frantically made by the South African business community, is also no longer seriously denied by significant sections of the Afrikaner political elite. A situation almost unique in National Party politics, the parliamentary caucus is more *verlig* than the cabinet.[92] The main policy differences in the National Party can no longer be described along conventional *verkrampte* and *verligte* lines. The National Party is in fact a coalition of at least three groupings. The conservatives (*verkramptes*) still accept the homelands as the starting point for any political solution. A broad middle group of *verligtes*, which includes P.W. Botha and most of his administration, support Botha's original reform programme, and the second reform strategy for the reintegration of the homelands along federal and confederal models. The pamphlet 'What About the Black People?' by Stoffel van der Merwe, one of the most influential voices of reform in the National Party, represents the direction of *verligte* thinking. A third group of about thirty-five 'New Nat' MPs want to conceptually move away from the protection of minority rights through the prescription of group rights in law, and towards the protection of individual rights through freedom of association.[93] These discussions, like those at the recent Transvaal Congress and Orange Free State Congress of the National Party, are usually accompanied by talk about a Bill of Rights for South Africa.[94] Sections of the Human Sciences Research Council (HSRC) report on intergroup relations (repealing Group Areas Act, Separate Amenities Act, one education system for all, abolition of influx control) and the most recent secret document by the Broederbond, under the 'New Nat' chairmanship of Professor Pieter de Lange, indicate the extent of this group's thinking on the abolition of apartheid, and the basis for political accommodation with the black majority.[95] The report gives greater importance to the allegations in the press that the Broederbond has already approached the ANC for talks, but was initially turned away.[96]

From this perspective, the policy direction of the Afrikaner political elite maybe a more important indicator of future developments than current government pronouncements and posturing (this is also true of the ANC). 'New Nat' thinking on politics and economics in post-apartheid South Africa is not insurmountably different from Oliver Tambo's recents statements on ANC policy.[97] The 'New Nats' believe the Afrikaner's exclusivity should be abolished and the best way of guaranteeing Afrikaner survival is through the promotion of black political and economic advancement. Both the 'New Nats' and the ANC acknowledge the inadequacy of capitalism to rectify the years of economic discrimination against the black majority.[98] The ANC also supports a Bill of Rights as the constitutional means of protecting individual human rights, but it opposes the protection of minority rights on the basis of the 'group rights' concept.

As put by Adam and Moodley (1986), 'The intellectual ferment in Afrikanerdom has . . . never been greater.'[99] The Afrikaners are the true survivors, and their ability to 'opt for being part of the future' should not be underestimated.[100] The Afrikaners may yet come to terms with reality. The tragedy is that greater levels of violence, perpetrated by all sides, and greater economic hardship will undoubtedly occur before all South Africans realize they have more to gain by living together than dying separately.

Notes

1. Steyn J.H., 'The options for South Africa'. *The Sunday Star*, 8 December 1985, p. 7.
2. Bowman, Larry, 'The Substate System of Southern Africa', *International Studies Quarterly* (1, no. 11, 1968), pp. 231–61; Shaw, T., 'Southern Africa: Co-operation and Conflict in the International Sub-system', *Journal of Modern African Studies* (12, no. 4, 1973), pp. 633–55; Davies, R. and D. O'Meara, 'The State of Analysis of the Southern African Region', *Review of African Political Economy* (no. 29, 1984).
3. *South Africa 1985*, Yearbook of the Republic of South Africa (Pretoria: Department of Foreign Affairs, 1985), p. 221.
4. Geldenhuys, D., 'South Africa's Regional Policy', in Clough, M., ed., *Changing Realities in Southern Africa* (Berkeley: Institute of International Studies, University of California, 1982).
5. Geldenhuys, D., 'Regional Co-operation in Southern Africa: A Constellation of States', *International Affairs Bulletin*, South African Institute of International Affairs (3, no. 3, December 1979), p. 51.
6. Chapters on these institutions in Falkena, H.B., Fourie, L.J., and W.J. Kok, (eds), *The Mechanics of the South African Financial System* (Johannesburg: Macmillan, 1984).
7. *South Africa 1985*, op. cit., p. 313.
8. *White Paper on Defence and Armaments Supply* (Pretoria: Department of Defence, 1984), p. 1.
9. *White Paper on Defence and Armaments Supply* (Pretoria: Department of Defence, 1986), p. 12.
10. Ibid., p. 13.
11. Price, Robert M., 'Pretoria's Southern African Strategy', *African Affairs* (83, no. 330, January 1984), pp. 11–32.
12. Lowenthal, Abraham F., 'The United States and Latin America: Ending the Hegemonic Presumption', *Foreign Affairs* (October 1976).

13. Botha, P.W., 'Swiss–South Africa Association', Zurich, 1 June 1984, *Southern African Record*, SAIIA, (no. 37, December 1984), pp. 53-8; cf. Botha, P.W., 'A New Beginning', 31 January 1986 (Pretoria: Bureau for Information, 1986), p. 3; 'Introductory Statement to the Federal Congress of the National Party by South African Minister of Foreign Affairs, Mr. R.F. Botha' Durban, 13 August 1986.

14. 'A New Beginning', op. cit., (Pretoria: Bureau for Information, 1986), pp. 3-4.

15. *White Paper on Defence 1986*, op. cit., p. iii.

16. 'Call for pan-African co-operation', *South African Digest*, 5 September 1986, p. 807.

17. Geldenhuys, D., 'South Africa's Regional Policy', The Golden Jubilee Conference of the SAIIA, Cape Town, 6-7 March 1984, p. 33.

18. In light of the violations of the Nkomati Accord, whether South Africa will stop supporting the insurgent Lesotho Liberation Army remains to be seen.

19. 'Bid to ease South Africa/Lesotho Tension', *South Africa Digest*, 17 January 1986, p. 35; 'South Africa/Lesotho talks continue', *South Africa Digest*, 24 January 1986, p. 54; 'South Africa/Lesotho links normalised', *South Africa Digest*, 31 January 1986, p. 81; 'Bill for joint water Projects', *South Africa Digest*, 25 July 1986, p. 675.

20. Grundy, Kenneth, *The Militarisation of South African Politics* (London: I.B. Tauris, 1986), p. 94.

21. The government's new direction is indicated in a National Party pamphlet by Stoffel van der Merwe, called 'What about the Black People?', *South Africa International* (16, no. 1, July 1985).

22. Hallet, Robin, 'ANC changes strategy to Iran pattern of Revolution', *Cape Times*, 25 May 1985; Whisson, Michael, 'Continuing Unrest—A Small Town Perspective', *Reality*, South African Institute of Race Relations (SAIRR), (March 1985); Cobbett, W., Glasser, D., Hindson, D., and Swilling, M., 'South Africa's Regional Political Economy: A Critical Analysis of Reform Strategy in the 1980s', *South African Review: Three*, South African Research Service (SARS), (Johannesburg: Raven Press, 1986).

23. Duff, Tom, 'Recent Political Developments', *South African International* (11, no. 3, January 1981), pp. 142-46; Cobbett, Glaser, Hindson and Swilling, op. cit., (1986), p. 138; Geldenhuys, D., *The Diplomacy of Isolation* (Johannesburg: Macmillan, 1984), pp. 36-7.

24. *South Africa 1985*, op. cit., pp. 224-7.

25. Maasdorp, Gavin, 'Co-ordinated Regional Development: Hope for Good Hope Proposals' in Giliomee, H., and Schlemmer, L., (eds), *Up Against the Fences* (Cape Town: David Philip, 1985), pp. 219-33. The government's 'planned urbanization' policy has made this failure explicit see,

'South Africa's Regional Political Economy', op. cit., p. 143.

26. The 1980 report of the influential Bureau for Economic Research: Co-operation and Development, (BENSO), *Rand Daily Mail*, 19 August 1980; cited in Geldenhuys, 'South Africa's Regional Policy', op. cit., p. 154.

27. Cobbett, Glaser, Hindson and Swilling, (1986), op. cit., p. 156; Van der Merwe, 'What About the Black People?', op. cit., pp. 10-12 critically makes this point.

28. Bell, Trevor, 'The Role of Regional Policy in South Africa', *Journal of Southern African Studies* (**12**, no. 2, April 1986); Forsyth, M., 'Federalism and the Future of South Africa', Bradlow Series no. 2 (Johannesburg: SAIIA, November 1984), pp. 15-27.

29. Geldenhuys, D., 'South Africa's Regional Policy', op. cit., p. 154.

30. For example, organizations of the UN system like the UNHCR and the Commissioner for Namibia have representatives in Gaborone, Botswana; see Dale, Richard, 'Botswana Foreign Policy: State and Non-state Actors and Small Power Diplomacy', in Picard, Louis, A., ed., *The Evolution of Modern Botswana* (Lincoln: University of Nebraska Press, 1985), p. 209.

31. 'Botha seeks solution to urban blacks' legitimate rights', *Cape Times*, 16 August 1985.

32. Ibid.

33. 'The Accord of Nkomati' (Pretoria: Department of Foreign Affairs, May 1984), p. 30.

34. South African Institute of Race Relations, *Survey of Race Relations 1984* (Johannesburg: SAIRR, 1985), p. 562.

35. 'Nkomati Accord "still operating" ', *SA Digest*, 29 August 1986, p. 789. This kind of functional cooperation has seemingly continued even though Machel discon-tinued Mozambique's participation in the joint security commission set up by the Accord. The repatriation of Mozambican workers, however, may finally end it.

36. 'Labour Representatives Appointed', *SA Digest*, 6 June 1986, p. 506; Robinson, Anthony, 'Pretoria administers first bitter pill to Front Line States', *Financial Times*, 10 October 1986.

37. *South Africa 1985*, op. cit., p. 959.

38. Ibid., p. 61.

39. *Survey of Race Relations 1984*, op. cit., p. 559.

40. Bell, 'The Role of Regional Policy in South Africa', op. cit., p. 291; Cobbett, Glaser, Hindson and Swilling (1986), op. cit., p. 138.

41. Cobbett, W., Glaser, D., Hindson, D., and Swilling, M. 'Regionalisation, Federalism and the Reconstruction of the South African State', *South African Labour Bulletin* (**10**, no. 5, March–April 1985), p. 89; Van der Merwe, 'What About the Black People?', op. cit., pp. 10-20.

42. Breier, David, 'Constitutional Accommodation for Blacks', *The South*

African Foundation News (**12**, no. 1, January 1986).

43. 'South Africa: Mainstay of Southern Africa' (Pretoria: Department of Foreign Affairs, September 1985).

44. This section draws heavily on Guma, X·P·, 'The Rand Monetary Area Agreement', *South African Journal of Economics* (**53**, no. 2, June 1985), pp. 166-83.

45. Gargano, Michael D., 'Withdrawal From the Rand Monetary Area: Swaziland's Prospects', *African Insight* (**16**, no. 2, 1986), pp. 79-82.

46. Ibid., p. 79.

47. Hanlon, Joseph, *Beggar Your Neighbours* (London: CIIR, 1986), p. 89.

48. Guma, op. cit., p. 166.

49. Gargano, op. cit., p. 79.

50. Matsebula, M.S., 'Swaziland: Economy', *Africa South of the Sahara 1987* (London: Europa Publications, 1986), p. 986.

51. Hanlon, op. cit., p. 89.

52. For a balanced assessment of the costs and benefits of the RMA before the recent Rand crisis, see Guma, op. cit.

53. Matsebula, op. cit., pp. 984-7.

54. Based on Matthews, Jacqueline, 'Economic Integration in Southern Africa: Progress or Decline?' *South African Journal of Economics* (**52**, no. 3, September 1984), pp. 256-65.

55. *South Africa 1985*, op. cit., pp. 959-66; 'Economic Interdependence in Southern Africa', *Africa Institute Bulletin*, Supplement (**26**, no. 4, 1986).

56. Matthews, op. cit., p. 257.

57. Lachman, Desmond, 'Import Restrictions and Exchange Rates', *South African Journal of Economics* (**42**, no. 1, March 1974), pp. 25-42.

58. *Survey of Race Relations 1984*, op. cit., pp. 546, 822-3.

59. Gargano, op. cit., p. 81.

60. 'Swaziland Privatizes Industrial Agency', *African Business* (September 1986), pp. 7-8.

61. 'Economic Interdependence in Southern Africa', op. cit., pp. 11-12.

62. Matthews, op. cit., p. 258; Matthews, J., 'The Third Lomé Convention and its Significance to Southern Africa', *Africa Insight* (**15**, no. 4, 1985), pp. 262-9.

63. *Survey of Race Relations 1984*, op. cit., p. 827.

64. 'Front Line States Summit', *ANC Weekly News Briefing* (**10**, no. 15, 13 April 1986), p. 23; 'SADCC and Front Line States Summits', *ANC Weekly News Briefing* (**10**, no. 34, 24 August 1986), p. 19.

65. Campbell, Kurt M., 'The Front Line States' Search for Security', *South African International* (**17**, no. 1, July 1986), pp. 1-8.

66. Ispahani, Mahnaz Zehra, 'Alone Together: Regional Security Arrangements in Southern Africa and the Arabian Gulf', *International Security* (**8**, no. 4, Spring 1984), pp. 152-75.

67.   Sessay, Amadu, 'The Roles of the Front Line States in Southern Africa',
      in Aluko, O. and Shaw, T., (eds), *Southern Africa in the 1980s* (London:
      George Allen & Unwin, 1985), p. 23.

68.   Jaster, Robert S., 'A Regional Security Role for Africa's Front Line
      States', Adelphi Paper No.180 (London: International Institute for Strat-
      egic Studies, 1983).

69.   Jackson, Robert H., and Rosberg, Carl G., 'Why Africa's Weak States
      Persist', *World Politics* (October 1982), pp. 1-24.

70.   Zimbabwe Survey, *The Economist*, 21 April 1984, p. 8.

71.   Sparks, Allister, 'The Frontline pulls back from (the) brink', *The Obser-
      ver*, 7 September 1986.

72.   Ibid.; cf. 'Non-Aligned Movement Meets in Harare', *ANC Weekly News
      Briefing* (**10**, no. 36, 7 September 1986), pp. 17-19; 'The Non-Aligned
      Movement', *ANC Weekly News Briefing* (**10**, no. 37, 14 September 1986),
      p. 18.

73.   Benson, Mary, *Nelson Mandela* (London: Penguin Books, 1986), p. 176.

74.   'International Seminar on Apartheid, Racial Discrimination and Colonial-
      ism in Southern Africa', Kitwe, Zambia, 23 July to 4 August 1967,
      Sechaba (**1**, no. 11, November 1967), pp. 14-16. In April 1979, a
      conference on the liberation movements jointly sponsored by Kaunda's
      UNIP and AAPSO recognized ANC, SWAPO, and the Patriotic Front in
      Zimbabwe; Kaunda, Kenneth, 'We are at the Forefront', *Sechaba* (July
      1979), pp. 20-4. At the FLS Summit in 1982 the ANC and SWAPO took
      part, Communiqué, *Sechaba* (April 1982), pp. 6-8.

75.   Brand, Simon, 'Economic Linkages', *International Affairs Bulletin* (**8**, no.
      1, 1984), p. 44.

76.   Jaster, Robert S. (1983), op. cit., pp. 27-8.

77.   See Olanrewaju, S.A. and Falola, Toyin, 'Development Through Integra-
      tion? The Problems and Politics of ECOWAS', Chapter 3 of this book.

78.   'EEC will back ACP projects to SA links', *Zimbabwe Herald*, 21
      November 1985.

79.   Legum, Colin, 'Neighbor states could lose billions if Pretoria retaliates',
      Christian Science Monitor, 15 July 1986.

80.   Cowell, Alan, 'South Africa's might belies a regional weakness', *New York
      Times*, 27 July 1986.

81.   Anglin, Douglas G., 'SADCC After Nkomati', *African Affairs* (**84**, no.
      335, April 1985), p. 179.

82.   'South Africa or SADCC, not both', *The Economist*, 22 January 1983,
      p. 60.

83.   'PTA', *Africa South of the Sahara 1987*. op. cit., p. 214.

84.   Anglin, Douglas G., 'Economic Liberation and Regional Co-operation in
      Southern Africa: SADCC and PTA', *International Organization* (**37**, no.
      4, Autumn 1983), p. 690.

85. Ibid., p. 691.

86. Zimbabwe Survey, *The Economist*, op. cit., p. 14.

87. Pakenham, Thomas, *The Boer War* (London: Weidenfeld and Nicolson, 1979), p. 577.

.88. 'Call for pan-African co-operation', *South Africa Digest*, 5 September 1986, p. 807.

89. Jaffee, Georgina, 'The Southern African Development Co-ordination Conference', *South African Review: One* (Johannesburg: Raven Press, 1983), p. 23.

90. 'Front Line States Summit', *ANC Weekly News Briefing*, op. cit., p. 23; 'SADCC and Front Line States Summits', *ANC Weekly News Briefing*, op. cit., p. 19.

91. Polhemus, James H., 'Botswana's Role in the Liberation of Southern Africa', in Picard, Louis A. (ed.) *The Evolution of Modern Botswana*, op. cit., p. 229.

92. Geldenhuys, D. and van Wyk, K., 'South Africa in Crisis: A Comparison of the Vorster and Botha Eras', *South Africa International* (**16**, no. 3, January 1986), pp. 135-45.

93. Braun, David, 'The "New Nats"—fact or fiction', *The Star* (WAE), 21 April 1986. The term was created by the Afrikaans Political journalist, Dries van Heerden, 'The New Nats', *Frontline* (Johannesburg, March 1986), pp. 35-7.

94. In April 1986, the Minister of Justice, Kobie Coetsee told the South African Law Commission to investigate the desirability of a Bill of Rights for South Africa. He told the Transvaal Congress of the National Party in September 1986 that a Bill of Rights was 'not a question of when, but how'. At the Orange Free State Congress of the Party, Botha supported the concept of a Bill of Rights as advocated by US Secretary of State, George Shultz. See Battersby, John, 'Advocating a Bill of Rights for South Africa', *Business Day* (Johannesburg), 8 November 1986; cf. 'Minister hints at a Bill of Rights', *The Star* (WAE), 5 May 1986; Cleary, Sean, 'The Utility of Bills of Rights in Culturally Heterogeneous Societies', *South Africa International*, (**16**, no. 4, April 1986), pp. 175-90.

95. Terblanche, Stephen, 'Secret Broeder plans to change the face of South Africa' *Sunday Times* (Johannesburg), 14 September 1986. The report argues that the exclusion of blacks from the 'highest level' of government 'is a threat to white survival'.

96. Waldmeir, Patti, 'Broederbond seeks meeting with ANC', *Financial Times*, 7 April 1986. On the role of the Broederbond under the Botha administration, see Geldenhuys, D., *The Diplomacy of Isolation*, op. cit., pp. 171-5, and Geldenhuys, D., and Kotze, H., 'Man of Action', *Leadership* (**4**, no. 2, 1985), pp. 41-2.

97. Mallet, Victor, 'Interview with Oliver Tambo: a lawyer in exile', *Financial*

Times, 27 October 1986.

98. See HSRC report on intergroup relations, *The South African Society: Realities and Future Prospects* (Pretoria: HSRC, 1985), pp. 103-6 for the inadequacy of the free market to care for 'the poorer groups' in South Africa. State intervention to care for 'poor white' Afrikaners during their migration from the rural areas to the cities, is just as essential as the handling of the needs of black urban migration today. The ANC's policies on nationalized industries found in the Freedom Charter, at least as they are explained by Mandela and Tambo, are not appreciably different from the economic policies of Afrikaner nationalism in the 1930s. For a copy of Mandela's 1956 article on the Freedom Charter, see *The Struggle is My Life* (London: IDAF, 1978), pp. 53-7. Comrade Mzala, 'The Freedom Charter and its Relevance Today', in the ANC publication *The Freedom Charter* (London: ANC, 1985), pp. 78-101, goes further than the pronouncements by Mandela and Tambo, arguing for a 'people's democratic republic in South Africa', and collective and state farms in agriculture.

99. Adam, Heribert, and Moodley, Kogila, *South Africa Without Apartheid* (London: University of California Press, 1986), p. 252.

100. De Wet, Hannes, 'A new Afrikaner slogan for the future', *The Star* (WAE), 30 August 1986.

6 The EC and development efforts in Africa

Christopher Stevens

Introduction

Europe claims to have a special relationship with Africa. Perhaps the most visible manifestation of this is the annual Franco-African summit for which a significant share of Africa's leaders regularly journey to France. But it is also evident in many more fundamental connections, not least the Lomé Conventions. Although these also cover the Caribbean and Pacific, there are many on both sides who regard Africa as taking pride of place. The EC institutions, and especially the Commission, have liked to see themselves as 'defenders' of Africa against the onslaught of the IMF and the World Bank (while conveniently overlooking the important role played by the EC member states in the formulation of these agencies' policies).

Claims are one thing; reality is something else. There is evidence, for example, that Africa is being marginalized in the European market.[1] No Black African state appears on the list of most important hosts for European foreign investment, nor is this likely to change in the foreseeable future.[2] Africa receives a large share of the official aid (ODA) provided by Europe but it is very rare for the EC, as opposed to its member states, to be either the largest or the most influential aid agency in a sub-Saharan African state.

What role has the EC played in development efforts in Africa? That is the subject of this chapter, which reviews the position of Africa in formal EC development policy and the evidence available on the impact of the Lomé Conventions' provisions for trade preferences and aid.

Lomé and its place in EC policy

Conceptualizing Lomé

Signed in 1975 following the accession of the United Kingdom to the EC, the Lomé Convention was very much the product of its times. It was negotiated in the aftermath of the first oil price increase and the rise in prices for some other primary commodities. It represented a balance between an extension of traditional economic relations between ex-colonies and their former metropoles, and an accommodation with the new forces that appeared to be emerging.

Despite much rhetoric, attempts to achieve substantial reforms to international economic and political arrangements—to create a New International Economic Order (NIEO)—had not achieved much success by the mid-1970s. The Lomé Convention appeared to offer an opportunity for a group of industrialized and developing countries to break out of the impasse created in the global negotiations by establishing a regional arrangement that would incorporate a number of the items on the NIEO agenda. This would serve both as a tangible advance in the politico-economic circumstances of the Third World signatories and as a model for others to follow.

That, at least, was the idea propounded by Lomé's supporters. But as European concern at the emergence of 'commodity power' in the South has dwindled so has the desire to build upon the non-traditional elements of the Convention. Lomé II (signed in 1979) and Lomé III (1984) follow very closely the pattern of the original Convention and have not introduced any more major innovations.

If it was not a step on the road to a NIEO, how should Lomé be conceptualized? In the early years after Lomé I was signed, the extravagant claims of its supporters brought forth a welter of counter-claims alleging that Lomé was nothing more than a neo-colonialist subterfuge, and pointing to the similarity between the new Convention and its Yaoundé predecessors.[3] The Convention's modest actual impact has undermined both the claims and counterclaims. Possibly a more fruitful approach to conceptualization is to examine Lomé within the framework of patron–client relations. The patron-client approach has been adapted by Ravenhill to describe the Lomé relationship.[4] Ravenhill argues that his concept of 'collective clientelism' is an alternative to dependency theory. In fact, it is compatible with any approach that, as a minimum, admits to individual Third World countries or sub-groups having some room for manœuvre to improve their position. Within a dependency framework, any palliatives obtained by developing countries through negotiations with industrialized countries would tend to be at the expense of other developing countries and be subject to severe upper limits. Within the classical, integrationist school these restrictions would not necessarily apply, but neither would they necessarily be ruled out.

Like patron–client analysis, the concept of collective clientelism deals with a situation in which a weak party negotiates with a strong party in order to obtain favours through an exchange of non-comparable resources. As an individual seeks economic favours in return for votes, so the ACP sought trade and aid preferences in return for a reinforcement of Eur-Africa (close links between Europe and Africa): the maintenance of a sphere of influence for Europe in the Third World (whatever that might mean), and the enhancement of its international public (self-)image. As expressed by Ravenhill,

Clientelship offers the weaker parties the opportunity to claim special advantages in the relationship on account of their weakness, which can also be used to ridicule the idea that their activities might pose a threat to the stronger parties . . . like all forms of clientelism, the collective variant typified by the ACP strategy in the Lomé Convention has its origins in scarcity and insecurity: the struggle of the weak to survive in an unpredictable world in which they are unable to compete on equal terms.[5]

EC policies affecting the Third World

The EC's development cooperation policy is only one vehicle for Europe's economic influence on the Third World and not necessarily the most important. European policy on agriculture, on industrial subsidies and on exchange rates, for example, can have a much larger impact on developing countries.

Europe's Common Agricultural Policy (CAP) has a particularly important effect given the dominance of agriculture in Africa's GDP. The transformation of the EC from a major importer of agricultural products to a net exporter of an increasing number of commodities must have had profound effects on the agricultural economies of Africa. The precise nature of the impact is not easy to identify since it depends upon the commodity composition of each country's imports and exports and also on the time period selected. The three main effects of the CAP of relevance to Africa are that: it has increased world supply (and hence reduced prices) of certain temperate commodities which African states currently import, most notably cereals; second, it has increased the instability of world prices for these very same commodities; and third, it has reduced market opportunities for some African commodity exports. The first effect—reducing world prices—has improved the terms of trade of African importing countries, which would normally be considered a beneficial effect. However, some critics would argue that this short-term gain is more than offset in the long term because it has enabled African governments to neglect their own agricultural development. The other two effects—increased instability and reduced export-market opportunities—have a negative impact on Africa. In addition to these direct effects, the Common Agricultural Policy has an indirect impact on the Third World because it has distorted European investment and, hence, has resulted in EC non-agricultural output being lower than would otherwise be the case.

Various attempts have been made to weigh up all these positive and negative features of the CAP. If the analysis is restricted to the agricultural sector, the general conclusion seems to be that Africa has gained more and lost less than most other Third World regions (because it has become such a major importer of cereals). In consequence, some analyses show Africa to have gained on balance, and even those that show a negative overall effect indicate that in Africa's case the adverse impact is quite small.[6] If the analysis is broadened to take account of the indirect effects then the consensus is that Africa has lost welfare as a result of the CAP although, once again, it has fared better than most other Third World regions.[7]

Apart from the CAP there are two other principal elements to Community-level policies affecting the Third World. They are the commercial policy (CCP) and the partially common aid policy. The existence of the common external tariff (CET) means that the foundations of Europe's foreign trade regime are established at Community level. The member states adopt a common position at meetings of the GATT and UNCTAD and have negotiated at EC level a host of bilateral and multilateral trade agreements with the Third World states. The CET's purity is reduced in practice as member states adopt to a greater or lesser extent national policies that influence trade flows. Most important are the growing number of non-tariff barriers (NTBs) to imports. Whereas the EC institutions have an unambiguous responsibility for setting tariff policy, their position on NTBs is much less secure. The member states have negotiated bilaterally numerous 'voluntary exports restraints' with developing countries. None the less, the most important NTB for the Third World, the Multifibre Arrangement (MFA) which limits LDCs' exports of clothing and textiles, is still negotiated at Community level.

Unlike trade and agriculture, aid policy is only partially common. There are three main strings to Europe's aid bow: multi-annual Community-level programmes, annual EC programmes, and member state national programmes.

The largest of the multi-annual Community-level programmes is financed outside the EC budget. It is the European Development Fund (EDF) which finances the aid provisions of the Lomé Convention. The EC also has financial protocols to its commercial agreements with a number of other Third World states, most notably those in North Africa and the Middle East. These provide a multi-annual commitment although the funds are drawn from the normal annual budget.

Second, there are annually-agreed aid programmes financed out of the EC budget. These include the food aid programme and the non-associates' aid programme that covers all countries lacking a specially negotiated multi-annual agreement. This substantial group includes India, China, ASEAN, and the whole of Latin America.

Finally, there are the member states' bilateral aid programmes. Some of these tend to reinforce the geographical and political bias of the EC's efforts, but with some member states the reverse is true. The French and Italian bilateral programmes, for example, have a similar geographical focus to that of the Community, but the United Kingdom has used its aid to offset the EC's geographical emphasis on Africa and its neglect of South Asia. The proportion of aid channelled through EC and bilateral programmes varies widely between the member states from 59 per cent of Italian official aid disbursements in 1979 to 6–9 per cent of those from Denmark, France and the Netherlands. Overall about 10 per cent of the Ten's official aid is channelled through Community aid programmes.

Although the Lomé Convention is one of the EC's most prominent regional preferential arrangements, it is not the only such European accord nor is it the only North–South package of its kind. The EC has a predisposition to favour formal trade and cooperation agreements partly because it establishes the legitimacy of Community as opposed to national action. The result has been a series of 'framework agreements' with different parts of the Third World. The Lomé Convention has also spawned imitative action by other countries. The most notable example is the USA's Caribbean Basin Initiative (CBI) which was openly compared to the Lomé Convention when first unveiled in 1982. Like Lomé it covers aid and trade provision, has sections on investment and has political overtones. The current Nordic initiative for a min-NIEO can also be seen as an attempt to emulate, and improve upon, the regional package approach of Lomé.

There are over twenty of these bilateral and multilateral agreements, that have been described as a 'pyramid of privilege' by virtue of the fact that those agreements at the 'top' provide more favourable treatment than those at the base. The countries at the top have preferences not only over developed countries but also over other LDC members of the pyramid. It is therefore a shifting pyramid, since improvements in the terms for some states can cut the value of concessions made to others.

The ACP are at the apex since they are granted a more liberal trading regime and more aid per capita than any other group. Next in the hierarchy come the North African countries. The trade provision of their bilateral agreements tend to be tightly tailored around past trade patterns so as to enable the countries to continue to export traditional lines even if they are potentially competitive with European production, but to discourage diversification into such lines. Their aid is detailed in quinquennial financial protocols to the trade agreements and is primarily in the form of soft loans from the European Investment Bank (EIB). The other non-EC Mediterranean countries tend to come further down the pyramid, although some have special relations with particular European member states, for example, Turkey with Germany and Cyprus with the United Kingdom. Most other developing countries benefit, on the trade side, only from the generalized system of preferences (GSP), and for aid from the catch-all 'non-associates' aid budget.

Hence, almost all the states of Africa are covered by framework agreements that are placed in the top two echelons of the pyramid of privilege. All independent Black African states are now parties to the Lomé Convention: until 1985, Mozambique and Angola were outside Lomé, but Mozambique participated in the Lomé III signing ceremony, and Angola joined subsequently. Most North African states are covered by bilateral agreements. The only African states with which the EC does not have a formal agreement are South Africa, Namibia and Libya.

ACP trade performance during Lomé I and II

But what have such concessions been worth? There is a common view that preferential trade agreements have conferred few, if any, benefits on their members and that these have primarily been the result of trade diversion rather than trade creation. The structure of trade preferences leads to an a priori assumption that any benefits conferred on the EC's partners are due, at least in part, to trade diversion. Many of the preference favour one group of extra-EC suppliers over another. Only a few remove or substantially reduce the protection that would otherwise be afforded to domestic EC suppliers. The decline in MFA tariff levels during the 1960s and 1970s has also lent support to the a priori expectation that tariff preferences are unlikely significantly to alter the competitive position of exporters.

Yet there are some trade creating preferences in the Lomé pack and preferences do not only cover tariffs. The Lomé Conventions have also covered non-tariff barriers (NTBs) and have included aid provisions likely to have some trade impact. Moreover, like most preference agreements, they are based upon relationships that have been built up over many years and cover a wide range of contacts. Hence preference agreements have to be interpreted as more than the provision of a few percentage points tariff reduction.

Identifying the impact of the EC's trade preferences on trade patterns involves a number of methodological problems, most notably disentangling the effects of the preferences from other economic changes. The problems are magnified because the ACP, and especially Africa, have experienced particularly sharp changes in their economic circumstances in the years during which the preferences have applied. The Lomé I and II periods coincided with substantial changes in world supply and demand for commodities that are important to the ACP, and also markedly different levels of economic growth in Europe compared to other actual and potential ACP trade partners.

The impact of the external environment on aggregate ACP trade flows is particularly large because this trade is heavily concentrated on a very small number of countries and of commodities. Almost 70 per cent of ACP exports to the EC are made by just eight members of the sixty-six country group. The eight principal products exported account for over 70 per cent of the total, by value. A similar geographical concentration is evident for ACP imports from the EC.[8]

The eight most important ACP exporting countries include two oil exporters—Nigeria and Gabon—whose exports to the EC have been heavily influenced not only by the fluctuations in world oil prices but also, more specifically, by the emergence of North Sea production during the Lomé I period. Three of the other major exporters are also countries which have experienced a markedly poor economic perform-ance over the period as a whole—Ghana, Zaïre and Zambia. Almost all of the major export commodities of the ACP have experienced sharp changes in world prices over the Lomé I and II period.

One approach to disentangling the 'Lomé effects' from other causes is to adopt a three-stage analysis: (1) analysis of changes in aggregate trade patterns; (2) identification of any sub-regional patterns that might be attributable to Lomé such as a shift in trade from formerly associated to formerly non-associated states; (3) analysis of the commodity compo-sition of trade to indicate any changes relevant to Lomé.

ACP trade shares

The most promising methodology for analysing ACP aggregate trade patterns in terms of a possible impact of the Lomé Convention is that developed by Moss and Ravenhill.[9] The methodology concentrates on an examination of changes in market shares rather than in the volume or rate of growth of trade. The data used are ACP figures on exports and imports. This has the advantage of 'controlling' for changes in local circumstances. Hence, if cocoa production in one ACP state falls sharply there is no reason to suppose that exports to the EC will be cut disproportionately to exports to other destinations. It is also possible to compare ACP performance with that of relevant control groups. These include both functional and geographical sub-groups of the ACP and non-ACP comparison countries.

The picture painted by this share-change analysis is not encouraging either for the ACP or for the proponents of Lomé as a significant influence on trade patterns. The Lomé provisions might have been expected to result in an increase in the share of ACP exports going to the EC. The ACP enjoy preferences over their competitors in the EC which they do not have in other markets. There might also be some expect-ation of an increase in the EC's share of ACP imports. Although there are no reverse preferences under Lomé, the Convention does require that all EC countries receive at least 'most favoured industrialized country' treatment, which in the case of several European states represents an improvement on the pre-Lomé regime.

Such expectations are not borne out by figures on trade to 1984 compiled and analysed by Moss and Ravenhill.[10] The EC's share of both ACP exports and imports fell during the Lomé I and II periods (see Table 6.1). The ACP were also markedly less successful than other

Table 6.1   EC–AP trade shares (per cent)

	Pre-Lomé 1970–4	Lomé I 1975–9	Lomé II 1980–4	Lomé I & II 1975–84
EC share of:				
Total ACP exports	45.6	38.7	36.7	37.7
Non-oil ACP exports	46.3	47.1	41.9	44.5
EC share of:				
Total ACP imports	41.9	42.5	38.5	40.5
Non-oil ACP imports	42.4	41.7	35.9	38.8
ACP share of:				
EC imports from LDCs	20.5	16.4	16.9	16.6
Non-oil ACP share of: EC imports from				
non-oil LDCs	27.3	22.8	20.1	21.5

Source: Moss, J. and Ravenhill, J., 'The Evolution of Trade under the Lomé Conventions: the First Ten Years', in Stevens, C. and Verloren Van Themaat, J., (eds), *Europe and the Changing International Association of Labour* (London, forthcoming, 1987).

LDCs in maintaining their share of EC imports. Hence, at an aggregate level, ACP–EC trade patterns have changed in the opposite direction to what might have been anticipated. Even if the analysis is limited to trade between the EC and non-oil ACP the results are not markedly different. Although the share of the EC in non-oil ACP exports fell only slightly over the Lomé I and II periods combined, this conceals a sharp fall during the Lomé II sub-period. A similar picture applies with respect to the EC's share of non-oil ACP imports.

The problem in interpreting these figures is to establish the counter-factual: what would have happened in the absence of the Lomé Convention? A large number of reasons can be adduced to explain the falling trade.[11] EC–ACP trade might have declined even further in the view of the poor economic performance of both partners. It is clear that the ACP performance during the period of the two Conventions has been disappointing overall. The ACP share of world trade increased during the 1970s, but has fallen in the 1980s. Between 1970 and 1979 the value of ACP trade with the world more than quadrupled, but between 1980 and 1984 it fell by an annual average of 7 per cent.[12] The benefits of the regional preferences in Lomé were insufficient to offset negative changes outside the Convention.

Sub-regional patterns

Although Lomé has not altered for the better the pattern of ACP trade at an aggregate level, the period since it was negotiated has been particularly turbulent. This failure may present an unduly bleak picture of the potential for regional trade preferences. It is important, therefore, to identify any other evidence that the preferences have had an effect on trade patterns.

A comparison of changes in trade shares between previously associated and non-associated countries provides a suggestive indicator. The 'previously non-associated' relations are between four groups of states:

— between the Commonwealth ACP and the original six members of the EC,
— between UK and the Yaoundé states,
— between Denmark and Ireland and all the ACP,
— and between the previously non-associated ACP and all the European states.

If the Lomé Convention had an effect on trade patterns one would expect to find a greater increase/smaller decrease in trade between previously non-associated states for which it resulted in a marked improvement in trade regime than between previously associated states. Evidence analysed by Moss and Ravenhill tends to indicate that previously non-associated groups performed better than others. Denmark and Ireland, for example, increased their share of non-oil ACP exports (compared with no change for the EC as a whole), and registered no change in their share of ACP imports (compared to the declining share of the EC as a whole). Trade between the original six countries of the EC (EC 6) and the Commonwealth ACP also tended to fare better than the average. Only British trade with the Yaoundé group failed to buck the trend, largely because of the poor economic performance of the United Kingdom and its growing self-sufficiency in oil.

A significant feature of the sub-regional pattern of trade has been the replacement of the United Kingdom by France as the ACP's principal European trading partner. In 1970 the United Kingdom accounted for 34 per cent of ACP exports and 36 per cent of imports, compared to France's 20 per cent and 25 per cent. The average shares for 1982–4 were 14 per cent and 21 per cent for the United Kingdom, and 27 per cent and 35 per cent for France. Although some other members of the EC increased their shares of ACP trade (notably Germany for ACP exports and Italy for ACP imports) these were not sufficient significantly to reduce the national market concentration of ACP trade.

Commodity structure and 'new' imports

Another possible indicator of the impact of the Lomé Convention is the commodity composition of ACP exports. The Convention's provisions are particularly liberal on manufactured goods (which have duty free entry) and on some temperate agricultural goods for which ACP preferences, while quota restricted, are more favourable than those for other suppliers. The aggregate picture is that there has been no major commodity diversification during the Lomé period, but at the margins there is evidence of rapid increase in the value of exports of 'new' products, although the absolute values are still very small.

Many of the ACP countries are either members of the least developed group or, if they are further up the development 'league table', they tend to be very small economies. One consequence is that it would be unrealistic to expect manufactured exports to develop on a large scale during the ten-year time horizon of Lomé I and II. If new manufactured, processed agricultural or temperate agricultural exports have emerged they are likely to be still small in absolute value terms. Hence, they are likely to be overlooked by analysis of aggregate trade flows. There is no expectation that such new exports will significantly alter the composition of ACP trade even in the medium term because of the very low absolute levels. But, it can be argued, if the Lomé Convention has had any effect on trade patterns, this is the place to look for it.

There have been two major analyses of ACP commodity diversification at the margins (Stevens and Weston 1984, McQueen and Read 1986).[13] These analyses start from an a priori identification of the type of exports most likely to have been encouraged by the Lomé Convention. This leads to an analysis of EC import statistics, mainly at the six-digit NIMEXE level, to identify which states have entered the market. The final step is to identify, wherever possible, the background to the development of new exports and the role, if any, of the Lomé Convention provisions.

The picture that emerges from this analysis is much kinder to the Lomé Convention than are the aggregate analyses described above. Not only have a significant number of ACP countries experienced a rapid increase in a wide range of new products, but also this trend has continued into the 1980s despite the difficult overall economic circumstances.

The Stevens and Weston analysis of trade data from 1975 to 1980 revealed eleven countries that had increased exports of manufactured, processed agricultural and temperate agricultural goods over the period at a rate faster than the IMF index of non-oil developing country export unit values. Some seventy-five product categories (at the six-digit level) were involved, roughly evenly split between agricultural and industrial products.

McQueen and Read have extended the analysis to include 1984 trade data. Their conclusion is that the pattern of diversification has continued. By 1984 the ACP had begun to record new exports in 128 categories. Particularly strong increases were found, both in the value of exports and in the number of ACP countries involved, for textiles, clothing, leather and leather goods, meat, fish and food preparations.

A notable feature of both analyses is that the ACP states involved in new exports include not only the middle income, Caribbean members of the group, but also a significant number of African states. The list includes Ethiopia (twelve new products), Mali (seven products), Zaïre (seven products), Tanzania (eleven products), Benin (six products) and Central African Republic (four products). Just over half of the sixty-six country group has been able to diversify into at least four new manufactured, processed agricultural or temperate agricultural goods (see Table 6.2).

Given the small scale of many of these new exports it is likely that in each case their development has been heavily influenced by country-specific factors. The most satisfactory way to identify the causal role of

Table 6.2   Non-traditional ACP exports into the EC showing significant changes 1975–80 and 1980–4

NIMEXE description	No. of exporting states 1980	No. of exporting states 1984	Value (Ecu mn) 1980	Value (Ecu mn) 1984	Per cent increase in value 1975–80	Per cent increase in value 1980–4
06 Plants, flowers etc.	4	12	10.6	19.7	75	86
16 Meat and fish preparations	9	18	82.4	176.6	108	114
21 Miscellaneous edible preparations	3	13	1.9	29.4	306	1,447
41 Hides and leather	7	17	5.0	56.6	225	1,032
42 Leather and articles	2	12	2.5	4.8	inf	92
55 Cotton yarn and fabrics	9	31	32.6	80.9	161	148
56 Man-made fibres and fabrics	1	1	4.7	6.1	inf	30
59 Ropes, special and industrial fibres	2	4	14.8	5.8	698	−61
60 Knitted garments	4	16	17.1	47.6	434	178
61 Woven garments	6	17	25.0	22.9	276	−8
71 Stones and imitation jewellery	4	21	3.3	2.7	inf	−18
85 Electrical machinery	4	18	4.8	1.2	96	−75
94 Furniture and bedding	4	20	4.2	2.5	2,276	−40
Total of above items			208.9	456.8		119
*Additional products**						
07 Vegetables			16.8	29.9		78
08 Fruit (grapefruit & melons)			6.4	11.4		78
62 Terry towelling			0.2	1.1		450
91 Watch movements			0	1.6		inf
Total of additional products			23.4	44.0		88
Percentage change in index of export unit values of non-oil LDCs					+79	−10.9

*   Additional products are those not originally listed by Stevens, C. and Weston, A., 'Trade Diversification: Has Lomé Helped?' in Stevens, C. (ed.) *EEC and the Third World: A Survey 4—Renegotiating Lomé* (London, ODI, 1984), p. 33.

Source: McQueen, M. and Read, R., 'Prospects for ACP Exports to the Enlarged Community', in Stevens, C., and Verloren Van Themaat, J., eds., *Europe and the Changing International Division of Labour* (London, forthcoming, 1987).

the Lomé Convention would be a series of country-level case studies. This has not been done because of the high resource cost involved. However, there have been two country case studies—of Mauritius and Côte d'Ivoire. In addition, McQueen and Read have examined the trade preferences granted by the Lomé Convention for most of the more important new exports to identify whether or not they provide a significant margin over other suppliers and hence, by implication, whether the preference appears to be a plausible influence on trade.

There seems to be clear evidence in the case of Mauritius that the Lomé Convention played a part in the development of new exports. A significant inward movement of capital and expertise occurred from Hong Kong in the mid-1970s which seems to have been attracted by the prospect of preferential access to the European market. This formed a symbiotic relationship with indigenous and other foreign capital and contributed to the initial stimulus to the development of exports. Since then, the rate of growth of new exports has slowed and Mauritius has been subject to some non-tariff restrictions. However, as discussed below, restrictions have been imposed more flexibly on Mauritius than on non-ACP suppliers and so the Lomé Convention has continued to provide some preference.

In the case of Côte d'Ivoire the Lomé Convention appears to have had a much smaller impact; however, this is because the country already enjoyed similar preferences in the original EC six, especially France, which remains its most important market for new exports. Hence, there was little change between the 'before' and 'after' Lomé situation.

The analysis of ACP preference margins (tariff and non-tariff) on new products suggests that they are sufficiently large to have had some effect in facilitating the new exports. The ACP benefit from a 50 per cent reduction in the CAP variable import levy for rice, for example. ACP exports of fresh beans are zero rated, compared to a CCT of 13 per cent plus a minimum levy of 2 Ecu per 100 kilos. ACP canned tuna exports benefit both from tariff free access (compared to a CCT of 24 per cent) and sympathetic treatment of rules of origin.

A significant preference which has benefited these new exports is the fact that they are either exempt from NTBs that apply to other suppliers, or the restrictions are imposed more sympathetically. The MFA, for example, is not applied *per se* either to the ACP or to a number of Mediterranean countries. The Mediterranean states (Cyprus, Malta, Morocco, Tunisia, Turkey and Yugoslavia) have signed bilateral restraint agreements which are similar to the MFA controls but, arguably, less stringent. Certainly, a number of these Mediterranean suppliers have been able to increase exports more rapidly than the average. The market share of Morocco, Tunisia, Turkey plus Spain and Portugal for example, increased by almost 50 per cent between 1976 and 1983.[14] The restrictions on ACP exports of clothing and textiles are even more flexible. Most comment has been attracted to the fact that the EC *does* impose some form of control despite the free access provisions of the Lomé Convention. VERs have been imposed on Mauritius' exports in the French and UK markets.[15] In addition, import surveillance has been introduced for ACP exports of MFA products. However, so far, these restrictions have not significantly hindered ACP exports of clothing. In a situation in which volume restrictions have encouraged super-competitive suppliers to move into higher unit value items, it could be argued that the differential treatment of the ACP provides them with some degree of protection against competition from other third-party suppliers.

Aid

Much was made at the time of the Lomé I signature of the EC's commitment to a five-year aid budget that it was 'contractually obliged' to spend, regardless of the political complexion of ACP governments. Allied to this was the formal responsibility of the ACP to select the projects that would be financed. The then EC Commissioner for Development Cooperation, Claude Cheysson, was fond of using words to the effect of 'this is your money—you may do with it what you will'.

Practice has diverged increasingly from theory. In important respects, the implementation of Lomé aid *has* been different from traditional donor–recipient relationships. But, as time has passed, the EC has increasingly tried to establish a more conventional donor–recipient approach. So far this has been achieved largely through administrative means, making use of the Commission's power under the Convention to take the final financing decision. Although Lomé accords to the ACP the responsibility for choosing projects, it also places with the EC responsibility for actually deciding to approve finance. This 'power of the purse' enables the Commission to delay approving a project until the ACP have agreed to make the changes required by the EC.

An attempt was made during the Lomé III negotiations to shift this

EC power from the *de facto* to the *de jure* level. This attempt was associated with the concept of 'policy dialogue', an imprecise phrase that has changed meaning over time.[16] The ACP regarded policy dialogue, probably correctly, as an attempt by the Commission to alter the formal balance of power for aid decision-making to give the Community a legitimate role in the selection of projects and the right to comment upon ACP sectoral policies relevant to the success of the project. They resisted this idea, and Lomé III does not contain any significant changes to the theoretical balance of power on aid decision-making. But it does continue the EC's 'power of the purse' and so the trend is likely to continue away from the spirit that pervaded the original Lomé towards a traditional donor–recipient relationship.

In the absence of any qualitative difference between Lomé aid and other forms of development assistance, an assessment of the Conventions has to be based upon the more prosaic criterion of whether the aid is administered well. On these, narrow grounds, Lomé aid has been heavily criticized. These criticisms of aid fall into two groups which are given different weights according to the critic. One is that the aid has been poorly used, too often financing projects that are either badly designed or nullified by a hostile policy environment. The other is that aid has been badly administered by the donor, with lengthy delays in spending.

The task of assessing the validity of the criticism that Lomé aid has been misapplied is made difficult by the absence of any systematic, comprehensive and rigorous evaluation of aid projects. While a little economic and a lot of financial evaluation does occur, the EC has no adequate counterpart to the World Bank's Operations Evaluation Department, with its independent power for in-depth examination of any project and its annual audit of project performance. However, a *prima facie* case exists that EC aid has been poorly applied, if only because there has been a generally low success rate with aid in Africa.

Not surprisingly given that Lomé aid accords the recipients an unusual degree of freedom in setting spending priorities, the few good, independent evaluations that have been made show that its impact has varied according to the characteristics of the recipient government. Where the recipient has a well-prepared, effectively implemented plan of action, Lomé's flexibility has made it particularly valuable; when governments have been self-serving or simply disorganized, the results have been less impressive.[17]

Critics of the EC's efficiency as an aid donor argue that it is slow and cumbersome, due to duplication of appraisal procedures, over-centralization, and the meddling of the member states. Lomé aid projects have to surmount three separate, and usually sequential, approval procedures: first by the EC's quasi-diplomatic delegation in the field, then by the Commission (DG VIII) and finally by a body representing the member states—the EDF committee.[18] Possibly the main lesson that Lomé practice provides is on the effect of aid bureaucratization. The sad fact is that, once negotiated, aid agreements are administered by a cadre in which innovation and risk taking are rarely rewarded, and failure through delay or over-control even more rarely punished.

Conclusion

When opening the negotiations for Lomé III in October 1983, the then Chairman of the ACP Council of Ministers, Botswana's foreign minister Archie Mogwe, complained that despite two Conventions, no ACP state had entered the league of newly industrializing countries. Hyperbole aside, one might well ask when comparing Africa's situation in the mid-1980s with the mid-1970s what the 'special relationship' with the EC has achieved. In the mid-1970s, the problem facing some African countries was how to absorb the burgeoning export revenue from oil, copper, coffee, tea or cocoa without distorting the economy. By the mid-1980s, the preoccupation of almost all states was how to adjust to sharp falls in the terms of trade and, often, a fall in real GDP. Yet, during this period of severe reversal, Africa was supposed to be enjoying the benefits of being in the EC's 'sphere of influence'.

There are three reasons for the failure of Lomé to live up to expectations. First, of course, external relations are only one set of factors influencing development; domestic African factors are also very important. Second, the EC is only one of the external influences on Africa, and the Lomé Convention is only part of its influence. Third, the Lomé Convention has not been implemented in the way that, in 1975, many ACP had hoped.

The relative importance of internal and external factors on African development is a complex and controversial area that is dealt with elsewhere in this book. It is not the purpose of this chapter to enter into the debate in any detail. However, it is sufficient to note that internal factors have some influence on development without having to take a view as to whether this influence is more or less important than that of external factors and, African states have themselves recognized that domestic policies have not been satisfactory in recent years. In its statement of *Africa's priority programme for economic recovery 1986-1990* the OAU has admitted candidly that, in their plans and budgets,

most African countries have tended to perpetuate and even accentuate the dependency of our economies through over reliance on foreign resources (financial and human) and have led to the misallocation of domestic resources through reduced shares for such high priority areas as agriculture, manpower, industry and massive expenditure on foreign consumer goods and non-productive investment projects.[19]

At the international level, the EC is the source of only one set of influences, and the Lomé Convention provisions form only part of this set. Since 1980 primary commodity producers have suffered from the deepest and most prolonged slump in world prices since 1945, and of all the Third World regions, Africa has been the most severely affected. The extreme volatility of exchange rates has greatly increased the difficulty of foreign exchange management and the severity of mis-management. The combination of deteriorating terms of trade, changes in exchange rates and the shift to higher levels of real interest rates compared to the mid-1970s has created a debt service burden for Africa compared to which Lomé aid appears puny. This can be illustrated by comparing the Lomé III aid budget of US$6 billion (over five years) with a debt service burden for sub-Saharan Africa of some US$11.6 billion per year over 1985-7.[20]

Finally, even within the narrow confines of the Lomé provisions, practice has not lived up to expectations. The first Lomé Convention was an ambiguous document and, with the receding threat of 'commodity power', the EC has shown no inclination to interpret it in a way that confers additional benefits on the ACP. Still less has there been a willingness to extend the provisions in subsequent conventions. This inertia on the part of the EC member states has been to the detriment even of EC Commission attempts to increase its formal power. During the Lomé III negotiations it could be argued that the EC member states were the most influential supporters of ACP interests because they did not wish to disturb the status quo.[21]

These gloomy conclusions do not mean that the EC has had no effect on development efforts in Africa, nor that the Lomé Convention has been a total failure. The EC has been able to provide palliatives to make

Africa's economic condition more bearable, but it has not been able to contribute to any fundamental structural change in Africa's situation in the world economy. More than this should not have been expected. Where Lomé has fallen short of realistic expectations is that the palliatives it has purveyed have been smaller, and Africa's economic distress greater than could have been envisaged in 1975.

Notes

1. Moss, J., and Ravenhill, J., 'The Evolution of Trade Under the Lomé Conventions: The First Ten Years', in Stevens C. and Verloren Van Themaat, J., eds, *Europe and the Changing International Division of Labour* (London, forthcoming, 1987).
2. Page, S., 'The Structure of Foreign Investment: Implications of Recent Changes for Europe and the Third World', in Stevens, C. and Verloren Van Themaat, J., (eds), *Europe and the Changing International Division of Labour* (London, forthcoming, 1987).
3. See for a review of these arguments, Shaw, T., 'EEC–ACP Interactions and Image as Redefinition of Eurafrica: Exemplary, Exclusive and/or Exploitive?', *Journal of Common Market Studies* (18, no.2, 1979).
4. Ravenhill, J., *Collective Clientelism: The Lomé Convention and North–South Relations* (New York, Colombia University Press, 1979).
5. Ibid., p. 23
6. Matthews, A., *The Common Agricultural Policy and the Undeveloped Countries* (Dublin, Gill and Macmillan, 1985).
7. See Burniaux, J.M., and Waelbroeck, J., 'The Impact of the CAP on Developing Countries: A General Equilibrium Analysis', in Stevens, C., and Verloren Van Themaat, J., (eds), *Pressure Groups Policies and Development* (London, Hodder and Stoughton, 1985); Bureau of Agricultural Economics (BAE), *Agricultural Policies in the European Community* (Canberra, Australian Government Publishing Service, 1985).
8. The eight main ACP exporting states are Nigeria, Côte d'Ivoire, Zaïre, Cameroon, Kenya, Ghana and Gabon. The most important commodities are, in order of importance (1980-4 average): crude petroleum, coffee, cocoa, refined copper, petroleum derivatives, non-coniferous wood, sugar and iron ore.
9. Moss, J., and Ravenhill, J., 'Trade Between the ACP and EC during Lomé I', in Stevens, C., ed., *EEC and the Third World: A Survey 3—The Atlantic Rift* (London, ODI, Hodder and Stoughton, 1983).
10. Moss, J., and Ravenhill, J. (1987), op. cit.

11.   Argwal, J.P., Dippl, M., Langhammer, R.J., *EEC Trade Policies Towards Associated Developing Countries—Barriers to Success* (Kiel, Kieler Studien, 1985).

12.   Moss, J. and Ravenhill, J. (1987), op. cit.

13.   Stevens, C., and Weston, A., 'Trade Diversification: Has Lomé Helped?', in Stevens, C., ed., *EEC and the Third World: A Survey 4—Renegotiating Lomé* (London, ODI, Hodder and Stoughton, 1984); McQueen, M., and Read, R., 'Prospects for ACP Exports to the Enlarged Community', in Stevens, C. and Verloren Van Themaat, J., eds., *Europe and the Changing International Division of Labour* (London, forthcoming, 1987).

14.   Teunissen, J., and Blokker, N., *Textile Protectionism in the 1980s: the MFA and the EEC's Bilateral Textiles Agreements with the Developing Countries* (CEPS Working Documents no. 15 [Economic], Brussels, July 1985).

15.   Stevens, C., and Weston, A. (1984), op. cit.

16.   See Stevens, C., *The New Lomé Convention: Implications for Europe's Third World Policy* (CEPS Paper no. 16, Brussels, 1985); Stevens, C., *Negotiating Lomé III: An Example of North–South Bargaining* (IDS Discussion Paper no. 215, Brighton, May 1986).

17.   Hewitt, A., 'Malawi and the EEC: The First Seven Years'; and Parfitt, T., 'EEC Aid in Practice: Sierra Leone' in Stevens C., ed., *EEC and the Third World: A Survey 4—Renegotiating Lomé*, op. cit.

18.   Stevens, C. (1984), op. cit.

19.   OAU, *Africa's Priority Programme for Economic Recovery 1986–1990* (OAU, Addis Ababa, 1985).

20.   World Bank, *Towards Sustained Development in sub-Saharan Africa* (Washington, August 1984).

21.   Stevens, C. (1986), op. cit.

7 The Commonwealth and development efforts in Africa

Olusola Akinrinade

Introduction

Cooperation for development in the Commonwealth is nearly as old as the broader, global context of international cooperation for development. Commonwealth countries are affected either as suppliers or recipients in many capital aid and technical assistance programmes, some purely intra-Commonwealth and some involving cooperation with non-Commnwealth countries or the United Nations and its agencies.

A small group of independent Commonwealth countries—Australia, Britain, Canada, India, New Zealand, Pakistan and Ceylon (now Sri Lanka)—met in Colombo in 1950 to launch the first post-war initiative in regional economic cooperation in financial and technical assistance in an area where the vast problems of poverty beg a description. The Commonwealth initiative fired the imagination of other non-Commonwealth countries in the region, which then joined the Colombo Plan. This led, in turn, to other Commonwealth initiatives like the Special Commonwealth African Assistance Plan in 1960, the Commonwealth Cooperation in Education Scheme and the Commonwealth Caribbean Assistance Plan. However, the Commonwealth was not, and has never been expected by any of its members to become, a self-contained aid 'bloc'.

While the Commonwealth is not an aid 'bloc', it can be seen as an important means for channelling aid, just as Commonwealth links can, and have, provided an important motivation for cooperation. The relative ease with which cooperation in the Commonwealth takes place rests upon several important foundations. Among these foundations are:

the ability to use a common working language; similarities in governmental institutions and administrative methods; a tradition of informality in intra-Commonwealth dealings; and a wide range of well-established contacts and friendly relationships through commercial interaction, universities, professional and voluntary associations. These important factors can be used to advantage in overcoming the complexities of international cooperation in technical assistance. All too often the machinery of assistance from wider international institutions is hampered by difficulties of language, by a lack of familiarity with institutions and/or the working of the machinery of government. The wide range of tangible and intangible contacts among Commonwealth countries and the advantages of background knowledge should be taken into consideration either in examining the practical possibilities of technical cooperation within the Commonwealth or in judging the effectiveness of such cooperation.

The possibility of economic cooperation within the Commonwealth framework, and of technical assistance from the more senior members of the association, can be isolated as one of the major reasons that prompted anglophone African states to become members of the organization. Kwame Nkrumah, the first leader of Ghana had urged the developed Commonwealth countries at the Prime Ministers Conference of 1960 to increase their flow of aid to Africa in order to strengthen relations with Western countries. At about the time of independence, some other Commonwealth African countries had expressed similar sentiments. Zambia[1] and Nigeria are two cases in point.

Commonwealth assistance to Northern Rhodesia (as Zambia was known prior to independence) had taken concrete forms in terms of funds, training facilities and provision of experts in many fields of development and scientific advancement. The governing authorities in the country considered that capital aid and technical assistance programmes provided through the Commonwealth association opened up new horizons for many developing countries and that a lot of economic advantages were likely to accrue from the commercial and industrial ventures being undertaken in developing states. It was expected that membership would enable Zambia to benefit from these programmes. Economic considerations were a significant factor in Nigeria's decision to remain a member of the Commonwealth on achieving independence. Douglas G. Anglin commented in a study in 1964 that, while economic factors had not been decisive in determining Nigeria's foreign policy, there were occasions when their impact was significant—one of these was Nigeria's decision to join the Commonwealth.[2] Nigeria's expectations of economic assistance from Commonwealth membership pre-dated independence and cut across party lines. The Prime Minister asserted that the country's economy was closely linked to the Commonwealth network and the intention was to strengthen those links to the mutual advantage of all concerned. In particular, it was hoped that the Commonwealth would develop into a closer trading community.

Although these two instances cannot be directly replicated for all Commonwealth African states, the overall pattern was similar for the majority of the states. Commonwealth assistance to these states started on a bilateral level with such programmes as the British Commonwealth Assistance Loans Scheme and the Canadian Commonwealth African Technical Aid Scheme. These schemes formed the framework for the development of the Special African Assistance Plan, which was the first Commonwealth-wide expression of support for Africa's development aspirations.

SCAAP: the bilateral phase of assistance

The economic development of Commonwealth countries in Africa was a subject of review at a meeting of Commonwealth Prime Ministers held in May 1960. At that meeting, it was agreed that the possibility of cooperative action between members of the Commonwealth in the form of development assistance should be examined at the next meeting of the Economic Consultative Council. The council subsequently met in September and considered recommendations made in a report prepared by senior economic officials. It noted that Commonwealth countries were already providing aid bilaterally and were also making substantial resources available through international organizations. In order to focus attention on this effort and to help further in meeting the urgent need for assistance in raising the living standards in the less-developed African Commonwealth countries, the Council decided to initiate a Special Commonwealth African Assistance Plan, hereafter referred to as SCAAP. The Plan was initiated with a view to expanding the assistance given to Commonwealth countries in Africa.

Under this initiative Commonwealth countries were to give all the assistance they could to the less-developed Commonwealth African countries. In part this would consist of capital aid, but it was expected that most countries would contribute mainly in the form of technical assistance of various kinds, including the provision of experts, training facilities and the sharing of experience gained in dealing with the problems of development. The provision of aid under the plan would not be channelled through any particular developmental institution, rather it was to be disbursed bilaterally along with increased support for existing aid-giving international organizations. In essence, the Plan was not set up to coordinate assistance from different countries, but to expand the overall total through negotiations between Commonwealth countries in Africa requiring assistance and those Commonwealth countries providing it.[3]

The assistance provided under the Plan fell into two broad categories: (a) capital aid, and (b) technical assistance. Both could be given under bilateral arrangements or through international agencies, particularly UN agencies, cooperating in the UN Technical Assistance programme. Capital aid was further divided into grants, loans and investments, and the supply of equipment. Technical assistance programmes included assistance with the recruitment of staff, the supply of experts, teachers and advisers, consultancy services, provision of scholarships, fellowships and other awards, and the provision of places in institutions of higher education. The technical assistance programme got a boost in the operating year 1961–2 when the British Overseas Service Aid Scheme (OSAS) was launched. Under the scheme, the services of expatriate officers working in the overseas civil service including administrators and professional officers (numbering some 13,000 in its first year) were to be retained, or recruited, for a period of ten years or for as long as their services were required. Already, the technical assistance programmes included the training of indigenous officers. An important result of the OSAS was that many African officers could now be trained on the job in their own countries.[4]

As anticipated by the Economic Consultative Council, the principal countries cooperating in the Plan were already providing technical assistance to these countries in various forms. The main participants were Britain and Canada, with contributions from Australia, New Zealand, India and Pakistan. Thus substantial participation was limited to countries outside the African continent, although there were instances of technical cooperation as between Nigeria and Kenya, Ghana and the Gambia, and Nigeria and Tanzania. Commonwealth African countries, while willing, were unable to provide much assistance to each other as all lacked the necessary resources because they were developing countries, all faced with the problems of development.[5]

From outside Africa, the capacity of the newly independent countries to give assistance was severely limited. These developing countries could not afford to give much assistance because they were themselves in need of assistance with their programmes for development and were equally urgently in need of capital aid and personnel. In spite of this, there were instances of offers of assistance. Malaysia was typical of the group of developing countries themselves requiring assistance. Throughout the lifespan of SCAAP, Malaysia was actively engaged in economic development programmes and although it was not in a position to contribute financial aid, it did consider sympathetically requests for technical assistance in the form of training facilities in such fields as rubber planting, land development and the cure of tropical diseases. Malaysia, together with other developing countries like Sri Lanka, Hong Kong and Malta, also made offers of scholarships under the Commonwealth Scholarships and Fellowships Plan (CSFP).[6]

Despite the severity of their own problems both India and Pakistan showed interest in the Plan and made appropriations for it in their regular budgets. Assistance was provided mainly in the form of supply of experts and the provision of training facilities including the provision of scholarships and fellowships and training places in institutions of technical and higher education. Assistance from Pakistan later expanded to include the supply of equipment. India's own contribution was especially felt in the area of educational development where assistance was rendered both on bilateral and multilateral levels. The bilateral programmes included a number of scholarships awarded under the CSFP and the Indian General Scholarships Scheme (GSS). While the number of scholarships awarded under the CSFP was small, India's own GSS enabled hundreds of students from Commonwealth African countries to pursue courses in that country. Multilaterally, the Indian government made contributions through the UNESCO Emergency Programme of Financial Assistance to African countries for Educational Development and the UNESCO African Fellowship Programme.[7]

The lack of New Zealand diplomatic representation in Africa made it difficult for that country to initiate its programme of assistance under which it intended to send experts to Africa and make grants of capital aid and/or equipment. Its initial offers of assistance were mainly for awards enabling African students to pursue a variety of courses in that country. To overcome the problem caused by lack of diplomatic representation, contacts, which later proved useful, were made with various bodies connected with aid administration, including UN agencies, and very soon the country was able to send its own experts on assignments to African countries.[8] Australian assistance was provided both bilaterally and by cooperation in international agencies and UN Technical Assistance programmes. It also participated in the Commonwealth Cooperation in Education Scheme. Assistance provided included the supply of experts and the provision of training facilities. Training was given under both the CSFP and special Australian schemes. Awards made under the Commonwealth Cooperation in Education Scheme included training awards to teachers, Visitors' Awards, and scholarships under the CSFP. Scholarships were also granted under the Australian International Awards Scheme. Included in the Australian programme was capital aid in the form of supply of books and the supply of equipment. Gifts of books were made to Ghana, Nigeria, Tanzania, Botswana and Swaziland among others.[9]

Canadian technical assistance to Commonwealth countries in Africa pre-dated SCAAP, although it increased thereafter. The Canadian programme was essentially a responsive one: the amount of aid given to a particular country was dependent largely on the nature of requests made. Requests were favourably considered if they were (a) clearly related to the social and economic development of the country and, where possible, to a planned programme of development; (b) supported by a clear statement of the objective of the particular project or programme for which assistance was required; and (c) for assistance of a type which Canada was well-fitted to supply. It was expected by the Canadian government that assistance programmes should be of a joint nature, with both the recipient and donor governments contributing to the success of the programme according to their capabilities. Recipient countries assumed obligations, for example, for the provision of counterpart personnel who could be trained to replace Canadian experts when they left, and to see that persons selected for training were properly qualified to benefit and were given an opportunity to put their training to use on their return. Canadian financial assistance was almost exclusively in the form of grants, but provisions were made for lending facilities to enable Canada to lend capital to developing countries on terms comparable with those of the International Development Agency. Capital aid consisted in the supply of materials, equipment, commodities and associated services and projects using such resources were undertaken in many countries.[10] Moreover, Commonwealth African countries, in their development plans assigned a high priority to educational and technical assistance, and Canada's aid programme concentrated on these sectors. Each year larger numbers of qualified Canadians were available to undertake assignments in Africa and the training programme involved even more persons. Scholars and Fellows under the CSFP came from almost all Commonwealth countries in Africa for courses lasting from six months to two years, in a great variety of subjects. An equal variety characterized the nationalities of, and the studies pursued by, the students enjoying awards under the Canadian SCAAP. The duration of courses under the latter ranged from three months to five years. Apart from these training programmes, places were also provided by the Canadian governments for students from Commonwealth African countries sponsored by the UN and its specialized agencies. The biggest contributor to the SCAAP, however, was the government of the United Kingdom.

In general, the nature of the British aid programme for Commonwealth countries in Africa reflected the pattern established before independence. The governments of many of these countries continued to look upon Britain as the major source of their external aid. Britain was the largest donor of capital aid. Grants were made to independent countries in support of development programmes—among the beneficiaries were Sierra Leone, Nigeria, Uganda and Tanzania.[11] Grants were, however, a minor part of British capital aid, a larger proportion being made in the form of loans. The interest charges on these loans were supposedly moderate and terms for repayment long.[12] Capital aid was also given in the form of equipment and books for universities and other institutions, such as those given to Nigeria and Ghana. Another form of capital aid came in the provision of budgetary assistance to some states. On the attainment of independence, the poorer ex-colonial territories found themselves confronted with serious difficulties in balancing their budgets. The very serious efforts made to develop their economies to the point of self-sufficiency led to increases in budgetary expenditure, which in the short term at least, went far ahead of practical increases in revenue. The problem was particularly acute in Malawi and the Gambia, and Britain provided budgetary assistance to both countries. Very substantial budgetary aid was also given to the southern African territories of Botswana, Lesotho and Swaziland.[13]

British technical assistance was usually provided in response to requests from the governments. High priority was given to technical assistance as it was seen as being a prerequisite of effective development. The most substantial part of this assistance was provided under the OSAS which enabled the governments of recipient states to retain and recruit administrative, professional and technical staff in Britain for their establishments until local staff could be trained to take over. The facilities were made available to all territories which had not become independent by 30 September 1960. Thus, the scheme applied to all Commonwealth countries in Africa except Ghana which was already independent by that date, along with Nigeria and Sierra Leone, both of which elected not to participate.[14] Independent Commonwealth African countries entered into mutual technical cooperation arrangements with the United Kingdom under which assistance was provided in a variety of ways: (1) specialist advisers or the services of British firms of consultants; (2) technical services from UK government funds and provided by such organizations as the Directorate of Overseas (Geodetic and Topographic) Surveys and Overseas Geological Surveys;[15] (3) education and training facilites in the United Kingdom; (4) university teachers, teacher training instructors and technical and secondary school teachers under the Commonwealth Cooperation in Education Scheme; and (5) scholarships and bursaries under the same scheme. The number of persons involved in these forms of cooperation was considerable.

Education and training was a major part of the United Kingdom's technical assistance efforts. For example, a substantial amount of British equipment was provided for educational, training and research purposes, often as part of combined schemes involving the provision of experts and/or training facilities.[16] Increased assistance was provided for universities and other institutions of higher education. Many of these universities had in fact been founded and developed with British capital aid. Financial assistance was also provided for research purposes. By far the largest part of the grants for research were disbursed in East Africa, with contributions in various degrees to Central, West and Southern Africa. Britain also supported research in a number of institutions in the United Kingdom aimed at solving various problems peculiar to Africa, and Commonwealth countries in Africa were regular users of the many special courses established at universities, training institutions and government departments in Britain to help in meeting the needs of developing countries, especially in the administrative, economic and social development fields.[17] The Institute for Development Studies (IDS) affiliated to Sussex University and established in 1967 is worthy of note in this regard.

Britain's institutional arrangements for administering overseas aid were reorganized in October 1964 with the establishment of the Ministry of Overseas Development under a minister. The new ministry assumed responsibility for all financial aid to independent countries previously administered by the Department of Technical Cooperation. For the remaining dependent territories, the Colonial Office remained responsible and it consulted with the new ministry, over the provision of budgetary aid. The Ministry, however, assumed responsibility for development aid to the dependencies, acting in agreement with the Colonial Office.[18] In order to make the most effective use of aid, developing countries normally need external technical assistance to help with its deployment. The establishment of the new ministry facilitated the provision of technical assistance in connection with individual projects of capital aid. In August 1965, a British government White Paper[19] on the work of the new ministry was published. The declared objective of the British aid programme was to help developing countries in their efforts to raise living standards. The special claim of developing Commonwealth countries upon British resources for aid, was acknowledged. Technical assistance was accorded the highest priority and new initiatives including the introduction of interest-free loans in appropriate cases were undertaken. Also included was the adoption of a policy of close coordination of technical assistance with financial aid in order to achieve maximum effectiveness. In order both to help recipient countries with their economic planning and to ensure that British aid was given in the most effective way, increasing use was to be made of British economic missions sent, in agreement with overseas governments, to examine the development problems facing these countries and to advise on measures necessary to overcome them. The missions were usually composed of experts drawn from the academic and professional fields, and their reports often formed the basis of discussions between the overseas governments concerned and the British government about Britain's future aid to the country in question. In Commonwealth Africa in 1965, such missions visited Lesotho, Botswana, Swaziland, the Gambia, Malawi and Tanzania; another went to Kenya to examine the land transfer plans of the Kenya government.[20].

Essentially, the programmes of the individual countries broadly outlined above formed the basis of their assistance to Commonwealth African countries under the Special Commonwealth African Assistance Plan which was in operation until the end of the 1960s. By 1967, however, the programme of African assistance within the Commonwealth had become a part of a larger framework of assistance to developing countries.

The multilateralization of assistance

The Commonwealth Programme of Technical Assistance

The 1964 Commonwealth Prime Ministers meeting launched a new phase in the development of the Commonwealth with the decision to establish the Secretariat as the administrative organ of the organization, transferring such duties away from the British Commonwealth Relations Office. The 'Agreed Memorandum' which set up the Secretariat has as one of the duties of the new organ, that it should 'assist the new member governments, at their request in advancing, and obtaining support for, development projects and technical assistance in a variety of fields on a multilateral Commonwealth basis, as appropriate'. The Secretariat started operations in 1965 with the appointment of its first Secretary-General, Arnold Smith, and the initial core members of staff. With the consolidation of the work of the Secretariat, technical and developmental assistance to African states became a part of an overall Commonwealth programme of technical assistance to less-developed members of the organization. Technical assistance in the Commonwealth, as already seen, was, until this time, essentially a bilateral affair.

Between 1964 and 1967, it was suggested at a number of Commonwealth meetings that it would be useful to examine the possible Commonwealth initiatives to supplement the existing programmes in the field of development assistance. Proposals were made for cooperative action in a number of fields at these meetings and, in accordance with a decision of Prime Ministers made in September 1966, a meeting of senior officials concerned with aid administration and development convened at Nairobi in May and June 1967.[21] These officials considered proposals which sought to achieve the aims set forth at the meeting of Heads of Government in 1964 'not merely to increase the economic strength and material well-being of recipients, vital though these considerations are, but also to strengthen the links between countries of the Commonwealth by encouraging their peoples to work closely together in a variety of ways'.[22] The meeting drew up a plan for Commonwealth Technical Assistance Programmes to give those governments which requested it expert assistance in assessing technical assistance needs, in formulating requests for assistance, and putting people in touch and finding people to meet these needs.[23].

The Commonwealth Technical Assistance Programme formulated at Nairobi was designed to cover areas in which the Commonwealth relationship gave special advantages. The scheme provided for: (1) assistance through the bilateral arrangements of Commonwealth governments; (2) a headquarters group in the Commonwealth Secretariat to be available to assist and advise governments on request; (3) third-party financing by which personnel could be drawn from a developing Commonwealth country for service in the headquarters group, or in another country, with a third country meeting all or part of the costs; and (4) Commonwealth teams to be organized by the Secretariat for missions to a Commonwealth country, the members to be drawn from other Commonwealth countries, but financed bilaterally or on a third-party basis.[24]

At the initial stages, the programme was expected to concentrate on meeting the planning, rather than the operational needs of governments. It was expected that it would develop pragmatically in the light of experience. The headquarters group was expected to build up a specialized knowledge of aid sources within the Commonwealth as it was expected that it would advise on sources of such assistance. The programme proceeded as expected and in the four years of its operation provided assistance that proved beneficial to almost all Commonwealth low-income countries, with most African members except Ghana, directly benefiting. At times the African states provided experts who served in other countries. Programmes executed in Africa included the technical assistance assignments carried out by two headquarters officers in the area of transport and communications in Kenya; visits made to Botswana by experts to advise on taxation and royalty matters and on the development problems posed by the prospects of a major mining industry. Sierra Leone, Uganda, Tanzania and the East African Community (now defunct), all received experts who came to advise or report on various issues including new industrial projects and technical needs in Sierra Leone, public administration in Uganda and Kenya, and the drawing up of a transport and communications plan for the EAC.

The Commonwealth Programme of Technical Assistance operated largely in the fields of planning including sectoral analysis, preparation of projects, plan execution, statistics, finance and public administration (particularly development administration), and cooperation in joint development programmes. The programme made an effective, albeit limited, contribution to fostering Commonwealth developmental cooperation. It added a new phase to international cooperation for development through the headquarters group, a team of four Secretariat

officers who undertook short-term technical assistance assignments in
various parts of the developing Commonwealth. It facilitated the
meeting of technical assistance needs on a 'third country' basis, financed
under bilateral programmes through arrangements made by the Secretariat. While third-party financing of programmes often proved
successful, it was recognized that the scheme proved administratively
difficult to operate.[25] But by this time there already had developed
in the Commonwealth, a spirit of voluntary partnership which was to
find collective expression in a new scheme called the Commonwealth
Fund for Technical Cooperation (CFTC).

The contemporary situation: the Commonwealth Fund for Technical Cooperation

The Commonwealth Programme of Technical Assistance functioned
from 1967 to 1971. Experience with the programme pointed to the
desirability of expanding its operational role, broadening its scope and
making it administratively more flexible. It was therefore agreed that a
Commonwealth multilateral fund should be established, to which all
members might contribute. Detailed proposals for the establishment of
such a fund were worked out at a series of meetings of Commonwealth
officials and endorsed by Commonwealth Heads of Governments at
their meeting in January 1971. The new fund, designated as the
Commonwealth Fund for Technical Cooperation (CFTC) was formally
set up on 1 April 1971, when a majority of Commonwealth governments
had agreed to participate and financial resources amounting to a quarter
of a million pounds had been pledged.

The CFTC was established as 'a collective contribution to raising
living standards, developing human resources and building the structures of modern society among a quarter of the world's peoples'.[26] It is
a cooperative undertaking designed to assist Commonwealth developing
countries to derive greater benefit from the human resources available
in other member countries in the pursuit of their national development
goals. The Fund demonstrates the value of a multilateral channel for
mutual assistance and also, complements existing Commonwealth bilateral aid schemes by responding to developmental priorities which are
not always met by such programmes or other multilateral aid arrangements. The Fund exists to undertake technical assistance projects in
developing countries of the Commonwealth. It basically assists in seven

ways. Firstly, by supplying experts where they are most necessary, at the specific requests of member governments. Secondly, by helping countries to build up their own expertise by enabling their personnel to be trained in other Commonwealth countries. Thirdly, by financing studies conducted by consultants, which can stimulate key sectors of a country's economy. Fourthly, by assisting countries in expanding their exports and earning crucial foreign exchange. Fifthly, by giving specialist advice to governments on legal, economic, financial and statistical matters. Sixthly, by helping in the establishment of new industries and in improving productivity in existing industries. And, finally, by supporting practical cooperation between countries in food production and rural development, education, law, health, women's affairs, science and technology, economic affairs and management development.

For organizational efficiency these activities have been grouped into three programmes, namely: the General Technical Assistance Programme, which covers the provision of technical assistance in a wide range of inter-related fields of economic and social development; the Education and Training Programme, which supports the training of personnel from Commonwealth developing countries in other Commonwealth developing countries; and the Export Market Development Programme, which provides for technical assistance geared to the expansion of exports and underwrites market research and trade promotion studies.

The General Technical Assistance Programme, operating in an area in which the Secretariat's aid functions began, has remained the mainstay of the Fund's activities. Under this programme, help and advice have been given in a wide range of developmental fields, including planning and plan implementation, statistics, finance, tourism, transport and public administration. African states have both been recipients and donors of assistance. For example, individual Ghanaian experts have been engaged to advise on public service reforms in Lesotho. An Indian expert provided the government of Ghana with statistical advice on national accounts, and advisers were also provided for the Gambian government for the development of national statistical services. Important national transport projects were undertaken in Zambia by Canadian advisers. Other projects have concerned such areas as the formulation of sectoral development plans (East Africa), the development of natural resources and tourism (Mauritius and Botswana), the establishment of new industries and hydro-electric power development

(Southern Africa). Several experts and consultants have been recruited from African countries to assist other developing countries on the continent or elsewhere.[27] Technical assistance for regional organizations has continued to assume increasing importance in the Fund's activities. This has stemmed from the conviction of the Fund that regional cooperation benefits several countries at once. Through the provision of staff for the organization and scholarships for the training of local staff, the CFTC helps a range of regional institutions to be of wider service to their regions. Training is also supported in cooperation with inter-governmental and non-governmental bodies.[28]

An off-shoot of the General Technical Assistance Programme is the Technical Assistance Group (TAG). The TAG provides consultancy services to member states in selected areas of high priority to governments. These include the development of petroleum and other natural resources, maritime boundary limitation and fisheries access agreements and statistics—areas in which the TAG's services are well-established. The TAG has been extensively involved in advising governments in designing the legal and fiscal frameworks within which petroleum exploration and development can successfully take place. Since 1983, TAG has provided advice on petroleum development to seven African countries—Ghana, Sierra Leone, Tanzania, the Gambia, Uganda, Seychelles and Mozambique (the last named not being a member of the Commonwealth). In five of these projects, TAG staff formed part of government teams negotiating with the oil companies.[29] In response to the balance of payments problems faced by many countries, the group has added a debt management capacity to its services to members.[30]

The Education and Training Programme is concerned primarily with the training of personnel from Commonwealth developing countries in other Commonwealth developing countries. The programme operates mainly through the provision of awards enabling countries to share their educational and training facilities more easily and thus to assist in each other's development. Requests for CFTC support for education and training projects are channelled through the agencies, including ministries and departments, which governments have appointed for this purpose. Priority is given to study or training programmes designed to contribute towards providing manpower skills that are required for economic and social development—for example, in agriculture, education, public administration, transport and communications. Within priority subject fields, particularly favourable consideration is accorded to proposals for the training of technicians and other middle-level workers in government, industry and commerce. Examples of awards made in this category were the training in Nigeria and Sierra Leone of agricultural extension workers from the Gambia. A number of awards are also made for first degree and postgraduate studies which have a clearly identifiable vocational or professional bias, or which could not be provided in the universities of the requesting countries. A particularly valuable feature of the Education and Training Programme is that it provides non-institutional forms of training that are not easily financed under many other aid programmes. Non-institutional or informal training programmes sometimes include study visits or temporary attachments, both in the public and private sectors, designed to enable trainees to gain first-hand experience of actual operations in other developing countries of the Commonwealth where expertise and new concepts have been successfully developed. Governments have sought support for study visits or training attachments in a number of fields, including in-service training in India for government officers from Kenya, in small-scale industries and internal marketing for small businesses, and a study tour of cooperatives in Kenya by a senior cooperative officer from Swaziland. The programme is able to give assistance for certain types of seminars or workshops in developing countries, provided that these have development orientation and include a substantial training element that is likely to enhance the professional competence or technical skills of participants, and that increased practical Commonwealth cooperation in education and training is likely to arise from them.[31]

Necessary as financial and technical assistance are, they are not by themselves sufficient. It is essential that developing countries are able to earn more foreign exchange. Increasing foreign exchange earnings has always been one of the most pressing problems of developing countries. Remedying this problem means more exports. Improved access to overseas markets is desirable but not enough, unless backed by effective marketing techniques. The highly sophisticated merchandising and promotional techniques that are normally necessary to open a new market in turn require sophisticated expertise and the early expenditure of foreign currencies, both in short supply in many developing countries. It was these thoughts that were behind a highly significant proposal made at a meeting of Commonwealth Trade Ministers for the establishment of a Commonwealth Export Market Development Scheme to use resources in the often neglected fields of market

development, market research, design and packaging advice, and
sophisticated trade promotion necessary to develop new export markets
for the products of the economically less-advanced Commonwealth
countries. This led to the formation of a Trade Promotion Study Team
which wrote a report for the consideration of Commonwealth Senior
Economic Officials meeting in London in June 1971. An enlargement of
the CFTC to embrace this new programme was recommended at this
meeting.[32]

As expected, the programme seeks to provide developing countries of
the Commonwealth with technical assistance in the field of export
promotion. The kind of activity that could be financed under this
programme is designed to lead to better export performance. For
example, technical assistance can be provided in packaging and labelling
for exports, export documentation, setting up of institutions for
standardization and quality control. Market surveys and research
studies can also be undertaken or commissioned in respect of products
with export potential. The changing world trading environment and the
varying priorities of national development plans have made it necessary
for the Export Market Development division of the CFTC to respond by
developing a number of project formats to suit the particular requirements of the country being assisted and the products being promoted.
Among the projects are the Buyer–Seller Meets, Contact Promotion
Programmes, Export Business Intensification Programmes, Integrated
Marketing Programmes and the conduct of market surveys and giving of
on the spot advice.[33]

Buyer–Seller Meets are large, single-country trade exhibitions,
backed by detailed supply and demand analysis and preparatory work
on product adaptation. Following intensive research in the supplying
country and the target market, the Buyer–Seller Meet presents a range
of carefully selected and adapted products from the supplier to potential
buyers in the market, with the object of achieving immediate orders and
developing long-term business. Follow-up action is taken to facilitate
and maintain contacts and monitor orders. Only a few countries have
benefited from this. Contact Promotion Programmes are smaller, highly
concentrated attempts to put sellers in direct touch with buyers, again,
after careful research in both exporting and importing countries. They
concentrate on a limited range of products on which research is followed
by the visit of a trade mission of exporters to the target market to contact
identified importers. Naturally, more countries have benefited from
the organization of these programmes. Export Business Intensification

Programmes are designed to maximize not only direct exports to a chosen market from all possible sectors in the country being assisted, but also explore possibilities for joint ventures for exports to the target market or to third countries and to provide short-term and long-term expertise to help improve export performance. The aim of the integrated Marketing Programme is to provide technical inputs in product design, quality control and export packaging for a particular product sector and to follow this up with an aggressive marketing strategy to promote sales to a selected market. Such integrated assistance, covering both product development and marketing, is expected to lead to optimum results through sustained increases in export earnings. Market surveys are undertaken to pinpoint import demand in overseas markets as well as any constraints to imports, and to provide appropriate marketing advice to assist the penetration of these markets. These surveys provide detailed market intelligence on which exporters can base promotional strategies or undertake product and packaging development to ensure that their products meet market requirements. Products which have been the subject of market surveys include those as diverse as rum, palm-oil, computer software and agricultural equipment, and almost all Commonwealth developing countries have benefited from this type of assistance.

The Export Market Development division of the CFTC also provides experts on short-term or long-term assignments to fill gaps in technical expertise and experience in government ministries, export promotion authorities or state trading organizations. Consistent with the CFTC philosophy of fostering technical cooperation among developing countries, experts are drawn from across the Commonwealth and are selected for their special knowledge of particular facets of export market development. For example, Tanzania had assigned to it a Sri Lankan export costing and pricing adviser while a Ghanaian timber marketing adviser was assigned to Belize. These advisers frequently form part of an integrated programme of export assistance to a particular country. Advisers help national export promotion authorities put into effect the recommendations of market surveys, or exporters to prepare for Contact Promotion Programmes or Buyer–Seller meets. Their assignments are sometimes a direct result of earlier project recommendations. The services of advisers have also been utilized to set up infrastructural facilities for export development such as export credit guarantee institution, export promotion councils, shippers' councils and standardization and quality control organizations. All advisers, as well as consultants undertaking market surveys or organizing Contact Promotion Programmes, Buyer–Seller meets and other projects, have attached to them a counterpart officer from the relevant ministry or export promotion authority of the recipient country, to ensure the transfer of information and expertise so that future work can be carried on by the counterpart at the conclusion of the adviser's term of service or the end of the export promotion project.[34]

Kenya is one country that has benefited from the organization of Buyer–Seller Meets. Except for one market study, Kenya had not received any Export Market Development Assistance until 1978. Kenya had already developed import substitution industries and these industries were in a position to work more than one shift, utilize potential capacity and expand into export production, provided markets were available. A Buyer–Seller Meet was first organized for Kenya in May 1978 in New York. This resulted in firm orders worth more than US$5 million in garments, furniture, sporting goods, chemicals and pharmaceuticals, ceramic products, canned foods, and so on. Subsequent Meets have been held for the country in Cologne, London and Tokyo. Kenya is also an established recipient of Contact Promotion Programmes and market surveys, among an increasingly wide variety of countries. Others that have benefited in Africa include Mauritius, Nigeria, Tanzania, Zambia and Zimbabwe.

The development-related programmes of the Commonwealth have not been exclusive to the CFTC. In varying degrees other divisions of the Secretariat are engaged actively in functional cooperation in a wide range of fields including rural development, food production, science and technology, health care, youth leadership, legal affairs and public administration. Over a number of years, the organization has witnessed a transformation as the socio-political balance of its membership has shifted in favour of developing countries. This has encouraged the organization to address itself increasingly to various issues relating to development at a time when the North–South conflict on the transfer of resources from the developed world to the developing countries is deepening in the international system. NIEO issues were first introduced into Commonwealth discussions at the Heads of Government meeting in 1975 in Kingston, Jamaica. Since that time the organization has been committed to the search for a more equitable international order. Different crises facing developing countries, including protectionist trade barriers, falling commodity prices, crippling international debt and food security problems causing famine in various parts of Africa with many Commonwealth countries being affected, have come to the attention of the Commonwealth. Various panels have been set up to look into these problems and make recommendations. The Secretariat has been involved in various international negotiations directed at creating the New International Economic Order.[35]

Moreover, the Commonwealth as a body, through the technical arms of the Secretariat, was an active participant in the various negotiations between the ACP states and the EEC on the side of the ACP group which contains an impressive number of Commonwealth countries, both in and outside Africa. This is in addition to the various reports the Secretariat commissioned on behalf of many of the members in preparation for negotiations. Although given their different levels of development members of the Commonwealth belong to different sides in the debates aimed at creating a new international economic order, the disagreements have not adversely affected the structure of the organization in a radical way, although it is difficult to say whether the impact of Commonwealth involvement in the negotiations has been more than marginal, even when the various reports commissioned by the body and its Secretariat are taken into consideration.

Concluding remarks

Given the constant crises that beset Commonwealth political relations and the constant threat to its survival as an international organization, it is noteworthy that the Commonwealth Secretariat has been able, mainly through the Commonwealth Fund for Technical Cooperation, to carve for itself a useful developmental role, especially in its attempt to utilize available resources in developing countries without necessarily having to depend on the developed countries for everything. One cannot but note the contributions of the various countries that participated in the bilateral programmes of assistance encompassed by the Special Commonwealth African Assistance Plan, although the usefulness of certain programmes is subject to doubt. In this category are the various loan 'assistance' programmes. As the years progressed, capital and interest repayments rendered this assistance meaningless, and eventually, more funds changed hands, but from the developing to the developed countries rather than the other way round. In many cases 'assistance loans' were given to 'help' potential defaulters meet repayment schedules and the value of such loans were indeed questionable.

The importance of this point is perhaps realized when it is known that a greater proportion of British capital assistance, the largest contributor of capital assistance to the programme, was in the form of loans.

The transition to multilateral assistance has brought the efforts of the Commonwealth into sharper focus Commonwealth-wide involvement in technical assistance has been transformed from mere consultation and planning to actual execution of programmes. Also, the CFTC was a pioneer in promoting the now widely accepted concept TCDC (Technical Cooperation among Developing Countries). Right from its inception, the CFTC has concentrated on enabling developing countries to help each other. This is consequent on its belief that experts from developing countries often have experience more relevant to their country of assignment than similarly qualified experts accustomed *only* to advanced countries. Equally, training is more effective the closer the environment is to the conditions in which the trainee will eventually work.

Over the years the impact of the organization's efforts has been felt. A few examples should suffice. Under the CFTC's programme for small countries, for instance, trainees from African countries have continued to benefit from CFTC sponsorship. Gambians, for example, have been trained in aquaculture, agricultural management and rural development, educational management, statistics, community development and small industry financing, promotion and management. Trainees from the small Southern African countries of Lesotho and Malawi have followed small industries' courses in India; Lesotho students have trained elsewhere in Africa in meteorology, post and telecommunications engineering, diplomacy, human resources management and accounting. Trainees from Swaziland have pursued courses in public accounts, film and television production and business administration in other African countries.[36]

The work of the Industrial Development Unit (IDU) is also worthy of note. The IDU has been most active in the field of agro-industries. When it is realized that most Commonwealth African countries are heavily dependent on agriculture and that food production is a key priority in these states, the importance of the unit's activities cannot be over-emphasised. Seventy-five per cent of IDU projects are related to agricultural development, either supplying agricultural inputs such as fertilizers, pesticides and farm implements, or processing raw materials from the crops, livestock, forestry and fisheries sub-sectors to meet basic needs for clothing, shelter, food products and educational materials. The IDU has assisted Sierra Leone to develop commercial fish-smoking, sugar, fruit and vegetable processing industries, and has assisted Nigeria in the manufacture of food-processing equipment. Other industries assisted include meat by-products in Uganda, edible oil in Zambia, and fertilizers, pesticides and farm machinery in the SADCC region. In the latter group of states, the IDU has played a significant part in promoting integrated industrial development. Apart from agro-industrial development the unit has rendered assistance in other areas of industrial development. For example, it has assisted Tanzania in small-scale industrial development with support given for the development of textiles, lime, solar salt, footwear, metal working and coconut products and engineering industries. Among projects in the pipeline to be assisted are the development of the leather tanning industry in Malawi, and agricultural bags and hand tools in the Gambia.[37]

The agro-industrial programmes are complemented by the agricultural and fisheries programmes. CFTC programmes are being geared to assist in increasing food production in the most affected countries. The body has a Food Production and Rural Development Division (FPRD), which has continued to assist countries to increase their food production capacity by organizing specialized manpower training courses in agricultural and rural development. Because drought has afflicted many parts of Africa, the efficient performance of agricultural and irrigation schemes, which is central to increasing food production in many of these countries, becomes very crucial. Largely to assist member countries in this important area, the FPRD designed a training course for senior agricultural and irrigation managers from Africa (and Asia) with responsibilities in their countries for staff training. Two courses were held, the first with twelve participants from Africa (and seven from Asia), at the Indian Institute for Management, Bangalore, in March 1984, and the second at Mananga Agricultural Management Centre in Swaziland in May 1985 with eighteen participants from Africa. The FPRD courses were only supplemental to the broader full-time and short courses and working attachments supported under the CFTC's Fellowship and Training Programme, of which rural development, fisheries and forestry have long been of importance. In 1983–5, trainees from a broad range of African countries, as well as Guyana, Cook Islands, Fiji, Solomon Islands, Papua New Guinea and Sri Lanka, were supported on agricultural management courses at the Mananga Agricultural Management Centre. African trainees have been supported to study rural development project management at the Eastern and Southern Africa Management Institute in Tanzania, the Pan-African Institute for Development in Zambia, where stress is placed on project evaluation, and a similar institute in Cameroon which specializes in integrated rural development.[38]

Finally, we may also note the CFTC's regional cooperation programmes which have proved to be equally useful to African countries. Regional cooperation benefits many countries at once. Among the most obvious of the programmes being operated in Africa is the support to SADCC—the Southern Africa Development Coordinating Conference. The IDU has given substantial assistance to the area's plan for integrated rural development. It collaborated with SADCC in organizing a workshop in 1984 which attracted substantial financial support for industrial projects from outside investors and a meeting of SADCC mining officials early in 1985. It is continuing to assist SADCC on request in securing finance and technical assistance for various projects relating to mining development. The IDU continues to give technical advice to SADCC's programme of industrial standardization and quality control. In the field of training, the CFTC maintains contact with SADCC's Regional Training Council, and has sponsored a seminar on the development of human resources in the region. In the area of food security, the CFTC is supporting a number of SADCC irrigation and fishery projects. Other CFTC projects have been directed at an increase in regional trade—a Contact Promotion Programme for Tanzania in Zambia and Mauritius provided an opportunity for an increase in trade between these countries, while a survey for Swaziland examined the potential for increased trade with five neighbouring members of the Eastern and Southern African Preferential Trade Area.[39]

Apart from the support for SADCC, the CFTC continues to support the Secretariat of the West African Health Community, the Regional Health Secretariat for East, Central and Southern Africa. It continues to support health activities and training in the regions as determined by health ministers, in health management and administration, personnel training, maintenance and repair of medical equipment, public health engineering and pharmaceuticals.[40]

But the extent to which its impact will continue to be felt is dependent largely on the amount of capital available to the CFTC. Although the body relies more on the utilization of human resources for the successful operation of its programmes, the importance of adequate funding cannot be over-emphasized. Given the vast size of the developmental problems confronting these states, the sum allocated to the fund is indeed very meagre, to say the least. The growth of the budget has not been impressive, having grown from a mere £0.2 million in 1972 to only £19 million in 1983–4. Out of this £19 million, Africa had the 'lion's share' with 41.6 per cent, or £7.904 million. The Caribbean and Atlantic region followed with 24.6 per cent or £4.674 million, while 13.8 per cent or £2.622 million went to the Pacific and Asia received 11.7 per cent or £2.223 million. The remaining 6.5 per cent or £1.235 million went to Pan-Commonwealth projects. Sectorally, the highest allocation of 26.7 per cent or £5.073 million went to Industry. Other allocations included 17 per cent or £3.230 million to International Trade; 14.4 per cent or £2.736 million to Administration and Planning; 8.5 per cent or £1.615 million to Finance and Taxation; 8.2 per cent or £1.558 million to Agriculture; 7 per cent or £1.33 million to Education; 5.1 per cent or £0.969 million to Health and Social Services; 3.7 per cent or $0.703 million to Transport, Post and Telecommunications; 3.5 per cent or £0.665 million to Legal Affairs; 1.9 per cent or £0.361 million to Energy; and another 1.9 per cent or £0.361 million to Mass Communication; while 2.1 per cent or £0.399 million was allocated to miscellaneous matters. These figures cannot really be regarded as impressive.

The problem of finance is compounded by the fact that contributions are voluntary. The extent to which a donor contributes to the Commonwealth fund will largely be a reflection of the importance it attaches to the organization. Unfortunately, the events of 1986 have been ominous and might even lead Commonwealth countries to attach less and less importance to the values of the organization. In turn, this may have an overall negative impact on the developmental role of the Secretariat. Meanwhile, we can only hope that the Commonwealth survives this phase of its development intact.

Notes

1. Legum, C., ed., *Zambia: Independence and Beyond* (London, Nelson, 1969), pp. 178–80.
2. Anglin, D.G., 'Nigeria: Political Non-alignment and Economic Alignment', *Journal of Modern African Studies* 2, no. 2, 1964), p. 258.

3. Commonwealth Economic Committee, *Special Commonwealth African Assistance Plan: Report for the Year Ending 31st March, 1962* (London, HMSO, 1963), p. 4.
4. Ibid.
5. SCAAP, Reports for various years between 1961–62 and December 1965.
6. Ibid.
7. Ibid.
8. Ibid.
9. Ibid.
10. One project that was executed over the years was the mapping and airborne geophysical survey of Nigeria; another was a study of the development and utilization of Nigeria's natural gas resources.
11. It should be pointed out that most of these countries produced grandiose national development plans that required foreign financial and technical assistance for their execution.
12. Five classes of loans could be distinguished: (1) loans under Section 1 of the Colonial Development and Welfare Act; (2) Exchequer loans made under Section 2 of the same Act for the development needs of dependent territories which could not raise external finance in other ways; (3) Commonwealth Assistance Loans, which were the normal form of British loan aid for development purposes to independent Commonwealth countries and were made under Section 3 of the Export Guarantees Act of 1945; (4) capital allocations for projects undertaken by the Colonial (later Commonwealth) Development Corporation (CDC) set up by the Overseas Resources Development Act of 1945; these were available for dependent territories (and later, in 1963, expanded to include independent ones) and for projects started during colonial period in countries which were already independent; finally; (5) special loams, such as the one granted to Tanzania for expenditure on the compensation of officers retiring from the services after independence and for the commutation of pensions, as well as other loans made available to Nigeria on an interest-free short-term basis to enable the Regional Governments to pay the advances of lump-sum compensation to certain officers. See, SCAAP: 'Report for the Year Ending 31st March 1962', op. cit., p. 13.
13. SCAAP: 'Report for the Year Ending 31st March 1965', pp. 13–14 and SCAAP: 'Report for the Year 1965' (March to December), p. 10.
14. SCAAP, Reports for the year 1961–62, pp. 13–14; year 1964–65, p. 14; and for calendar year 1965, p. 12.
15. The Overseas Surveys Directorate operated for many years a continuous programme of field survey and mapping out in all countries in Commonwealth Africa and, where necessary, arranged for specialist firms to carry out aerial photography. It also undertook land use and ecological surveys

and provided training for draughtsmen and surveyors. The Overseas Geological Surveys Directorate provided parallel services in geological matters, including staff and facilities for surveys and extensive laboratory determinations. SCAAP: 'Report for the Year Ending 31st March 1964', p. 15.

16. Ibid.
17. Ibid., p. 14 and SCAAP: 'Report for the Year Ending 31st March 1965', p. 16.
18. Ibid. (March 1965), p. 12.
19. Cmnd. 2736 (London, HMSO, 1965).
20. SCAAP: 'Report for the year 1965', pp. 7–8.
21. 'Third Report of the Commonwealth Secretary-General' (London, Commonwealth Secretariat, 1971), p. 35.
22. *Flow of Intra-Commonwealth Aid, 1966* (London, Commonwealth Secretariat, 1967), p. 8.
23. Ibid., p. 9 and 'Third Report of the Commonwealth Secretary-General', pp. 35–6.
24. 'Third Report of the Commonwealth Secretary-General', p. 36.
25. Ibid., and 'Fourth Report of the Commonwealth Secretary-General', p. 23.
26. Commonwealth Fund for Technical Co-operation, *Commonwealth Skills for Commonwealth Needs* (London, Commonwealth Secretariat, 1985), p. 1.
27. 'Fourth Report of the Commonwealth Secretary-General', op. cit., p. 25.
28. Ibid., p. 27.
29. *Commonwealth Skills for Commonwealth Needs*, op. cit., p. 4.
30. Ibid., p. 4.
31. Ibid.
32. 'Fourth Report of the Commonwealth Secretary-General', op. cit., pp. 28–9.
33. Ibid.
34. Commonwealth Secretariat, 'Export Market Development', *Notes on the Commonwealth Series* (London, 1986).
35. *Commonwealth Skills for Commonwealth Needs*, op. cit., p. 1.
36. Ibid., pp. 5–6.
37. Ibid., pp. 10–11.
38. Ibid.
39. Ibid., pp. 25–6.
40. Ibid.

8 'Francophonie', culture and development: the experience of the ACCT

Kaye Whiteman

France must fulfil her mission as a world power. We are everywhere in the world. There is no corner of the earth where, at a given time, men do not look to us and ask what France says. It is a great responsibility to be France, the humanizing power *par excellence*.

> President de Gaulle, Bordeaux,
> April 1961

Today, many thinkers and researchers are more and more convinced that a conception of development that sacrifices culture to economic growth, qualitative to quantitative, can only provide an incomplete development. That is why, today, as yesterday in the 1930s, I said with all the militants of negritude and francophonie, not to mention Arabite: 'speak of culture first'.

> Leopold S. Senghor, in a speech made
> during a visit to the headquarters of the
> Agence pour la Coopération Culturelle
> et Technique (ACCT) in Paris,
> September 1985.

The ACCT has become an essential instrument in the development of relations between the francophone countries of the North and of the South, and an example of solidarity and complementarity in our countries.

> Abdou Diouf, at the 10th General
> Council of the ACCT, Dakar,
> December 1985.

It is curious, but not surprising, that the only multilateral organizations for French-speaking countries should be what are usually referred to as cultural, rather than strictly developmental. The mechanisms of French aid are another story: there are a number of French inspired and run vehicles for French financial assistance, notably the Fonds d'Aide et Coopération (FAC) and the Caisse Centrale de la Coopération Econom-ique (CCCE). Although the ministers of the franc zone meet regularly, all apart from the French representative are from Africa south of the Sahara, and the French still fundamentally make the rules which govern the zone's operation.

There is a school of thought that appears to have been growing in recent years that seeks to merge the notions of culture and develop-ment. It is a trend that found favour in the last negotiations for the renewed Lomé Convention (Lomé III), signed in December 1984, which includes a chapter on Cultural Cooperation. Although this part of the convention has no funds specifically allocated to it from the European Development Fund, the strong implication is that culture infuses all development, and therefore Lomé aid projects and pro-grammes should take into account, 'the cultural and social dimension' (to quote the text of the convention).[1]

The notion that culture is the basis of all human activity is one that is particularly associated with one of the founding fathers of the movement to further *francophonie*: Leopold Sedar Senghor, poet–politician, first President of the Republic of Senegal from 1960 to 1980. There are various sayings of his about culture which are often quoted,[2] most particularly on the subject of the supremacy of culture over all other subjects: one of the most recent is cited at the beginning of this article. In an important essay 'La Française, Langue de Culture', published in a special issue on 'French in the World' of the review *L'Esprit* in Novem-ber 1962,[3] he argues that in Africa culture and politics go together: 'the African mind does not permit dichotomy'. The same line of thinking was applied in the 1970s to a matter which increasingly came to preoccupy him, the oneness of culture and development. His seventieth birthday celebrations in October 1986 were held under the sign of 'culture and development'.

In writing of the Agency for Cultural and Technical Cooperation (known either by its initials, ACCT, standing for the Agence de Coopération Culturelle et Technique, or by the acronym AGECOOP), which was set up in 1970 as a vehicle for cooperation between French-speaking states, one is acutely aware of the relatively minor role accorded to what the non-francophone world would see as properly developmental activities, that is, those related to economic develop-ment. Much depends on the role of education, which has always featured strongly in France's own aid programmes, and although the educational aspect of development is undeniable, France's great stress on it has a strong 'smack' of self-interest. The purpose of sending so many French teachers to developing countries, the stress laid on teaching the French language there, the proper inspection of the way it is taught, so that standards can at least be aspired to, has undoubtedly done more to further French influence than to promote development. That the one may ensue from the other, and it is by no means certain that this will always happen, is simply a bonus.

The seeds of the AGECOOP lie in the whole concept of *francophonie*. Xavier Deniau, a French parliamentarian who has been a great apostle of *francophonie*, states that the word was coined by a French geographer Onesime Reclus (1837–1916) who popularized the phrase in the late nineteenth and early twentieth centuries, in the heyday of imperial enthusiasm.[4] In a series of works he developed a theory of the division of the world according to language. In one book, *Le Partage du Monde* (1906) he stressed the possibilities that the future of the colonial era offered to the spread of the French language. An earlier book called *Lâchons l'Asie, Prenons l'Afrique* (1904) stressed particularly the especially fruitful ground that Africa offered for the spread of French.[5] Significantly the phrase 'Lâchons l'Asie, Prenons l'Afrique' became a slogan in the 1950s, when the failing war in Indochina gave it an altogether more poignant reality. The dropping of Asia, and the 'taking' of Africa, at least south of the Sahara, was indeed what came to pass.

The name 'francophone', however, did not enter into current usage until the early 1960s. Deniau traces the exact moment of its renaissance to the special issue on 'French in the World' in November 1962, more precisely to the article in the issue by Senghor on 'La Française, Langue de Culture' which has already been cited, and is subsequently reproduced in the book of essays, *Liberté 1*. He then began to use the term regularly and as enthusiastically as if he had coined it himself (the remark 'I did not invent *francophonie*, it already existed' is attributed to him).[6] But it was in 1965 that the concrete proposal for a Commonwealth *à la Française* was evolved, and here new ground was broken by President Habib Bourguiba of Tunisia during an African tour in the latter part of the year.[7] The idea was taken up by Senghor, who made a formal proposal on the subject to a summit in Tananarive of the Afro-Malagasy Common Organization (OCAM), a grouping of francophone African countries that had evolved from the so-called 'Brazzaville group', that was sometimes seen as a sort of nucleus of *francophonie*.

The idea was slow to germinate. Although President Hamani Diori, who became Chairman of OCAM in Tananarive, was mandated to promote the idea in Algeria, Tunisia and Morocco, only Tunisia produced a favourable response, and that had already been certain. It was clearly an idea for which time was not entirely ripe. The Organization of African Unity had just been created, and the francophone African states were already on the defensive about resuscitating their own cooperation organization, OCAM. President Senghor, in particular, was aware of this aspect, and said after the Tananarive summit that Africa's first political loyalty was to the OAU, that *francophonie* would be non-political, and would concentrate in the first instance on education.

He made frequent references at this time to the way the British had been able to organize their former dependencies into a 'Commonwealth' and now, in his view, the same thing was desirable for the francophones. The example of the Commonwealth may, however, have been what caused some hesitation on the part of France. In the mid-1960s it was easy to observe how much trouble the Commonwealth was giving Britain in the wake of the Unilateral Declaration of Independence (UDI) in Rhodesia. One of Senghor's undoubted motives was to ensure that France was somehow tied down by structures into a continuing relationship with Africa: he often expressed fears that the former colonial powers could lose interest in Africa. This was arguably the only reason why President Hamani Diori, leader of the impoverished and landlocked country of Niger, became involved.

It was often said that President de Gaulle himself was doubtful of the value of *francophonie* and was suspicious of some of Senghor's 'woollier' concepts. A political pragmatist, de Gaulle instinctively avoided anything that might limit his room for maneouvre, and held in considerable and well-publicized disdain international organizations such as the United Nations or the European Community. Officially, he was non-committal on *francophonie*, and this was often interpreted in a positive light. Xavier Deniau, for example, writes:

General de Gaulle himself was always discreet on *francophonie*. Remember the only question which he refused to answer in his press conference of 20 October 1966, posed by a Dahomeyan journalist, was on the subject of *francophonie*. He did not want to mark the idea with his imprint by personalizing it: it should be the possession of all francophones.[8]

There was no doubt, however, that in his more mystical moments, he appreciated the value of the French language as an essential instrument

of what he was wont to call the *rayonnement* [influence] of France. His
emotional view of the francophones of Quebec seen in his celebrated
cry of 'Vive le Québec Libre!' during his visit there in 1967, sustains
this view. The establishment of the High Commission for the
Protection and Expansion of the French Language happened in de
Gaulle's presidency, even if the architect was very much the Prime
Minister Georges Pompidou. Likewise, two of the main existing
multilateral organs grouping francophones were also established in
the de Gaulle era: L'Association des Universités Partiellement ou
Entièrement de Langue Française (AUPELF) was established in
Montreal in 1961, greatly stimulated by the Canadian francophone
universities; and in 1967 there was established in Luxembourg, with
European, Canadian and African support, a francophone parliamentary
organization called L'Association Internationale des Parliamentaires de
Langue Française (AIPLF).

Interestingly, one of the principal leaders of francophone Africa,
President Houphouët-Boigny,[9] spoke of *la francophonie* as 'L'idée
fumeuse de Senghor' (the nebulous idea of Senghor). Baulin adds: 'he
always considered it as a marginal, low rank affair, and in any case
without practical utility on the African level, and probably condemned
to memorable failure'. After the establishment of AGECOOP, however,
the Côte d'Ivoire played a full part in it, and Houphouët-Boigny
attended the first francophone summit in 1986.

It was at this period that Philip M. Allen produced a remarkable
article in *Africa Report*[10] that equated *francophonie* with a religion,
complete with pope, prophets, church militant, heretics, holy writ and
'educational sacraments', in which he made the key observation that the
'hard-knuckled' priests who 'intrepidly extend *francophonie's* frontiers
. . . rejoice in having assembled a congregation of 200 million souls,
whereas the more aesthetic deem barely one-third of these worthy
according to the tests of their linguistic order'. This draws attention to
the fact that countries that are described as *francophone*, above all in
Africa, are in fact very far from containing a majority of people with a
reasonable command of French. Twenty years later, despite considerable educational efforts, it is doubtful that the ratio has changed, so that
as the population of the countries that are touched by *francophonie* has
grown to some 300 million, the number of true francophones is probably
little more than 100 million, which still makes it the smallest of the so-
called 'world languages' (English, Spanish, Portuguese, Arabic, Russian
and Chinese being the other principal languages). Nevertheless, the

resilience of *francophonie* as an idea or a movement would no doubt surprise the sceptical Allen. Maybe the religious analogy he detected is a clue to its survival power.

Despite the doubts raised by the idea, it was clear that by the late 1960s a movement was under way to provide a greater institutional framework for *francophonie*. The creation of the AIPLF in 1967 ensured a much greater mobilization of the lobby at the level of the countries most likely to provide the financial backing, namely France, Belgium and Canada, and their 1968 meeting at Versailles specifically called for the agency to be set up. The case of Belgium is an interesting one, as the 1960s was a period of considerable linguistic turbulence in Belgium, a country divided almost equally between French and Flemish speakers. Linguistic legislation of 1962–3 did not appease the tensions and before the end of the decade the great bone of contention of the University of Louvain was settled by splitting the establishment into two separate linguistic units. The increasing defensiveness of the francophone community (the Walloons) meant that any project to reinforce international francophone solidarity received their enthusiastic support, and it was from Belgium that the idea came of holding a francophone Biennial conference (the first was held in Namur in 1967).[11]

More than anywhere, however, the catalyst for setting up the AGECOOP came from Canada. It so happened that the 1960s was also a period of turbulence for the francophone minority in Canada, mainly concentrated in the province of Quebec. The year 1960 saw the creation of the Rassemblement pour l'Indépendance Nationale (RIN) and the growth of openly separatist sentiments, demonstrated in its most extreme form in terrorist attacks by the more radical groups. At the same time French interest in the province grew as appeals for francophone solidarity increased and, in 1965, cultural cooperation agreements were signed between France and Quebec, under the vigilant eyes of the federal government in Ottawa. The defeat of the liberals in the 1966 election, and the coming to power of the Union Nationale of Daniel Johnson, brought a more separatist-minded regime to power. This was followed a year later by de Gaulle's famous visit. In this atmosphere any attempt at an international francophone structure was bound to be surrounded by diplomatic minefields. On the one hand campaigning francophones from Quebec, such as the journalist Jean-Marc Leger, the then Secretary-General of AUPELF, who had advocated a French-speaking community as early as 1962,[12] were pushing hard for a separate *Québécois* role, while on the other the Canadian government was extremely nervous at anything that gave Quebec a separate international personality.

Thus, in taking on the rather vague mandate from the OCAM summit at Tananarive to pursue the establishment of *francophonie*, President Diori probably did not quite know what he was taking on. As Jacques Baulin, an adviser to Diori, recounts in his book *Conseiller du Président Diori*,[13] the problem soon came high on the agenda of the Niger president, and was one cause, according to Baulin, of differences with both the French and the Ivorian President, who had been Diori's political mentor. Baulin goes as far as to say 'the support of Niger for Canada showed itself decisively in the two conferences in Niamey which gave birth to *francophonie*'. These were the conferences, the first in February 1968, the second in March 1970, which gave birth to AGECOOP.

Although the enthusiasm for Quebec, and of the Quebec lobby in Paris for *francophonie* was an important factor in helping it to be established, if the Canadian government had opposed it, the project could easily have been aborted. From the beginning in Tananarive, the stress was on the cultural nature of the project (that is, there was no serious politics involved, which perhaps may have provided some reassurance to the 'Anglo-Saxon' elements in Canada). This did not prevent a major diplomatic *brouhaha* being caused by the invitation sent directly to Quebec to attend the meeting of francophone African education ministers in Libreville in February 1968. This may be perhaps attributed to the naïvety of President Bongo, then very newly arrived in power (in December 1967), but most sources, including Baulin, ascribe it to the influence of the Quebec lobby, using contacts among the heavy presence of French advisers in all ministries in Gabon. The result was the temporary suspension of diplomatic relations with Gabon by Canada, because the Quebec Minister of Education Jean Guy Cardinal had attended the meeting as if Quebec were a sovereign state with the fleur-de-lis flag of the province flying outside the conference hall aongside other national flags.[14]

Diori, already aware of the possibilities of an expansion of Canada's aid programmes in francophone Africa, deployed considerable efforts to avoid such a *débâcle* at the planned 'first conference of partially or entirely French-speaking countries'. Baulin reveals[15] that in November 1968 Diori told Canadian Premier Pierre Trudeau at a meeting in Ottawa that the French were pressing for the invitation to be sent to Quebec only, and would boycott the meeting if, as Diori had at first suggested, the invitation was made to Canada. The Niger President suggested, therefore, that both the federal government and Quebec should be invited, with a copy of the latter invitation being sent to Ottawa—a compromise that Trudeau reluctantly accepted. Baulin's account suggests that up to and during the conference in February 1969 a bitter cold war ensued between France and Canada marked particularly by French 'harassment' of the Canadian government.

During the Niamey meeting itself (February 16–21), this was most conspicuously observed in what came to be called the 'Ballet of the Flags'. The Quebec delegate insisted that the provincial flag be flown alongside the Canadian flag, but when this duly happened the Quebec flag proved to be much bigger than the Canadian flag, which was 'rather bedraggled after it became entangled in a tree'. The other Canadian provinces which have francophone populations, New Brunswick, Manitoba and Ontario and had representatives in the Canadian delegation, protested, so their flags had to be flown too, and when the Quebec flagpole was found to be higher than the rest, all the poles had to be adjusted to the same height. The other provincial flags contained Union Jacks, an 'unexpected spectacle', says Baulin.[16]

The meeting itself, however, was counted a success, if only because it was agreed in principle to establish the planned structure for *francophonie* in the shape of an agency for cultural and technical cooperation. The drawing up of the statute to create the agency was entrusted to a provisional Executive Secretary, Jean-Marc Leger, working under the direction of President Diori. It was also requested that President Diori host another meeting the following year, which would approve the definitive establishment of the agency. Baulin cites a letter that President Diori received after the meeting from General de Gaulle congratulating him on the 'very remarkable results of this meeting' as a sign that de Gaulle wanted to distance himself from the antics of the Quebec lobby. It does appear, however, that the sessions of the conference were not easy, not just because of the Quebec issue, but because of a struggle for control over the future structure between France and Canada with Quebec on the side of the Canadians. This was in part due to the ambition of Jean-Marc Leger, who had made the project very much a personal affair, but there is no doubt that the traditionally *dirigiste* and centralizing French could not conceive of a division of power in a structure like this, especially since it concerned the sensitive area of French influence in Africa. According to Corbett:

In its desire not to appear in the forefront in the creation of the OCAM sponsored union, Paris overplayed its hand. In the final sessions at Niamey in 1969, its pique at Jean-Marc Leger surfaced. He seems to have given no more weight in elaborating his idea of an administrative structure, to 'suggestions' from Paris than to the recommendations of other interested countries. The French delegation flatly refused to accept his proposal, calling it too rigid, although the other participants considered it satisfactory. The French view prevailed . . .[17]

At this stage the overall enthusiasm of the African francophone countries for the idea was difficult to gauge. Apart from Diori, Senghor and Bourguiba, the bulk of the remainder seemed content to go along with a project that might mean more assistance for them. The sudden resignation of de Gaulle in April 1969 and his replacement as President by Georges Pompidou a month later introduced a subtle change into the relations of former French territories with France, as if to say that the age of paternalism was at an end. Criticism of France, almost unheard of in former French Africa since the departure of Sekou Touré's Guinea from their number, seemed permissible, and several countries began to call for a renegotiation of economic and military cooperation agreements.

Records indicate the presence of thirty-three delegations from twenty-nine countries (including five Canadian delegations—Federal, Quebec, New Brunswick, Ontario and Manitoba) at Niamey I. A year later, at Niamey II, the numbers were down slightly to thirty delegations from twenty-six countries. Too much should not perhaps be made of this—with small countries, attendance at international meetings is sometimes difficult, and there were some specific circumstances (neither the Central African Republic nor Congo–Kinshasa were present at Niamey II, apparently for the transient reason that their Union of Central African States (UEAC) had temporarily distanced themselves from the francophone orbit). It is worth noting, however, that apart from Tunisia and Lebanon, some Arab states that could be designated as francophone (Syria and Mauritania) were absent from both, that Algeria attended Niamey I as an observer and has subsequently had nothing to do with AGECOOP, and that Morocco attended both as an observer. There is no doubt that the pull of Arabic as a rival linguistic grouping adds to the doubts in the Arab world on *francophonie*. Bilingual Cameroon also expressed some reservations, but ended up a member. In Asia, though Laos[18] and South Vietnam attended, North Vietnam refused its invitation, and Cambodia was present only as an observer and withdrew after the Lon Nol coup which occurred during the meeting.

The positions of France and Canada on the Quebec question also did not improve between Niamey I and Niamey II. The Canadian position had hardened, as they now did not wish any separate invitation to be sent to Quebec, to which the reaction of France was first of all to say that if that was the case they would boycott the next Niamey meeting. Again, President Diori had to work out a formula with the Canadians, under which invitations to all provinces with francophone populations, however small, should all be physically sent to the federal government in Ottawa, which would then process them. Although, according to Baulin, there was a rearguard action in favour of Quebec involving pressure on the Niger president from a diversity of French personalities, including the powerful and mysterious adviser at the Elysée on African Affairs, Jacques Foccart, Diori stuck to his ground, and maintained his agreement with the Canadians. His last word on the subject was contained in a 'glacial' communication to Jean de Lipkowski, Gaullist Secretary of State for Foreign Affairs (a junior minister in the Quai D'Orsay) of 20 February 1970 saying that relations between Canada and Quebec were the 'affair of Canadians, and Canadians alone'. He told de Lipkowski that he had invited Canada to the conference and had 'advised the authorities of Quebec in view of their active participation within the Canadian delegation'.[19] Baulin's account, it is true, is written very much from Diori's point of view, but many observers at the time were able to note the maturity of Diori's attitude, faced with what were effectively cowboy tactics emanating from certain quarters in Paris, and after the consolidation of AGECOOP at Niamey II the lesson seems to have been at least partially learnt in Paris.

Even during the meeting, there were arguments between the French and the Canadians centred on Quebec's participation in the agency. France had argued that 'governments' (that is, Quebec) could take part in the work of the agency. When this was rejected, the French suggested that 'Associations' could participate instead, but the Canadians also saw this as a loophole, arguing that it was wrong to put associations on the same level as states. In the end all four Canadian provinces signed the charter along with and as part of the federal Canadian delegation. The French also reportedly had misgivings about the confirmation of the appointment of Leger as substantive Secretary-General of the organization (they were disappointed at his unwillingness to defy the Ottawa government on the Quebec issue), and there were reports of corridor charges of 'Canadian penetration of *francophonie*'. There is no doubt that Leger received general approval from the conference because of the hard work and extensive travelling in francophone countries that he had already engaged in.[20] Likewise, there was general agreement that the headquarters of the new Agency should be in Paris.

In the Convention and Charter[21] which were approved by Niamey II (prepared by Leger and his staff working closely with the Niger government), the objectives of the agency were stated to be 'the affirmation and development between its members of a multilateral cooperation in domains relating to education, training, culture, science and technical matters, and to observe strict neutrality in questions of an ideological and political nature'. The Charter also specifically mentions the agency's collaboration with various international and regional organizations, and its need to take account of 'all forms of existing technical and cultural cooperation'. This almost amounts to a warning not to duplicate work already being done, since by this time there was already an awareness of the proliferation of a variety of regional and sub-regional organizations, all with the potential for burgeoning bureaucracies. The Convention begins with a preamble saying that the signing states are 'aware of the solidarity that links them with the use of the French language', but the words 'French' and *'francophonie'* do not appear in the objectives as stated in the Charter, and scarcely indeed, throughout either Convention or Charter. But then, it was not really necessary for them to do so. French was, of course, specified as the working language of the agency. Leger himself, from the beginning, stressed that the agency was dedicated to 'cooperation and multilateral technical assistance and is not an instrument for the diffusion of French'. The catch-all expression usually used, from Niamey through to Versailles in 1986 is 'countries having in common the use of French', a phrase both vague and flexible.

Article 2 of the Charter list the 'functions' of the Agency, which are described as 'study, information, coordination and action', having been granted the following powers: making periodic inventories of the resources of the francophone world; pooling of some resources in order to propose joint development programmes; finding the means to spread information in the fields of science, teaching and technology; the pooling of complementary means for training; contributing to the creation of common instruments of scientific and technical research, and exploitation of that research; functioning as a meeting place between specialists in diverse disciplines and national officials in education, culture, science and technology; supporting concentration of efforts and means in research, technology, education, training, and communication as well as in the study of development problems; encouraging mutual knowledge of peoples through mass communications, teaching and exchanges; facilitating governments' access to sources of bilateral and multilateral cooperation; and maintaining liaison with associations working within the agency's domain. These, it will be seen, place the emphasis in highly practical sectors, such as education, research, science and technology, with at least two references to the word 'development', even if not economic development. The remaining sections of the Charter set out conditions for membership (a complicated formula is spelled out to cover all those countries where a 'government' may wish to participate in the work of the agency, using the expression subject to 'the approval of the member state where lies the territory over which the participating government concerned exercises its authority'. Observer countries may also be admitted on request. Again, in none of these rules is the word 'francophone' actually mentioned. Over the years, considerable fexibility has been adopted in admitting countries, either as members, associates or observers, and a fairly wide net has been cast, so that from the twenty-one who signed the original charter in 1970, membership of ACCT had increased to thirty-six by 1986, with seven associate members.

In the beginning the ACCT was granted an extremely modest budget, perhaps as an indication of the caution with which the French, the largest donor, initially regarded it. The total budget for 1970, a 'running-in' budget, was 1,566,000 French francs (approximately £150,000 at the 1970 rate of exchange), of which half was to go on administration and recurrent costs. This increased in 1971 to a budget of 10 million francs as various programmes got under way, but resources for the agency were still fairly limited. No country was allowed to contribute more than 45 per cent, and the rate of contribution was determined as follows: France 43 per cent, Canada 33 per cent, Belgium 12 per cent, and all other member states 10 per cent. The minimum contribution was fixed at 0.36 per cent. These proportions were later modified with France's contribution (raising slightly the maximum ceiling) increased to 46 per cent, and Canada's increased to 35 per cent (with Quebec and New Brunswick contributing 4.5 per cent to that total). Belgium remained at 12 per cent, which meant that other members contributions shrank to 7 per cent. The budget itself increased tenfold in fifteen years to a little over 100 million French francs in the 1987 budget.

In the first budget the most important share was allocated to training, a priority which has largely continued. It was re-emphasized as part of the educational priority outlined at the Mauritius meeting of 1975. From the beginning there has been a useful allocation for scholarships, and the agency rapidly set up its own training institution, the International School in Bordeaux. The decision to set it up was made at a meeting of francophone public service ministers in Lomé in 1971, and the school, housed in a converted convent (with the chapel as a library) was set up in 1972. It specializes in courses for civil servants (what the francophones call *perfectionnement des cadres*), and over the years it has found it more useful to have shorter courses for a greater number of people. The main specialization has been in different forms of administration and management, but from 1982 a series of more development-orientated courses have been introduced. The example of the Bordeaux school as far as orientation towards development is concerned can be seen in the whole range of activities of the ACCT.

In the early years, despite the solid work done in the training field, it was the cultural and information activities of the agency which attracted attention. There was, for instance, almost from the beginning, a stress on the cinema. France's own attitude towards the development of the cinema in developing countries with which she was closely related has always been positive, especially in the provision of funds and facilities, so that in both North Africa and francophone sub-Saharan Africa, the development of cinema, and a school of new directors, has outstripped what has happened elsewhere in Africa. The setting up of the ACCT gave this whole movement added impulse, and it has organized from 1970 onwards a series of competitions—for scenarios, encouragement of young talent and for short films (*courts-metrages*), as well as establishing a francophone film festival. There are similar activities in the field of literature and the distribution of books, and also in the sector of 'Oral Tradition and Protection of Cultural Patrimony', a UNESCO-orientated theme dear to the hearts of some ACCT members. The question of oral tradition draws attention to another more surprising activity of the ACCT—its involvement with the promotion of national languages. This became one of the priorities which emerged from the 4th General Conference at Port-Louis in Mauritius in 1975, which marked the first turning point in the history of the organization for a number of reasons. Official documents of the ACCT make a point of stressing that in the first

article of the Convention signed in Niamey in 1970 it is specifically
stated that the aim of the agency is to 'promote and spread the cultures
of the contracting High Parties, and to intensify cultural and technical
cooperation between them'. This has a slightly different emphasis from
the objectives as laid out in the Charter, annexed to the Convention
(quoted previously), but it certainly justifies a policy on national
languages, which are specifically referred to in the convention's preamble alongside 'respect for the sovereignty of states'. Although there
might be a kind of logic in the Senghorean position of supporting the
spread of the French language in Africa because in practice French has
furthered unity, its very strength is sometimes seen as an obstacle to
African unity as such.

However, while such a provision in the rules governing an agency
which has from its inception been associated with *francophonie* might
seem like a piece of cosmetic over-compensation, the fact remains that
the theme of 'national languages' is there in the statutes. Accordingly
after the Mauritius meeting underlined this priority, a special meeting
attended by ten African states as well as France and Canada was held in
Cameroon in December 1976. This established two commissions, for
West Africa and for Central Africa, both of which came up with a variety
of projects in the field of atlases and dictionaries, with one project for
the promotion of the regional languages Fulfulde and Mauding in West
Africa. There are, however, many in Africa who would still be suspicious
that all this is 'tokenism' and similar to other 'crumbs' that have been
directed to African languages from France over the years, while the
chief French emphasis and interest, from the colonial period onwards,
has been the spread and maintenance of the French language, which
other activities of the ACCT aid and abet. But it is at least a measure of
the discomfort, often concealed, which the idea of *francophonie*,
despite all assurances of innocuousness, can encourage.

The other important orientation which was decided on in Mauritius
was to introduce a stronger development priority into the activities of
the agency. We have already noted that Senghor was increasingly
concerned about the culture–development equation. As Hymans says
'his increasing concern for social problems was symptomatic of his
growing awareness of the poverty of Africa'. The same concern came
increasingly to find voices within the agency, especially after the
first African became Secretary–General. This also took place at the
Mauritius meeting, when Dankoulodo Dan Dicko, a former teacher from
Niger took over from Jean-Marc Leger. Dan Dicko spoke a somewhat

different discourse from Leger, more heavily impregnated with development language. He initiated the creation of a special multinational unit called the PSD (Programme Spécial de Développement), which became operational at the end of 1977, and consciously targeted itself towards projects in national development plans. Some of this might look like a simple rearrangement of budget headings (national languages, science and technology and so on) but the range of projects widened, and in fact the PSD was funded from voluntary contributions from members, associates or even from outside. In 1978 the PSD funded some thirty 'projects' and by 1982 the number had risen to 200. Again, examination of the details of the projects would seem to indicate that they fell generally within the priorities of the ACCT as already established, especially in the field of training and technical assistance, but with heightened developmental criteria.

The Bordeaux school also introduced the subject of economic and social development into its curriculum in 1982, with such courses as the 'identification, preparation and evaluation of development projects' and 'the role of credit policy in development' and 'the organization and administration of rural cooperatives'. A conference of francophone ministers of agriculture and rural development was held in 1981 in Paris.

One function of the agency has been to coordinate the activities, what Corbett calls the 'capstick', with the various organizations connected to *francophonie*. The AIPLF and the AUPELF have already been mentioned, as has the Haut Comité de la Langue Française. There are also the various conferences of francophone ministers, pioneered by those of education, but growing gradually to include youth and sport, health, justice, culture, some only meeting very occasionally. There is also a francophone group at the United Nations (where the French are very proud of their language being a working language), which watches particularly over such issues as job allocations to francophones within the UN system (from 1987 the ACCT has obtained observer status at the UN). There is also a long list of professional associations, some of which go back well before the Second World War, such as the Association des Ecrivains de Langue Française (ADELF) created in 1926. Scientists, philosophers and lawyers as well as computer specialists all have their groupings, and there are many others, some encouraged by the ACCT, which in a modest way fulfils the function of the Commonwealth Foundation in London in relation to such organizations. France itself also has its own structures such as the Prime Ministerial

Francophonie Committee set up in 1973, and an Inter-ministerial Committee set up a year later.

The agency has not been without its institutional upsets. In its seventeen years of existence it has had four secretaries-general, an indication perhaps of the acute struggle for influence that the agency seems to generate. Leger had already been marked as controversial and, moreover, managed to upset the French, so it was not surprising that in 1979, after only two years, he was replaced, especially as there was pressure for the job from African states who felt that they had played a particularly significant role in the agency as its principal beneficiaries. Dan Dicko proved more durable and survived for eight years, but even his departure involved some recrimination. From 1981 the Secretariat has been the preserve of the Gabonese, first with François Owono-Nguema, and then, when his term expired, with Paul Okumba d'Okwat-segue. The latter prevailed in spite of a determined but misguided attempt by the French government to insert a Socialist minister Georges Fillioud[22] in the post, an idea that, it is interesting to note, met with strong resistance from most African countries.

Considering the criticism that surrounded its birth, from such quarters as President Sekou Touré in Guinea or the Algerians, the ACCT has been surprisingly uncontroversial from a political point of view. There has been lack of enthusiasm, no doubt partly occasioned by the fairly small scale of the operations. Enthusiasts of *francophonie* have even identified a problem here. Xavier Deniau notes in 1983 that *francophonie* was still little known, and this was a major problem for its further enlargement.

It may have been awareness of a certain marking of time or even of sclerosis that led President Senghor in the year 1980, at the end of which he retired as President of Senegal, to press once again for the completion of the original Senghor–Bourguiba project for a French Commonwealth. The arrival on the scene of the Franco-African summits in 1973 (another initiative of President Hamani Diori) had somehow taken the wind out of the sails of the original idea of francophone summits, which would in any case have re-opened the sensitive Quebec dossier. The Franco-African summits had also, incidentally, helped to hasten the decline of OCAM, the organization which had attempted to group together the francophone African countries. Although it struggled on in a half-life to the mid-1980s, the summits became less and less frequent and less and less well attended, in spite of an attempt to give it a voice in support of poorer, smaller, land-locked countries.

The original idea of a 'Commonwealth *à la Française*' floated by Presidents Senghor and Bourguiba in 1965 had certainly envisaged a full-dress francophone summit as the centre-piece for all of the other organizations relating to *francophonie* (see above). The Franco-Canadian row, plus French reservations, plus the distraction of the Franco-African summits, had only served to leave the idea simmering on the back burner, but as *francophonie* seemed to be gaining an ever more solid appearance, it was only a matter of time before it was raised again. President Senghor brought it up at the Franco-African summit in Dakar in 1977, and was given a mandate to explore the subject. He made a new proposal for an 'organic community'[23] to both the Franco-African summit in Kigali in 1979 and Nice in June 1980. At a meeting of legal experts in Dakar in October that year the project fell foul once again of the problem of how Quebec was to be represented at the meeting. Thus even a planned preparatory meeting for foreign ministers of AGECOOP countries could not take place. The problem would have to wait until a formula could be found that would meet France's need to see Quebec represented at the meeting, and Canada's requirements of sovereignty. As Deniau writes, Quebec with 10 million francophones is the second largest francophone community in the world after France, so its absence would remove the francophone character of the summit. Thus Senghor's dream of seeing a francophone Commonwealth realized while he was still President was dashed, though he continued to work for it.

The arrival in power of the Socialist leader President François Mitterrand in May 1981 gave a new impulse to the ideal of *francophonie*, as not only was he a man with considerable interest in culture and education, with real affection for the French language, who took evident delight during African visits (for example) in being among French speakers outside France, but he had fewer reservations about the difficulty of controlling an 'organic community' *à la* Senghor. His background in the Socialist party made him more at ease with high-minded talk about the Third World and North–South dialogue (though his predecessor Giscard d'Estaing had also been capable of such rhetoric, it had certainly not been in the style of de Gaulle), which had now become an increasingly important part of *le discours francophone*. The tying down of France to overseas aid commitments, which de Gaulle had seemed to fear, was not something that would give Mitterrand a problem.

Preoccupation over the future of French had already led, in Giscard's last year of presidential office, to the establishment, in December 1980 by the National Assembly (with support from both Socialists and the right-wing parties), of a Commission of Inquiry into Policy on the French Language, to 'analyse the difficulties the language encountered in the world, to determine the nature and extent of the threats to it in France, and to define its situation in the world', as well as to study methods of diffusion, means available, conditions for teaching overseas, and so on. As one might have expected, the Commission made many recommendations for reinforcing government action in the direction of maintaining the standard of French taught and used in France, but also in reinforcing the effort to maintain French where it exists and spread it elsewhere in such fields as teaching, books, newspapers, news agencies and radio. Institutionally it called for *generalisation* of meetings of francophone ministers, with a permanent secretariat to coordinate them (possibly using the secretariat which existed already in Dakar which services meetings of ministers of education, youth and sports), and for a variety of actions that would have the effect of reinforcing *concertation* among francophones.

President Mitterrand, on assuming office, made a number of declarations indicating his sympathy with the idea of a wider concert of francophone nations.[24] He received support from Senghor's successor as President of Senegal, Abdou Diouf, at the Franco-African summit in 1982. Also in November of the same year the growing interest of Canada in *francophonie* (which had been reflected in the considerable growth over the years of Canadian interest in francophone Africa, an interest reflected in its aid distribution) was symbolized by the visit of Premier Pierre Trudeau to the headquarters of AGECOOP. Trudeau, however, having lived through the whole de Gaulle experience and its aftermath early in his premiership, retained a basic suspicion of French designs on Quebec, and it was really only under his successor Brian Mulroney, who won the premiership in the general elections of 1984, that the situation on *francophonie* became unfrozen. This was not without ironies as Trudeau was of French descent with a plainly francophone name, while Mulroney was of Irish descent, though he happened to be *Québécois*, with some sympathy for the peoples of the province.

Mulroney soon made it clear that he was not opposed to direct and 'privileged' relations between Paris and Quebec, while obviously maintaining respect for Canada's sovereignty, and by mid-May 1985, Foreign Minister Joe Clark was able to announce that France would soon be convoking a francophone summit. This was confirmed by the Paris visit

of Quebec premier René Levesque (earlier a thorn in Trudeau's side) at
the end of the same month. At the end of his visit he indicated that 'the
government of Quebec and the federal government understand each
other more and more on the form which the participation of Quebec
could take at an eventual francophone summit', and Quebec would be a
'participating government'.

The nuances here seemed so slight compared with the way in which
participation has been organized at ACCT meetings, that most observers attributed the new hope for the summit more to the change of
political climate within Canada than anything else. When the meeting
was finally called the invitations still passed through Canada, and
the Canadian delegation included delegations from Quebec and New
Brunswick (the idea of delegations from Ontario and Manitoba where
the francophone population is small, and which had been included
partly to 'drown' the separateness of Quebec, had been dropped).

At a certain stage President Mitterrand developed a personal interest
in the holding of the summit before the parliamentary elections of
March 1986, as the Socialists were likely to lose power then, and
Mitterrand was anxious to be able to stage the first francophone summit
not just in his presidency but while his party was still in office. All the
main parties would appear to feel there are votes in *francophonie*, as
seen by Chirac's decision immediately he came to power as Premier
immediately after the same elections, to appoint a Secretary of State
within the Foreign Ministry specifically for Francophone Affairs and
give the job to a Martiniquaise, Lucette Michaux-Chèvry.[25]

The summit itself was held 17–19 February 1897 in Paris, after a solemn
opening session with pomp and ceremony at the Palace of Versailles.
It was given the cumbersome title of 'Conference of heads of state and
governments of countries having in common the use of French', and
after a great many speeches, and several working sessions of experts
they produced 'twenty-eight practical decisions', almost all in the areas
of communications and education, including the creation of an international francophone television agency; the use of the new French cable
channel TV5 for North Africa and Africa; francophone programmes from
1987 on France's four television channels; a working group on linguistic
data banks; study of the use of video discs for medical teaching; an
exhibition of francophone books to be held every two years in Paris; an
international prize for linguistic innovation; a francophone bacca-
laureate, and so on. One of the interesting things about this list of
decisions was that many of them had quantifiable sums of money

attached to them, drawing attention to the main reason that various African leaders had gone along with the *francophonie* idea—not only would it help maintain France's interest in its former colonies, but it could be a way of consolidating and perhaps increasing financial flows. Here the Canadian angle was also important: the Canadians certainly took the opportunity of the summit to publicize their various aid programmes.

Some of the speeches at the summit, notably those of Mitterrand, Mulroney and Diouf, drew attention to a concern which seems to have given the whole idea of *francophonie* a new impetus, that modern developments in the field of information technology were giving an increasing advantage to the English-speaking world (mainly because of the thrust in that direction both in the United States and Japan), and that they could bypass the French language unless conscious efforts were made to promote the use of French.[26] The Canadians felt particularly strongly about this issue (although there is some ambivalence in Paris as to whether the Canadians are not playing the role of Trojan horse for American companies), as evidenced by the exhibition of French language computers from Quebec which occupied one third of the press room at the conference centre in Avenue Kleber.

Canadian interest in the summit was very high, as witnessed by the large body of journalists, both federal and Québécois, covering the conference, receiving their own briefings at their own press conference with the publicity-conscious Mulroney immediately after the official closing press conference with Mitterrand and several other personalities. Several French journalists noted that media interest in Paris was lukewarm[27] (apart from the way the Chad crisis impinged on the meeting in the form of tit-for-tat air raids by French and Libyans across the 16th parallel there). This draws attention to a phenomenon pinpointed by Deniau, that in spite of the espousal of the cause of *francophonie* by French political leaders (who believe it has votes), enthusiasm for *francophonie* in France is lukewarm. He attributes this to lack of awareness and information: 'The French live at the centre of the language without it posing a problem, as it does for the *Québécois* or the Walloons'.[28]

The African enthusiasm for the summit deserves some comment. Cynics might observe that African leaders need no pretext for rushing to Paris, even in sub-zero temperatures, and even though they had already been in Paris two months previously at the Franco-African summit. The vast majority of francophone African leaders felt they could not afford to miss this event. The Cameroon leader Paul Biya was conspicuously absent, without a delegation, because it had been a question of principle for Cameroon, a bilingual state, not to attend summits that favour one language (although Cameroon is an 'associate' of the ACCT). Although leaders of Marxist people's republics like the Congo and Benin were present, the current *enfant terrible* of francophone Africa, Captain Thomas Sankara of Burkina Faso, only sent a minister, with a message for the meeting that 'the French language is only one means of expressing our realities' and that it must 'accept other languages'. French was 'first of all the language of the colonizer', but today Burkina uses it 'no more as the vector of whatever cultural alienation, but as a means of communication with other people', so it was 'attending the summit to contribute to the enrichment of universalized French'.

This was a fairly adroit way of meeting the undercurrent of criticism of the whole exercise that undoubtedly still exists in unofficial francophone Africa. What is surprising is that it is currently so rarely articulated. It is a reflection of the harsh climate of the 1980s that the protests, often of a largely rhetorical nature that might have been made in the age of the first flush of nationalism, are very muted. The Algerians are still hostile, and occasional blasts still come from elsewhere in Africa outside the francophone group; but the kind of blasts of opposition that in the old days would have come from Sekou Touré and those around him now only find voice in, for example, the pages of Mongo Beti's, *Peuples Noirs, Peuples Africains* ironically published in French and in France. But the contradiction of *francophonie* (whatever advantages it may bring, even in contributing to unity within countries and to regional cooperation) with aspirations to African unity is bound to remain a permanent irritant that is sure to resurface, even within the francophone countries as the generations change.

The fairly mundane decisions listed above scarcely convey the elevated atmosphere which surrounded the first summit, especially at Versailles. Senghor disclosed later that it was one of the three happiest days of his life, and some of the speeches almost seemed influenced by the grandeur of Louis XIV's great chateau. The Tunisian Prime Minister M'Hamed Mzali even managed to convey the impression, perhaps to tickle French sensibilities, that Versailles was a symbol of French values. Mitterrand, always capable of great loftiness, put the issue squarely as one of cultural identity, a 'profound and powerful will to exist [which] each one of us here feels profoundly'. *Francophonie*, he said was a 'vital reflex against the mortal abolition of differences', in other words, it would be deadly if everyone spoke English.

One interesting question raised at the summit was the extent to which what was being created was really a French version of the Commonwealth, a line much pursued by the Canadians, who see the question very much as one of parity. Thus the offer by the Canadians to host the summit in Quebec in 1987 has been seen as an attempt by Mulroney to make it coincide with the Commonwealth summit which the Canadians also hosted in October 1987 in Vancouver. President Mitterrand, however, seemed to want to play down the comparison in his opening speech, and several observers stressed the fact that in *francophonie*, even in its very name, linguistic identity is much stronger and more openly expressed than in the Commonwealth, where it is taken for granted.[29]

Where does the ACCT fit into all these developments? There had been some expectation that the conference would be the decisive impetus that would help convert the agency into a francophone equivalent of the Commonwealth Secretariat. The summit itself had said that it was important that 'the ACCT, principal intergovernmental organ of *francophonie*, should adapt its orientations and actions to the decisions of the summit', but it gave the responsibility for follow-up to the Comité de Suivi (with its sub-committees on francophone organizations, culture and communications, training and education, and science and research) under the Canadian Senator Leprette. One concern of the countries involved has been to avoid giving the ACCT too much power too quickly, and to avoid the expansion of a costly bureaucracy. These concerns were seen in a special ministerial meeting of the ACCT in December, which had been billed as a meeting where the new vocation of the agency would be spelt out, but which largely focused on budgetary adjustments. These were not without significance—the administrative budget was cut to 40 per cent from over 50 per cent of the total, so that more could be spent on the programmes, giving the Secretary-General in fact more say in recruitment and more flexibility of operation to meet the challenges of the immediate future. But this is still far from widening the mandate of the agency (the only new powers granted were in the increasingly innovative sector of communications).

In fact the 1986 summit gave a tremendous new psychological impetus to the ACCT. After the summit it was taken for granted for the first time that the agency would have responsibility for all the subsidiary meetings connected with *francophonie*, including ministerial ones,[30] which reinforced its mandate to liaise with all the diverse francophone professional organizations. Under its present Secretary-General, the former Gabonese Foreign Minister, the most overtly political holder of that office there has been, the ACCT seems to have more wind in its sails. But a major moment of truth will still come at the Montreal summit, when it will have to decide whether or not the Comité de Suivi will continue, or whether its functions will be handed to the ACCT.

The political and administrative debate on its future, and the rhetoric surrounding the launching of the summit, as well as the new 'communications'-based drive to keep abreast of modern technology, have temporarily eclipsed concentration on the developmental role of the agency. For the Senghorean 'all-culture-is-development' school of thought it is patently an inappropriate debate, in any case. But the limited headway already made at the ACCT in devoting a portion of its resources to economic development shows that concern in African states for the continent's most urgent priorities is likely to keep emerging through the no doubt beneficial, but lower priority activity in the cultural sector. Africa, more or less coterminous with that part of *francophonie* that lies in the developing world, which played a vital role in spawning the concept, could yet materially help to determine its future orientation.

Notes

1. For the text of the Cultural Cooperation chapter of Lomé, see, *The Third ACP-EEC Convention signed at Lomé, 8 December 1984 and Related Documents* (Luxembourg, Office for Official Publications for EC Council of Ministers, 1984).

2. See, Hymans, Jacques-Louis, *Leopold Sedar Senghor—An Intellectual Biography* (Edinburgh, Edinburgh University Press, 1971), chapter on 'Politics and Culture', pp. 153–4. Senghor's insistence on the primacy of culture (see, most recently the quotation printed at the head of the chapter) was sometimes seen by radicals as making him lukewarm about political issues like independence. However, it could sometimes lead him into utterances that could be interpreted as ultra-radical, such as 'we must understand that true independence is cultural independence' (Hymans, p. 153), which could be taken as a slogan by those who were suspicious of letting *francophonie* take too strong a grip.

3. Reprinted in Senghor, L.S., *Liberté 1: Negritude et Humanisme* (Paris, Editions du Seuil, 1964). According to the official organ of the ACCT,

AGECOOP-Liaison, (no. 84, January–February 1986), Senghor is cited as having first raised the prospect of a 'francophone community' at a summit of the Afro-Malagasy Union (UAM), the precursor of OCAM, in Bangui on 25 March 1962. But his first use of the word *'francophonie'* appears indeed to have been in the article in *L'Esprit*.

4.   Deniau, Xavier, *La Francophonie*, Que-Sais-Je Series (Paris, Presses Universitaires de France, 1983). See also, Viatte, Auguste, *La Francophonie* (Paris, Librairie Larousse, 1969), and de Monetra, Hyacinthe, and Campion, Xavier, *Dictionnaire de le Francophonie* (Paris, Association de Solidarité Francophone, 1969).

5.   Ossito-Midiouhan, Guy, 'Portée, Idéologie et Fondements Politiques de la Francophonie', *Peuples Noirs, Peuples Africains* (no. 23, January–February 1985), spotlights these works and criticizes Deniau for not citing them since they cast a somewhat different light on the views of Reclus whom Deniau simply presents as a model of republican virtue.

6.   Hymans, op. cit., p. 153.

7.   At the University of Dakar in December 1965, he called for a 'French-style Commonwealth' which would be able to 'give the enormous means necessary for the progress of our elites, that is to say, of our states'. Quoted by Decraene, Philippe, *Le Monde*, 18 February 1969.

8.   Deniau, op. cit., p. 54. He goes on to say that the only time that de Gaulle was heard to utter the word was on hearing of the death of the Quebec leader, Daniel Johnson: 'What a great loss for all of *francophonie*', he said.

9.   Baulin, Jacques, *La Politique Africaine d'Houphouët-Boigny* (Paris, Editions Eurafor-Presse, 1980).

10. Allen, Philip M., 'Francophonie Considered', *Africa Report* (June 1968). Allen, like many students of French culture from outside it, seems to have a love–hate relationship with his subject matter, which gives his elegantly written article additional piquancy.

11. See, Viatte, op. cit., pp. 9–25, and *Dictionnaire de la Francophonie*, *passim*.

12. Cobbet, Edward, *The French Presence in Black Africa* (Washington, Black Orpheus Press, 1972).

13. Baulin, Jacques, *Conseiller du President Diori* (Paris, Eurafor-Presse, 1986), pp. 53–82. This is an absorbing but not entirely disinterested study.

14. 'Griot' column, *West Africa*, 9 March 1968, p. 285.

15. Baulin, op. cit., p. 61.

16. 'Matchet's Diary' *West Africa*, 24 March 1969, p. 244.

17. Corbett, op. cit., p. 80.

18. Laos, in the end, remained with observer status.

19. Baulin, op. cit., p. 81.

20. 'Francophonie's Founding Fathers', *West Africa*, 4 April 1970, p. 357.

21. *Convention and Charter of the Agence de Co-operation Culturelle et Technique* (Paris, ACCT, 1983).

22. I understand the move to accommodate Fillioud came from the French Socialist party, and not from Mitterrand himself who opposed it, aware of the views of African governments, in particular.

23. Dealt with at length in Valantin, Christian, 'A Propos de la Communauté Organique: Francophone et Dialectique', *Revue des Parlementaires de la Langue Française* (no. 40, October 1980), p. 120.

24. In 1984, he announced the creation of the *Haut Conseil de la Franco-phonie* as an international forum to discuss matters related to *franco-phonie*, to which he appointed mainly cultural personalities such as Euzhan Palcy, Martiniquaise film-maker of *Rue Cases-Negres*; Francis Bebey, Cameroonian musician and composer; Edouard Maunick, Mauritian poet; and others, mainly from Africa, the Caribbean and the Arab world. Senghor, almost inevitably, was the Vice-President and the French President was ex-officio President of the Conseil.

25. This was a belated recognition of the important *francophonie* component in the French Overseas Departments and Territories, which had been invisible at Niamey I and II, and in the early years of the agency.

26. Mulroney quoted the French academician Maurice Druon as saying that 'all progress must express itself in French', because, said Mulroney, 'the South like the North, is in danger of by-passing French if it should cease to assert itself as an instrument of scientific and technical communication. It is the fate that other languages have known when they ceased to live in their time. Let us make sure it does not happen to the French language'. Quoted in *West Africa*, 3 March 1986, p. 448.

27. An editorial in *Le Monde*, 21 February 1986, quoted a Quebec delegate as saying that the French media had paid less attention to the summit than they would to any fashion-show of women's underwear.

28. See, *West Africa*, 3 March 1986, p. 449.

29. The insistence on parity was reportedly upsetting Commonwealth officials early in 1987, because the Quebec summit is only five days, so the normally ten-day Commonwealth summit is being cut down to the same length.

30. The Dakar Secretariat for Education, Youth and Sport has now been wound up.

9   South–South cooperation: Africa's Brazilian option

Mark S.C. Simpson

Introduction

In the last decade a number of attempts have been made in the development literature to construct a model of South–South cooperation between developing countries as a means of achieving a more equitable New International Economic Order (NIEO).[1] Running parallel to these intellectual exercises and directly related to the deepening of the international economic recession, there has been a tendency on the part of Third World statesmen to call for greater interaction amongst LDCs.[2] It is possible to identify a number of recurrent underlying assumptions common to all these efforts.

One central concept is that of partial delinking. Due to the present deadlocked state of the North–South dialogue and a general consensus that this is unlikely to be broken in the foreseeable future, it is argued that the South should now examine the possibilities of collective self-reliance. Another powerful reason for the South to attenuate its dependence on the North as a source of growth stimuli is that, while Third World countries (it is generally held) need growth rates of at least 6 per cent to have any serious impact on poverty, the OECD growth rate has more or less stagnated at around 3 per cent. The industrialized countries are therefore incapable of serving as the engines of growth for Third World economies, which should look to each other as counter-vailing options. As one analyst has argued, the development of a South–South nexus should be seen as the key intermediate position between the 'unrealistic and undesirable de-coupling of the fledgling economies of the South from the North on the one hand and sinking further into the tight embrace of asymmetrical North–South interdependence on the other'.[3] South–South relations are therefore seen essentially as a means whereby the periphery can speed up its own development process.

Added to these immediate and direct economic benefits arising from South–South cooperation, some view the development of horizontal linkages as enhancing the Third World's bargaining power *vis-à-vis* the North through the establishment of a common front on the part of the LDCs.[4] This idea is not new, dating back in fact to the 1950s and 1960s with the formation of the Non-Aligned Movement, the Group of 77 in UNCTAD and other attempts to create a united Third World position on international issues. As many have argued, little change will occur in the present unequal relationship between North and South unless the South begins to organize its countervailing power on the economic and political front.[5] By developing the collective self-reliance of the South, it is believed that the stalemate in the North–South dialogue can be broken, the rationale being that the increased economic strength of the Third World will permit it to take retaliatory action against the North, forcing the latter to come to the negotiating table to discuss fundamental structural reforms to the international economy.

In the debate on South–South therefore, it appears there are two time-frames as well as two closely linked objectives. The first objective is the short-term one of developing links between LDCs as an alternative to the restrictive and exploitative existing North–South trading patterns. Immediate economic benefits for the participants are thus seen to be the main driving force behind intra-South trade. The second objective is longer-term and more strategic, namely to bring about a NIEO through a strengthening of LDC economies and the Third World's collective bargaining power via cooperation amongst its members which will then have a positive impact on North–South relations.

The means whereby these intra-South ties can be created, or where already in existence, strengthened, are those of exploring areas of possible complementarity in trade, financial cooperation, examining the viability of joint ventures in certain sectors and sharing technology. At the 7th Special Session of the UN General Assembly in 1975 for example, a resolution was adopted concerning 'Development and International Economic Cooperation', which dealt with the question of cooperation between developing countries, calling for an increase in mutual assistance at all levels. A belief common to this and subsequent UN statements on this subject is that all developing countries were basically similar in terms of the structural features of their economies and the positions they occupied in the international economic system. It followed from this that their relations with each other would be more symmetrical and less exploitative than their traditional pattern of contacts with the industrialized countries, an imbalance which arose from the qualitatively different economic structures found in the latter. Due to this suggested essential similarity between LDCs, exchanges of goods and technology were likely to be more adequate in terms of the satisfaction of the needs of the respective parties than the existing North–South flows. At the same time, cooperation on an intra-South basis would permit the developing countries to pursue policies of mutual specialization and comparative advantages in trade, thus strengthening their economies on an individual basis.

In sum, it has been argued by advocates of South–South cooperation that this will, by allowing the creation of an integrated Third World market, permit individual countries to exploit economies of scale, increase productive capacity within the South as a whole, protect it to an extent from fluctuations in the Northern economies and increase the Third World's bargaining power *vis-à-vis* the industrialized countries through a reduction in the degree of dependence of the former on the latter.

The newly industrialized countries as initiators of South–South relations

The 1970s saw a number of fundamental structural changes in the international economic system. Amongst the most important of these was the rise of the Newly Industrializing Countries (NICs), which began to challenge the traditional North–South relationship by increasing their contacts with other LDCs. These NICs, such as Brazil, Mexico, Taiwan, South Korea and India, had all built up sizeable industrial capacities and were capable of substantial exports of manufactured products. In important areas these NICs have already taken over or are beginning to take over the traditional role of the developed countries as suppliers of industrial products and technology to the Third World.[6] These NICs have been challenging the old international division of labour which excluded the possibility of extensive contacts within the South, since all Third World economies were tied in through vertical linkages with the industrialized countries. This process of 'hierarchization' and differentiation within the Third World, resulting from the

restructuring of the international division of labour which occurred
during the 1970s, has permitted the development of new economic
linkages within the South. The traditional division of the world into two
distinct blocs, North and South—or in the terminology of the neo-
Marxists, the centre and periphery—is in the process of being substi-
tuted for a new tripartite division of the international economy, with the
addition of a new, third, middle category of states—the NICs or semi-
periphery.

The formation of the NICs has been the subject of a number of in-
depth studies which are worth reflecting upon in order to fully
understand why it is that these countries are the prime movers behind
the growth of South–South contacts.

Wallerstein argues that in a highly inequitable system such as the
prevailing international economic set-up, a safety valve is required
through which steam can be let out. The semi-peripheral countries are
seen to perform this function.[7] It is argued that the structural crisis
of the international economy in the 1970s, characterized by falling
aggregate demand, led capital in the industrialized (or core) countries to
explore new possibilities for its own continued expansion. Running
parallel to these developments in the core countries, certain peripheral
countries were in the process of obtaining, or already possessed, a
number of important prerequisites for continued industrialization. The
most important of these were a relatively high degree of technological
sophisticiation as compared to most of the Third World, some basic
infrastructure and semi-skilled work-forces, all the products of the
import-substitution industrialization drives undertaken by these countries during the 1950s and 1960s. The semi-peripheral countries helped
to solve the problem of core capital, arising out of the fact that
productivity gains were less than wage increases, by allowing core
capital to relocate in certain Third World countries which had basic
industrial capacities and cheaper semi-skilled labour forces. It is these
countries which have become the NICs.

These NICs have been the initiators of South–South relations and
their expansionist drive towards establishing commercial contacts with
other Third World countries must be analysed in the light of economic
considerations. Like all capitalist economies, the semi-peripheral countries need to expand their markets but are faced with a peculiar
dilemma. The state is unable to permit substantial wage increases since
this would destroy the advantageous wage differential the particular
NIC enjoys *vis-à-vis* the core countries. Low wages are maintained

since priority is given to cost minimization in order to continue attracting core capital. The option of granting wage increases in order to widen the domestic market and raise the level of internal demand is thus precluded. As Marini, the Brazilian political economist who developed the concept of 'sub-imperialism' argued, semi-peripheral capital is thus faced with problems of realization. The solution is found in the development of export markets in the Third World, the commercial contacts with the periphery providing new conditions for the capital accumulation process in the semi-periphery.[8]

The barriers to South–South contacts are enormous. The vertical links established with the North over centuries of interaction are extensive, entrenched and extremely difficult to break. This is particularly obvious if one recognizes the nature of the transport networks which run along a North–South axis and militate against intra-South trade. One could add to this the relative ignorance amongst LDCs of each others capabilities and needs as compared to the knowledge of Third World markets that the industrialized countries possess. At the same time, there are social groups within each individual LDC whose interest lies in the maintenance of existing patterns of exchange.

If one accepted the UN's characterization of the Third World as being composed of fairly homogeneous units this, rather than encouraging intra-South trade, would tend to militate against it. If we assume that all Third World countries share a number of basic structural features, (that is, they are all primary commodity producers with limited industrial capacities), there would be no rationale for peripheral countries to sell goods to each other, especially in view of a general desire to protect their own employment opportunities.

There has been an upsurge in South–South trade since the mid-1970s but not according to the pattern suggested by the UN model. The impetus arises precisely from the fact that Third World countries are far from homogeneous in terms of their levels of economic development. South–South links have tended to involve NICs on the one hand and other developing countries on the other. The most salient of these relationships has been the one between Brazil and Africa.

Brazil–Africa trade

Trade between Brazil and Africa has shown remarkable growth over the last two decades. From less than US$20 million in 1960, it had soared by

1981 to US$2.6 billion. Just taking the Southern African region (exclud-
ing South Africa), imports from Brazil grew 1,500 per cent between
1974 and 1980 from US$12.2 million to US$191.7 million. On the other
hand, by 1982 Nigeria alone was importing Brazilian goods and services
to the tune of US$245 million, making it easily Brazil's largest trade
partner in Africa, followed by Zaïre with US$146 million. In relative
terms exports to Africa as a percentage of Brazil's total exports rose from
2.3 per cent in 1972 to 4.5 per cent in 1979.[9] Despite sharp oscillations,
both in value and volume, the trend has been continually upwards.
What factors lie behind these figures?

It is clear that the initiative came from the Latin American partner. As
mentioned above, Wallerstein and Marini have provided structural
explanations for the expansion in NIC exports to other Third World
countries. In the Brazilian case, however, there have been a number of
conjunctural factors which also help to throw light on the tendency for
LDC markets to grow in importance for Brazilian exporters from the
mid-1960s onwards. The years of the so-called 'Brazilian miracle' from
1968 to 1973, with the country achieving an average growth rate of
around 10 per cent per annum, also increased Brazil's vulnerability to
external shocks through a trebling of the external debt which jumped
from US$4 billion in 1968 to US$12.5 billion in 1973. At the same time,
the country's dependence on oil imports was exacerbated, a reflection of
the development model that was chosen with its heavy emphasis on
industrial production.[10] With the onset of the 1973 oil price rises, Brazil
was faced with serious balance of payments problems and great stress
was laid by the state on the necessity of a more aggressive export
performance as a means of overcoming the balance of payments
constraint on growth. Continued growth required the maintenance of
the country's import capacity at all costs, particularly in reference to
capital goods. A central element in the government's strategy since 1973
has been to encourage the growth of manufactured exports to help offset
the external imbalance and service external debt. These pressures to
find new markets were compounded by the growth of protectionism in
North American and West European markets in the early 1970s.
Conscious of the country's vulnerability to an oil embargo from the
Middle East as a result of the 1973 OPEC action, the government also
began to press for a diversification of the country's fuel suppliers.

The convergence of all these factors resulted in the choice of Africa as
a partner that could help Brazil to overcome its difficulties.[11] This is
evident when one examines the composition of Brazil–African trade,

dominated as it is by exchanges of African petroleum for Brazilian industrialized products. In 1980 for example, 87.9 per cent of African purchases from Brazil were manufactured and semi-manufactured goods. Nigeria took manufactured products as 99 per cent of its purchases in the boom year of Brazil–African trade (1981), when the country became Brazil's second largest export market after the United States, accounting for 5.4 per cent of Brazil's total manufacturing sales. Brazilian exports to Africa quadrupled between 1972 and 1974 and were given significant boosts in 1977 and 1981. In 1985, with the signing of a US$1 billion countertrade deal between Brazil and Nigeria, it became clear that this particular case of South–South trade was here to stay.[12]

Brazilian imports from Africa on the other hand were dominated by crude oil which accounted for an average of 70 per cent of total imports from Africa in the period 1975–8. By 1982 this figure had risen to 90 per cent, the principal suppliers being Nigeria, Gabon, Libya, Angola and Congo. The remaining percentages have been taken up by Brazilian imports of phosphate from Morocco and copper from Zaïre.

In contrast, African imports from Brazil have been much more varied. These have ranged from foodstuffs (sugar, meat and cereals), to goods which one would expect an NIC to produce, that is, those that require intermediate technology such as synthetic fibres, chemical fertilizers, agricultural equipment (tractors, harvesters and processing equipment), consumer goods such as refrigerators, televisions, air-conditioners and CKD ('completely knocked down') vehicle parts for reassembly in Africa.[13]

Brazil–African trade, therefore, appears to be characterized by straightforward commercial transactions and apart from those which have been made on the basis of countertrade agreements, they would appear to be no different from traditional North–South exchanges, that is, manufactured products for primary commodities. A number of arguments could be put forward, however, to counter the view that Brazil–African trade simply replicates North–South relations on a South–South axis. Firstly, intentionally or otherwise, it is clear that in the context of the existing conditions of recession experienced by the world economy, added to the protectionism in Western markets, the growth of Brazil–African trade has permitted the partners to achieve higher levels of production than would otherwise have been the case. Brazil and Africa were able therefore to use each other as compensatory mechanisms to counter the difficulties in their trade with the West. Secondly, in the longer term, the establishment of such intra-South trading links will also go some way towards insulating the partners from the upswings and downswings of the Western business cycles of the future. Finally, an even stronger argument in favour of Brazil–African trade is that, in contrast to North–South exchanges, the relationship has been responsible for the transfer of appropriate technology from Brazil to Africa.

'Tropicalized' technology

Technology is an important variable in the development equation. It should not be treated as an immutable element incapable of adapting itself to other factors such as the availability of capital and labour skills. This has often been the case with technology imported from the North, which requires adjustments in other factors in order to accommodate it. It is increasingly accepted that developing countries require new and specific technologies which take account of the scarcity of capital, managerial and operative capabilities, their particular raw material endowments and their distinct climatic conditions.

An argument increasingly forwarded by Brazilian firms as part of their marketing strategies is that their products are somehow more suited to African conditions than their Northern equivalents since they have been 'tropicalized' during their process of adaptation to Brazilian conditions.[14] Brazilian industrialists point out that they are interested in selling precisely what Africa needs, namely intermediate technology products, and possess an understanding of the peculiarities of African socio-economic conditions gleaned from their own experience of having to tailor their products to suit the predominantly low-income Brazilian market. It is also argued that, because they produce on a smaller-scale than their competitors from the industrialized countries, they are more adaptable and willing to introduce modifications into what they sell to fit in with the requirements of the buyer.

The claims would appear to have some validity and seem to be borne out by experience so far. In contrast to the NICs of the Far East for example, which opted for a development path based on the production of high-technology consumer goods aimed at high-income markets in industrialized countries, Brazil underwent a process of import-substitution industrialization which reflected its own largely Third World domestic market. As a result the range of goods it now produces would seem ideal for Third World socio-economic as well as geographical and climatic conditions. Consequently the natural outlet for exports of these products will be the Third World itself.

Examples abound in Africa of the positive attitudes towards products carrying 'Made in Brazil' labels. African farmers for example, using Brazilian-made Ford and Caterpillar tractors, have found them simpler to operate, better-suited to African soil conditions and therefore longer lasting than Northern equivalents.[15] It is clear that this comparative advantage of the Brazilian machines arises out of the fact that they were developed taking into account the low level of skills of the average Brazilian farmer and so as to be used more intensively all year round as a result of the longer agricultural cycle of the tropics, as compared to the temperate zones of the North.[16] Brazilian-made buses, trucks and cars have also been found to be sturdier and better-suited to African road conditions than Japanese, American and West European models. Likewise in the field of consumer durables, favourable comments have been passed on the ability of Brazilian export houses to supply such things as kerosene refrigerators to African markets for use in non-electrified areas, products developed firstly with a view to a particular section of Brazil's domestic market.

The idea of Brazil's comparative advantage in appropriate technology has been used as a trump card especially by those firms dealing in the export of services to Africa, while the fact that close to fifty Brazilian firms at present operate in Africa, indicates a high degree of receptivity to Brazilian expertise.[17] In the area of civil construction and road engineering for example, a number of African countries have been or are at present hosts to projects undertaken by Brazilian companies. Road building in particular has been a favourite for Brazilian engineering firms operating in Africa and it is clear that Brazilian technology, expertise, adaptability and cost competitiveness have proved decisive in firms clinching contracts. As one commentator has put it, Brazilian firms are better equipped than many competitors from the industrialized world to undertake 'labour-intensive projects using local raw materials, in operating under close cost constraints and in being more flexible and able to provide "simple" approaches'.[18]

Having gained unique experience building highways, railways and hydro-electric power stations in the inhospitable Amazon and the semi-deserts of the Brazilian North-East, these engineering firms possess the expertise with which to tackle similar projects under equally difficult climatic and topographic conditions. The most spectacular example of Brazilian know-how applied to the African context was the 800 mile

Rodovia da Esperanca (Highway of Hope), cutting across the Sahara desert in Mauritania, built by a leading Brazilian engineering firm, Construtora Mendes Junior. The benefits accruing to Mauritania were not only connected to the competitive pricing of the Brazilian bid (though to a cash-strapped economy such as the Mauritanian this was not an insignificant factor, although a short-term one) but also produced longer-term benefits from the type of technology employed by the firm, which had significant employment effects. This was a result of the firm's willingness to establish links with local partners through sub-contracting which helped to create some backward linkages in the otherwise disconnected Mauritanian economy. At the same time, Mendes Junior undertook to train nationals in the skills necessary for maintaining the road so that when it left the country upon termination of the project, it left behind a workforce of skilled technicians and labourers, an important developmental by-product.

Another Brazilian construction company, Norberto Odebrecht, is at present responsible for a hydro-electric project on the Cuanza River in Angola, estimated to cost US$1 billion. This project is of particular interest in that it is a joint venture, with the Soviet Union providing the turbines and the Brazilian firm handling the construction. Odebrecht undertook to contract half its work-force amongst nationals, who are being trained *in situ*. When eventually completed, the dam will be the second largest in Africa. Andrade Gutierrez, another Brazilian engineering concern, is at present involved in the construction of a 200km highway in the Congo (linking it with Zaïre), which cuts straight through tropical jungle. It is interesting to note that this particular company had accumulated a great deal of invaluable experience of operating in isolated and difficult terrains in Brazil, one of its past projects having been participation in the construction of the Trans-Amazon highway.

The record so far suggests therefore a number of reasons for the growing receptivity of African countries to bids from Brazilian construction firms. As they often do in Brazil for similar reasons, namely the unavailability of a pool of semi-skilled and skilled labour in the area of operation, the companies are prepared to take on unskilled workers and train them on the job, a valuable by-product to any such projects. This is in contrast to Western and even South Korean firms which tend to import Pakistani or Indian labour. Added to this is their already mentioned unequalled experience in dealing with the logistical problems inherent in such undertakings, namely tenuous communications, a hostile environment and poor local materials. Whereas concerns from the industrialized countries tend to approach such projects with a great deal of highly expensive machinery and material, the Brazilian companies have shown that they are willing to improvise on the basis of what is available in the host country. They are therefore able to win contracts on the basis of price-competitiveness, to the advantage of the African country in question which is likely to be suffering from a lack of foreign exchange.

Other examples of the transfer of technology include the sale of Brazilian alcohol as fuel technology to Zimbabwe as well as help in building a methanol plant (a joint venture between a Brazilian company and the Bank for Housing and Construction of Ghana), setting up plants to produce ceramic tiles, while another firm is helping Accra in its project to build a brick factory in each of Ghana's ten regional capitals. In another joint project, a state mining company is involved in a coal-mining venture in Mozambique, supplying the know-how while OPEC is providing the financial backing. The Brazilian Pao de Acucar super-market chain has set up a number of outlets in Angola and has been working closely with the Angolan government and state supermarkets in order to help overcome the distribution problems in Luanda.

This trade in technical services is particularly prominent in Brazil's dealings with Nigeria. Linked to the high levels of public expenditure during the 1970s as a result of the oil boom, Brazilian companies won a number of civil engineering contracts for low cost housing projects, the building of the new federal capital in Abuja (Brazilian experience from the building of Brasilia being invaluable in this context), as well as for telecommunications systems and railways. While many have been turnkey projects with Brazilian expertise and technology being used to set up plant (completed projects which were then handed over to Nigerians), a number of Brazilian–Nigerian joint ventures have been established. The most notable of these has been the factory producing nuts and bolts set up in Kaduna by Cotia, Brazil's largest private trading company, in partnership with the Nigerian Bank for Commerce and Industry. Both partners have 25 per cent of the shares, the remainder being held by Nigerian nationals.[19]

These transfers of technology have not been limited to the industrial sector. Brazilian companies have participated in a number of Africa's agricultural projects, the most impressive being Cotia's involvement in the Côte d'Ivoire.[20] In 1978 Abidjan decided to integrate the target of food self-sufficiency in its development programme and set up an

enormous agro-industrial project known as the Soya Project with
Brazilian help. Under the supervision of Cotia, engineers, agronomists,
agricultural economists and equipment were transported from Brazil to
the Côte d'Ivoire. The Brazilians were involved in all stages of the
10,000 hectare project—clearing of the land, preparation of the soil,
sowing, harvesting and storage of the soya, rice and corn produced by
the scheme. They were also responsible for setting up a seed bank
which produced the various strains considered suitable for the conditions in the Côte d'Ivoire.

Once the scheme had been successfully completed, Brazilian involvement was not terminated. The Brazilian firms involved in the project
subsequently set up Procampo (the Brazilian Programme for Technical
Cooperation in Agriculture), which retains 40 per cent ownership of the
scheme, the remainder belonging to Lair Financière of the Côte d'Ivoire.
The Brazilians are now responsible for the commercialization of the
products and Cotia has used its undertaking in the West African country
as a 'demonstration model' with which to win new joint ventures in
other African countries. Brazilian agronomists are also currently
involved in a number of other countries. In Ghana, for example,
Brazilians are helping in a project which aims to revitalize the country's
long neglected live-stock sector through the introduction of both
Brazilian artificial insemination as well as live-stock raising techniques,
the building of silos and of small dams to increase irrigation. In Gabon,
Brazil is helping the government set up a Centre for Agricultural
Technology and Training costed at CFA Francs 13.5 billion (approximately US$4.5 million at current 1987 exchange rates), the financing of the
project being divided equally between Brazil and Gabon.

It is clear therefore that a number of African countries judge Brazil's
agricultural experience to be of some relevance to their own situations.
From the Ghanaian example mentioned earlier it seems that one
particularly promising area for the transfer of Brazilian know-how lies in
live-stock raising. Most of Brazil's herd is composed of Zebu, the
humped animal originally imported from India and held to be highly
appropriate to African conditions. Added to this is the fact that Brazilian
farmers have over the years been able to improve the meat-yielding
capacity of their stocks as well as their resistance to diseases common to
both Latin America and Africa. Pest and disease control is another field
in which Brazilian farmers have made significant progress, with their
crop losses being significantly lower than the African average. Due to
the coincidence of both food crops (cassava, rice), and cash crops (coffee,

cocoa), grown on both sides of the South Atlantic, there is obviously scope for the transfer of Brazilian know-how in this field to Africa.

The Brazilian state has itself become heavily involved in technological cooperation with Africa and inter-governmental agreements have been signed with the Côte d'Ivoire, Gabon, Ghana, Mali, Nigeria, Tunisia, Angola, Cape Verde and Mozambique which allow for the training of Africans in Brazil in a variety of fields ranging from hotel management and agronomy to computer science and medicine. The Lusophone (Portuguese-speaking) African countries have been especially privileged in this respect, with linguistic and cultural affinities facilitating such exchanges. Petrobras, the state oil company, has set up a course in the University of Luanda to provide training to Angolans in the fields of geology, engineering and exploration and production technology. This transfer of Brazilian petroleum technology is part of a joint venture exploration agreement between the Brazilian company and Angola's state-owned Sonangol for the development of Angola's reserves on its continental shelf. Other Brazilian state corporations have been involved in the training of Portuguese-speaking Africans such as the national airline, Varig. It is interesting to note that, both for reasons of experience and the language factor, UNESCO is currently using Brazilians in its literacy campaign in Mozambique. The programme, based on the transmission of lessons to isolated centres of population via the radio, has drawn on Brazilian 'know-how' accumulated from the extensive MOBRAL (Brazilian Literacy Movement) compaign under-taken by successive governments under very similar conditions to those operating in Mozambique.

Countertrade as a survival mechanism for Africa

Brazil's potential for cooperation with Africa is arguably best illustrated not through the appropriateness of Brazilian goods, the transfers of Brazilian technology or the establishment of joint ventures but through the recent countertrade deal between Brazil and Nigeria mentioned earlier.

Due to mounting foreign debts on both sides of the South Atlantic and a resultant shortage of foreign exchange, the years 1982–3 saw a contraction in trade between Brazil and Africa, though the reciprocal demand for goods had not diminished. The solution was to reverse the downward trend in bilateral trade through countertrade deals, the most important being that signed in 1984 with Nigeria and estimated to have been worth US$1 billion. The package deal, once again coordinated by Cotia and agreed upon at an inter-governmental level, involved the exchange of Brazilian manufactured goods (cars, agricultural equipment, chemical products, food and iron ore), for Nigerian crude oil.

The use of countertrade exchanges helped both countries to by-pass the international system as far as the financing of the exchanges was concerned by avoiding the use of hard currency at a time when the foreign exchange reserves of both countries were already dangerously low. This was of particular importance to Nigeria, at the time under a great deal of pressure from creditor banks to reach an understanding with the IMF on an agenda of internal economic reforms before negotiations on rescheduling of its foreign debt could be initiated. From the history of IMF policies in Africa, the Nigerians were aware that the conditions of the Fund would have been monothematic, involving a devaluation of the Naira, the removal of government subsidies on a number of basic consumer goods and a liberalization of the existing foreign investment code, all remedies bound to result in social discontent. At the same time, Nigeria's room for maneouvre was also limited by her quota arrangement with OPEC, thus excluding the option of overcoming her balance of payments difficulties and debt-servicing shortfalls through an increase in oil exports. The 1984 countertrade deal in effect allowed Nigeria to escape from being 'blackmailed' into accepting IMF conditionality in its negotiations on external debt. In the past this had been a route followed by many African countries with declining import capacity coinciding with maturing debt repayments, the bitter medicine of the Fund's austerity measures always leading to recession.[21]

For Brazil on the other hand, the deal allowed it to continue exporting without having to show its foreign exchange earnings which would have had to be turned over, at least in part, to its foreign creditors. The guaranteed supply of Nigerian crude oil, it could be argued, also allowed the country to maintain its level of economic activity, enhancing the strength of Brazil's debt negotiators by denying the IMF the use of the threat to withdraw its standby credits which would have been used partly for oil imports.

The financial crisis of 1982–4, in both Africa and Brazil, had begun to constitute an obstacle to the South–South relationship, with Brazilian exports to Africa falling by over 20 per cent and trade in the other direction dropping by nearly 100 per cent, the latter figure a reflection of the deep recession prevailing in the Brazilian economy, with its concomitant decline in the demand for fuel. It is arguable that Brazil's interest in Africa up till then had been based on a mercantilist concern to generate foreign exchange to service its external debt, through exploiting short-term export opportunities offered by capital-surplus African oil producers. With the worsening debt profile of African countries such as Nigeria, however, the parties were forced to base their relationship increasingly on complementarities and shared interests as evidenced by the countertrade arrangement.

It is noteworthy that even before the 1984 deal was signed, Brazil had been operating another unique arrangement with Nigeria, signed between the Nigerian National Petroleum Corporation (NNPC) and Petrobras. NNPC provided the Brazilian concern with 110,000 barrels of oil per day. Out of this Petrobras processed 50,000 barrels per day. The fuel derivatives were returned to Nigeria with Brazil retaining a proportion of the end products equal to the total value of the crude oil. The mechanism proved highly advantageous to both sides. Brazil was able to make use of its under-utilized refining capacity, a result of its own highly successful alcohol as fuel programme, as well as protecting jobs in the petro-chemical industry. The benefits to Nigeria arose from the lower processing costs of Petrobras. It appears that the percentage Petrobras retains from the deal is lower than that which would have been taken by Western oil companies. For both countries there were obviously foreign exchange savings as well.

Not surprisingly, both arrangements were strongly condemned by the IMF, since they did not produce the hard currency with which to meet foreign debt obligations. There may, however, have been more deep-seated objections, since countertrade, as part of a wider strategy of South–South cooperation, does pose a potentially serious long-term threat to the Western-dominated international economic system, if LDCs were to continue to make an effort to find solutions to their needs and problems from among their neighbours rather than from the North.

What countertrade does show is that during times of economic difficulties, Africa now possesses an alternative source of help to the Western-dominated international financial institutions and more importantly, one that will not dictate policy prescriptions.

Problems and prospects

That Brazil has a great deal to offer Africa in terms of its development needs is clear from the above exposition. The Latin American country now occupies a somewhat ambiguous position in the international economic system: a member of the Third World yet an aspirant to the status of developed country; the eighth largest economy in the capitalist world and by far the most powerful one in the South, but with a per capita income that stands at just over US$2,000 per annum, as well as a foreign debt of over US$130 billion. It is precisely this ambiguity, however, that has and could continue to rebound to Africa's benefit and these factors that make Brazil an ideal development partner.

Having opted for an industrialization drive based on massive imports of Western technology and capital during the 1960s and 1970s, Brazil was able, through a learning process based on trial and error, to adapt these factors of production to its own particular needs and socio-economic conditions. Over this period, therefore, Brazil developed a whole range of unique technological skills both in industry and agriculture, which it can now offer to Africa and the record so far indicates that this know-how is of great applicability to the African situation. Africa could continue to use Brazil as a source of adapted technology and expertise to solve some of its development problems. By so doing, Africa would be able to skip stages in its learning process and avoid mistakes that it can ill afford.

That the relationship is asymmetrical should not constitute an obstacle. South–South trade would not even get off the ground unless one of the participants was a technological innovator since, given the generalized desire to protect employment opportunities, there is no logic in LDCs exchanging goods that could feasibly be produced by any Third World country. Therefore, while the Brazil–African relationship apparently replicates the North–South model, transferring it to a South–South axis, with Africa serving the traditional role of supplier of raw materials and market for Brazilian exports of industrial goods and services, there is an important qualitative difference characterizing the horizontal links, namely their cooperative element.

Due to the increasing debt problems and internal economic difficulties that are common to both Africa and Brazil, the relationship has gradually become one between 'partners in trouble' and as such is characterized by a search for complementarities and modalities of economic interaction that maximize mutual benefit. This is in contrast to traditional exchanges between the developed world and the LDCs, where the balance of influence that determined the distribution of benefits from trade was tilted firmly in favour of the former group of countries. On the assumption that there is unlikely to be a short-term solution to, or even improvement to, the Third World's debt problem, the very lack of disposable foreign exchange on the part of both Africa as a whole and Brazil will tend to increase the cooperative aspects of their relationships and force them to search for new mechanisms for dealing with their common problems.

This is not to say that a strengthening of trans-Atlantic ties will be easy. Many factors militate against closer relations between Third World countries.[22] Probably the most significant immediate challenge to be faced concerns the interpretation of their respective national interests. A narrow definition of national interest and a strict adherence to its counterpart, sovereignty, will only serve to obstruct the development of South–South relations. The participants will have to widen their definition of national interest and refrain from treating international trade as a zero-sum game. The sacrificing of possible short-term gains will be necessary in some instances in order to consolidate patterns of trade in the long term. With the recent drop in the price of oil there is obviously the temptation for Brazil to cancel its agreement with Nigeria and return to the international market in order to satisfy its energy needs. This would, however, be a myopic act, destroying any chances of Brazil becoming a preferential supplier of manufactured goods as well as services to the African country.

As an alternative development path for Africa, South–South cooperation has already shown great promise. It remains however a modality of economic interaction that is still in its infancy and its full potential is yet to be discovered. Africa needs to seek out other extra-continental partners who may, like Brazil, have something unique to offer in terms of Africa's development needs. Although not within the scope of this chapter, India immediately comes to mind. India is a country that has made great strides in the field of appropriate technology, attempting to reconcile the exigencies of increased productivity and efficiency with the reality of a labour-surplus economy and Indian science has also come up with answers that may be applicable to the African situation. Like the Brazilian alternative, this option requires further exploration on the part of African policy-makers.

A longer-term challenge for both Brazil and Africa, and one which will only be solved on an incremental basis, is how to attenuate their vertical links with the North in order to develop their horizontal ties. The strength of these vertical relations is best seen in the ties between Africa and Western Europe as embodied in the Lomé Convention, which effectively ensures the continuation of colonial patterns of trade and investment.[23] Through various mechanisms which guarantee both markets and minimum receipts for African exports of raw materials, the arrangement in effect forces African countries to continue gearing their economies to the satisfaction of the needs of the ex-metropoles. The tortuous nature of the negotiations preceeding the signing of Lomé III in 1985, which reflected the growing disillusionment of the African countries with the arrangement, increases the attractiveness of the Brazilian option.

Notes

1.   Carlsson, J., 'The emergence of South–South relations in a changing world economy', in Carlsson, J., ed., *South–South Relations in a Changing World Order* (Uppsala, Scandinavian Institute, 1982); Laszlo, E. (ed.), *Cooperation for Development — Strategies for the 1980s* (Dublin, Tycooly International Publishing Limited, 1984).

2.   Nyerere, J., 'The South–South Option', Address on the occasion of receiving the Third World Prize, New Delhi, 22 February 1983; Ramphal, S., 'South–South: Parameters and Pre-conditions', *Third World Quarterly* (7, no. 3, July 1982).

3.   Laszlo, E., op. cit., p. 15.

4.   Manley, M., 'Third World Under Challenge: The Politics of Affirmation', *Third World Quarterly* (11, no. 1, 1986), pp. 28–34.

5.   Ul Haq, M., 'Beyond the Slogan of South–South Co-operation', *World Development* (8, October 1980), pp. 743-51.

6.   Tyler, W., *Advanced Developing Countries as Export Competitors in Third World Markets: The Brazilian Experience*, (Washington, DC, Georgetown University, Centre for Strategic and International Studies, 1980); Campos, R., 'Prospectives of the New Industrial Countries — Brazil', paper presented to the International Conference on Old and New Industrial Countries in the 1980s (Sussex European Research Centre, University of Sussex, 1980).

7.   Wallerstein, I., and Hopkins, T., eds., *Processes of the World-System* (London, Sage, 1980); Wallerstein, I., *The Capitalist World Economy* (Cambridge, Cambridge University Press, 1980).

8. Marini, R., *Dialectica de la Dependencia* (Mexico, Ediciones Era, 1973); Marini, R., 'Brazilian Sub-imperialism', *Monthly Review* (no. 9, 1972), pp. 14–24.

9. D'Adesky, J., 'Intercambio Comercial Brasil–Africa (1958–1977): Problemas e Perspectivas', *Estudos Afro-Asiaticos* (no. 3, Centro de Estudos Afro-Asiaticos, Rio de Janeiro, Brazil, 1980); d'Adesky, J., 'Penetracao Brasileira na Africa Austral: Perpectivas Politicas e Entraves Economicos', *Estudos Afro-Asiaticos* (no. 10, 1984); 'Brazil and Africa Survey', African Business (no. 85, September 1985); Hoffman, H., 'Towards Africa? Brazil and South–South Trade', in Carlsson, J., op. cit., pp. 55–72.

10. Martinière, G., 'Politique Africaine du Brésil', *Problèmes d'Amerique Latine* (no. 67, Paris, 1978).

11. Ibid.

12. *African Economic Digest* (23 June 1985), pp. 31–2.

13. *Relatorio*, Banco do Brasil, Fundacao Centro de Estudos do Comercio Exterior.

14. 'Brazil and Africa Survey', op. cit.

15. *Africa Guide* (1979), p. 31.

16. Fragoso, J. 'Tratores: Novo Campo de Exportacao para a Africa', *Conjuntura Africana* (no 2, 1985, Rio de Janeiro, Brazil).

17. *Afrochamber*, published by the Brazil–African Chamber of Commerce, Sao Paulo.

18. Collins, P., 'Brazil in Africa: Perspectives on Economic Cooperation Among Developing Countries', *Development Policy Review*, (3, 1985), p. 28.

19. Collins, P., ibid.

20. Roque, A., 'Brasil e Africa: Tecnologia e Cooperacao', *Conjuntura Africana* (no. 3, Rio de Janeiro, 1985), p. 6.

21. Miguel Lourenço, S., 'Countertrade: O Drible Nigeriano', *Conjuntura Africana* (no. 6, Rio de Janeiro, 1985), p. 1; 'Brazil and Africa Survey', op. cit.

22. Ogwu, J., 'Africa and Latin America: Perspectives and Challenges', paper presented to the Congress on Africa and Latin America (Rio de Janeiro), 1981; 'Nigeria and Brazil: A Model for the Emerging South–South relations?' in Carlsson, E., op. cit., pp. 102–21.

23. Perona, N., 'Os Convenios de Lomé e a Sua Influencia no Comercio entre a America Latina e a Africa', *Estudos Afro-Asiaticos* (no. 11, 1985), pp. 30–7; Simpson, M., 'Relacoes Euro-Africanas e a Convençao de Lomé', *Conjuntura Africana* (Rio de Janeiro, no. 2, 1985), p. 1.

10 Crisis management: solving Africa's debt problem?

Matthew Martin*

Africa faces many development crises in the mid-1980s.[1] Famine, population growth, ecological destruction and refugees are all major problems, and debt cannot claim to be ahead of them in the queue for solutions. But for many nations, debt is *the* immediate crisis, because if its burden is not reduced rapidly and in an orderly way, it can have catastrophic effects on development through to the end of the century.[2]

An African debt crisis? Anyone who takes the slightest interest in international affairs must know about the Latin American debt crisis. But few people outside African governments are aware that Africa has any debt, let alone a crisis. Admittedly the size of African debt is not very large. The exact size is disputed, with estimates for sub-Saharan Africa ranging between US$80 billion and US$135 billion, and for the whole of Africa between US$125 billion and US$180 billion.[3] This amounts to no more than the debt of three of the major Latin/South American debtors (Brazil, Mexico and Argentina) added together. The ignorance of African debt is also explained by its composition: more than 75 per cent of sub-Saharan debt is owed to international institutions such as the World Bank, IMF and African Development Bank, or to OECD governments. The amount of debt owed to the commercial

* I am grateful to the ESRC for funding me through my current doctorate research programme. Special thanks to Susan Strange, Chris Stevens, Tony Killick, James Mayall and Dennis Austin. Thanks are due also to the many officials in international organizations and creditor/African governments, the journalists and the bankers who have helped me but would not wish their names to be known.

banks is only US$19.8 billion, and does not account for a significant percentage of the lending of any of the major banks[4] For this reason, African debt is not seen as a threat to the international financial system, is not the subject of hundreds of detailed academic studies, and is not covered every day in the press.

Yet the size of the debt is irrelevant. What is important is the burden this debt imposes on African economies in retarding and even reversing their development processes, and what the international financial community is doing to reduce that burden.

How debt affects development

A debt service ratio (the percentage of foreign exchange earnings from exports of goods and services payable to debt service) is generally used as the best measure of the burden of debt on the economy, and one over 30 per cent is commonly regarded as a serious drain on the economy. Latest estimates suggest that seven African nations have 1986–7 ratios over 50 per cent and nineteen are over 30 per cent.[5] The figures mean little without showing how debt affects development. High debt service ratios bring about crisis by draining the economy of badly-needed resources and by causing other sources of finance to dry up.

The debt service drain

Debt service drains the economy in the following ways: first, as debt service rises, so an increasing percentage of foreign exchange earnings is diverted from paying for imports to paying the creditors. This reduces the 'import capacity' of the economy. For African economies this is particularly serious: their industries and agriculture are highly dependent on imports for their capital goods such as chemicals, farm machinery, pesticides, industrial machinery and plastics, which are needed to increase or even maintain productivity. The cutback in imports therefore brings about 'import strangulation', reducing productivity in the vital export sectors (and thereby further cutting import capacity). This strangulation extends into the non-export sectors as the government tries to concentrate resources on exports in order to earn foreign exchange. The import strangulation can also hit imports of capital goods designed to increase food production, thereby decreasing the prospects

for any agriculture-based self-reliant development and prolonging
dependence on foreign finance. In the most extreme cases, the shortage
of foreign exchange can lead to cuts in food imports, exacerbating famine
or creating severe shortages and high prices. It should also be noted that
a cut in imports generally means a cut in exports from OECD creditor
countries. For example, Nigeria, once regarded as the foremost export
market in Africa, has had its import budget cut from US$17 billion to
US$3 billion between 1982 and 1986.[6]

Second, debt service also drains the government budget. This
generally forces cuts in other spending. These cuts may hit immediately
productive investment in industry, agriculture, or infrastructure
(though some uneconomic infrastructure projects such as dams and
airports may also be hit). Or they may hit longer-term investments in
'human capital'—spending on health, education or housing. Either way
they retard development of the economy and increase hardship for the
people of the country. The alternative for the government is to try to
borrow more, both domestically and externally, to be able to continue
with its spending plans: this generally results in the prelude to the crisis
described below.

Third, debt service is also likely to drain the government's foreign
exchange reserves. This makes the country much more vulnerable to
delays in export earnings or sudden increases in debt service or capital
flight, because either of these will cause delays in payment for its
imports (which will reduce creditor confidence in the country and
accelerate the decline into debt crisis). Again, many governments have
tried to borrow their way out of this problem, with the consequences
described below.

Finally, in extreme circumstances, governments may be forced to
introduce restrictions on use of foreign exchange. Bans on certain
imports (food crops or consumer items) may cause immediate hardship
for consumers. Restrictions on the repatriation of investors' profits will
also reduce investor confidence in the country, leading to a slump in
new investment and exacerbating the foreign exchange shortage.

Cuts in new finance: the prelude to the crisis

The prelude to the crisis comes as creditors realize the extent of the
debt service overcommitment of the country. While the country is
trying to borrow as much as (or more than) before, the banks are

becoming increasingly reluctant to lend new medium/long-term loans (of more than one year) and switching to short-term loans, which are due for repayment in less than one year, in order to protect themselves from the risk of default or rescheduling. The next step for the banks is to begin cutting down the length of time for which they are prepared to 'roll over' (renew) even the short-term loans, and to increase the interest rates and fees due on the loans. This period is also commonly marked by reduction in the number of banks willing to subscribe to new long-term, medium-term or short-term loans.

The decline of new loans brings a fall in project finance, hitting infrastructural/industrial projects, and a fall in programme finance, which can hit import capacity or increase the government budget deficit. Worst of all, it hits trade finance, the money which the government relies on for day-to-day financing of imports. This comes from two sources: export credit agencies of exporting countries, and banks in exporting countries. Export credit agencies go 'off cover' (that is, suspend the normal guarantees they give for new private loans) when any country gets into arrears on its payments of 'official' debt (that is, debt to OECD governments). They may also suspend cover when facing extreme delays in trade payments for imports. This cuts off access to those lenders who are worried about the risk of lending to the country: by the time the export credit agencies suspend cover, loans are generally available only with cover! Meanwhile the commercial banks, which have been financing lines of credit to the country to pay for imports (with or without an OECD government guarantee), begin to cut back the lines, refusing 'unconfirmed' letters of credit and ultimately (in the case of Nigeria in 1986), making the credit lines conditional on prior release of foreign exchange by the central bank. This defeats the whole purpose of letters of credit, which is to enable the African country to buy imports on credit.

These two moves force the African country either to make further cuts in imports immediately, or to use its foreign exchange reserves to finance imports. Since the level of reserves is usually extremely low by this stage, the country is likely to go into arrears on its debt payments.

Management of the crisis

It is at this point that debt management by the international financial community begins to operate, when the position of the economy is

already critical. The effect on development of the debt service burden
has been extensively examined, but the ways in which the debt
management process helps or hinders development have not. This
article will concentrate on the two major multilateral fora for the
management or 'rescheduling' of debt: negotiations with the 'Paris Club'
of official creditors, and negotiations with the 'London Club' of
commercial creditors.[7] Rescheduling is the process of stretching out
debt service payments falling due in a given period over a longer period,
so as to reduce the immediate burden on the economy. The aim of this
article is not to describe the functioning of the rescheduling process.
Many other authors have done that.[8] The aim is a critical analysis of that
process, in order to gauge its efficiency in achieving the stated aim of its
advocates: to restore the African nations to a path of healthy development and to credit-worthiness for international banks and investors.[9]

Paris Club rescheduling

The 'Paris Club' is an *ad hoc* meeting of OECD creditor nations. It is
responsible for rescheduling direct government-to-government loans,
and suppliers or buyers credits for exports from the OECD country
which have been guaranteed by the export credit agency of that
country. Participation is open to any creditor country with an export
credit agency which has sufficient debt owed to it by the debtor to make
it wish to attend the meeting. It has expanded in recent years beyond
the OECD countries to include several centrally planned economies
and devloping countries such as Brazil and India.

Until 1974, the Paris Club had no formal secretariat, but since that
time a handful of civil servants from the French Treasury have handled
the administrative formalities of setting up meetings. The justification
for the lack of any permanent staff before 1974, and for the low level of
staff since then, has been that a large permanent secretariat would
encourage nations to apply for rescheduling. In the rush of reschedulings in the late 1970s and early 1980s, the staff level has been increased,
but not enough for it to play any independent role in the negotiations
beyond that of paperwork and communication.

Preconditions before meeting

The debtor country is responsible for applying to the Paris Club for a rescheduling of its debts when it feels it can no longer repay on schedule. However, there are two conditions which need to be fulfilled before the Paris Club will agree to a meeting: first the debtor state must be facing imminent default, with arrears on its Paris Club debts. This condition is justified by the need to avoid the 'moral hazard' of countries asking for rescheduling before they are absolutely desperate. It causes serious problems for the African economy: unless the government is able to 'plan' arrears on its Paris Club debts without getting into arrears on commercial debt service or IMF/World Bank repayments, it will have to pay heavy premiums on all its commercial transactions and may face suspension of IMF programmes or World Bank loans, before it can apply to the Paris Club. Paris Club failure to agree to new rescheduling requests has often led to the collapse of previous rescheduling packages.

Second, it must be negotiating seriously for an agreement with the IMF, and before a final Paris Club agreement can be reached, the IMF must have agreed to a standby loan. This duplicates the previous condition by guarding against 'moral hazard', but the domestic political criticism the African government will face if it goes to the IMF is sufficient deterrent to stop any government asking for a rescheduling before it is desperate. There can be no justifiable reason for retaining the first precondition.

This condition also reinforces the central position of the IMF in the rescheduling process. The IMF is often responsible for pushing the African government into applying for a rescheduling (for in reality many governments are determined to keep up repayments in order to maintain their good name and credit-worthiness). It then helps the government to decide what level of relief it will ask the Club for and advises it on the details of procedure in the Paris Club meetings. Depending on the previous experience or other independent expertise available to the government in deciding the terms it will request and its negotiating tactics, the IMF advice may determine almost the whole African presentation to the Club. Although they deny that there is any conflict of interest between the Fund's position as a large creditor in many countries and its role as adviser to the debtor, my research has shown that those governments relying on the Fund to prepare their submission to the Club have generally asked for less (and therefore received less) than other more independent governments. The hands of these governments have thereby been tied in advance of the negotiations. Other participants in the rescheduling process therefore see an urgent need for more independent advice and training being made available to Finance Ministries and Central Banks, particularly in smaller countries with smaller budgets and less manpower.

It is also significant that the IMF generally agrees with the debtor country an outline of the amount of foreign exchange it will save by rescheduling debt, and of the foreign exchange it can expect to receive in new aid from donors, in order to draw up the adjustment measures for the standby programme. The relatively close correlation between this preliminary estimate and the final amount of foreign exchange made available during the rescheduling process seems to negate the public assertion by the IMF, the Paris Club (speaking on behalf of the OECD creditors) and some OECD creditors themselves that one forum, in which all reschedulings and aid commitments would be decided, is impossible because it would be too complex. It is evidently possible to have one document, if it has been compiled with the help of the IMF (or the World Bank), but not to have one negotiation.

The Paris Club meeting

Between the request to the Paris Club for rescheduling and the formal meeting of the Club, there is a period of between two weeks and two months during which most of the terms are agreed in outline form during a series of preliminary discussions. The debtor government circulates a paper laying out the amount of relief needed, and the Paris Club creditors consult among themselves to determine their approximate response. Some have criticized this period as too short for a detailed enough assessment of the needs of the debtor, but this is not the primary aim of the consultations. They aim instead to resolve political differences among the creditors over the amount of relief they are prepared to grant the debtor country. It is a rare country that has its debt relief decided on the basis of its economic needs. The most important factors in the negotiations are the amount of money owed to each Paris Club creditor, and the wider political, strategic and economic ties between the creditors and the debtor. Factors such as the quality of economic management by the debtor state (in the view of the creditors), or the need for more extensive economic reforms, only exacerbate the hardline position of some creditor governments.

This preliminary consultation enables the actual meeting to be extremely short, ranging between 3–4 hours and a formal maximum of two days (though some negotiations have needed to 'stop the clock' and pretend that the third day is still the second). This period of time is too short to explore all the facets of the economy of the country involved or the different positions of the creditors. It therefore takes the form of a written report by the African delegation on the reason for the debt problem, what policies are being undertaken to overcome it, the medium-term to long-term prospects for the economy, and the amount of relief requested. This report is a formality, deviating little from the paper circulated in advance, and unless the presentation is totally inadequate, it has little effect on the outcome of the negotiations.

Next come the presentations by representatives of the IMF, the World Bank and UNCTAD. The least important is the UNCTAD presentation: while it may be of the same quality as the others, UNCTAD is seen as the friend of the debtor, and is therefore generally ignored by the creditors. The importance of the IMF and World Bank varies, depending on the attitudes of the creditors to the economic management of the debtor. If it has an excellent track record of fulfilling IMF and World Bank conditions, then the IMF statement will be largely a formality, stating its good relations with the country and reinforcing its request for relief. After this come the views of the World Bank: if the creditors are prepared to be more lenient because they have no strong political antipathy towards the debtor, they will consider the rescheduling request in the light of the medium-term development needs of the debtor, as explained by the Bank. However, if the debtor has a bad track record of breakdowns of IMF/World Bank programmes, or of protracted unresolved negotiations, then the creditors are most interested in the IMF's assessment of the debtors commitment to economic reform.

Yet the IMF's role is always predominant, in preparing the debtor submission, in reporting on the short-term to medium-term (two to three years) balance of payments prospects for the economy, and in using this projection as the basis for its assessment of the debt relief needed by the country. If there is any disparity between the amounts of debt relief assessed as necessary by the African government, the IMF and the World Bank, the creditor representatives are likely to take the IMF assessment as gospel.

Now the creditors move into a closed session (sometimes calling in the IMF for further advice) where they iron out their differences over rescheduling terms. These are usually due to political factors, as over the Cote d'Ivoire in 1983 or the Sudan in 1983–5.[10] Having resolved these problems, they return to the plenary session and present their terms to the debtor. There have been several cases where the more confident and experienced debtors have disputed the terms, and another closed session has revised them, but no recorded cases where the meeting has broken down. Most meetings reach agreement immediately (after the first closed session), and spend the rest of the meeting discussing data on the debts and drafting the agreed minutes and the standard communiqué for the press.

The bilateral meetings

The reconciliation of creditor and debtor data on debt, the decision as to which debts should be included in the rescheduling, and the negotiation of the interest rates on the rescheduled debt, are left to subsequent bilateral meetings between the debtor government and each one of its official creditors, no matter how small their debt. The debtor nations also have to talk separately with different agencies of the same creditor government, such as the Eximbank, USAID, and the CCC in the United States. This reflects a rivalry among the creditors (and their agencies), looking to grant political favours to their allies in Africa by agreeing to lower interest rates than those prevailing in the creditor financial markets. Each creditor country is obsessive about hiding the interest rates and the total amount of debt rescheduled from its fellows, until it is forced some months later to report the figures to the Paris Club secretariat, because this enables it to maintain this political leverage (and may help to get new contracts in the African country). African governments are also conscious of the ability to play off creditors against each other, but there are clear problems with this process.

  The first relates to the fact that the concessions gained in the bilateral talks are mostly so small, that several African governments have calculated that the cost of travelling to all the bilateral negotiations (which is paid by the Africans) virtually cancels them out. Secondly, these negotiations cause interminable delay. Though the agreed minute sets a deadline for them, this is often exceeded, more often than not because of creditor bureaucracy. Indeed, by the time one round of bilateral negotiations is over, it is often time to start the next multilateral round. There is no enforcement mechanism to prevent this delay.

Finally, the smaller the government, the more these myriad simultaneous negotiations tax its manpower. Several governments have simply given up on devising negotiating plans and proposed the same interest rates to all governments, which cancels out the benefits of these bilateral talks to the debtors, and gives the creditors a stronger bargaining position.

London Club rescheduling

The 'London Club' is also an *ad hoc* body, composed of creditor commercial banks, and responsible for rescheduling commercial bank loans. Its coverage is wider than that of the Paris Club, because it deals with restoration of bank trade credit lines, interbank lines which provide short-term finance to banks in debtor countries, and new bank loans (these wider categories are dealt with later on in the chapter). The London Club had no formal secretariat (in order to discourage applications for rescheduling) until 1983, when the Institute of International Finance in Washington, DC, was formed to fulfil the role of co-ordinating the creditor banks.[11]

Preconditions before rescheduling

The two preconditions before a Paris Club meeting also apply to the London Club, as do the criticisms voiced on them. While arrears are not a formal condition, in practice banks are reluctant to agree a meeting before arrears, and the need to coordinate large numbers of creditors causes delays in accepting the need for rescheduling. The financial penalties (cuts in credit lines/interbank lines/new loans) imposed on the early-applying debtor are great enough to deter rescheduling until the debtor is desperate. There is no record of the London Club agreeing to reschedulings without IMF approval. However, they do agree to negotiate with the debtor country before the final signing of the IMF loan: all but the signing of the London Club agreement may be completed before the IMF gives final approval. In practice, the length of the London Club negotiating process means that no country has received a London Club rescheduling until at least six months after an IMF loan (unless the IMF loan broke down and there was a new loan in the interim).

The procedure of the London Club differs from that of the Paris Club: instead of one formal meeting there are several meetings. Their number varies with the size of the debt and with difficulties in reconciling the debt figures of the two sides and in negotiating an agreement. The stages of negotiation may be loosely divided into: forming committees; gathering information; negotiating the draft agreement; and negotiations among the commercial banks to turn the draft into a final accord.

Forming committees

The initial meeting between the debtor state and its creditors is designed to establish a steering committee of a few selected banks to represent the multitude of commercial creditors. This procedure has the advantages of simplifying the negotiations by reducing the number of direct participants in them, of making the steering committee responsible for providing information to the other banks (therefore giving the creditors some of the work to do), and of acting as a point of contact for the IMF and World Bank. But there are a number of problems with the committee system, the first of which has to do with the composition of the committee. On the committee, places are allocated to the banks with the largest exposure, while trying to ensure a fair geographical representation on the committee. Yet both the Nigerian and Ivorian committees have been the subject of dispute among banks, and with creditor and debtor governments, because some banks were thought likely to be softer or harder on the debtor than others. These disputes can sour the atmosphere before the formal negotiations with the African government begin. Secondly, the debtor government pays the expenses of the committee, even though the rescheduled debts are subject to new fees. Thus any delay or complication costs the debtor money.

Furthermore, the heterogeneity of the nationalities, opinions, negotiating abilities, interests and power of the committee members makes consensus very slow and difficult to achieve, and means that very minor issues can cause severe disputes and delays. Finally, the extent of the mandate of the negotiators also varies widely. Some can commit their banks, but others have to spend long periods in consultation with their head offices.

Gathering information

The steering committee generally forms sub-committees, of which the primary purpose is to gather information (and later to reconcile the positions of the committee members on individual issues). They may include some or all of the following:

1. An economic sub-committee to analyse government economic policy and debt management, and to liaise with the IMF. This is not simply a duplication of the functions of the IMF, because the economic sub-committee has in some cases reported more favourably on the African economy than the IMF and therefore recommended more lenient rescheduling terms. However, the recommendations of these committees have usually been ignored or watered down into very minor concessions, and therefore the expense and the delay while the committee composes its report must be questioned.

2. The other committees, for debt owed by the private sector in the LDC, for trade credits, for interbank lines, and for legal matters, are more obviously necessary, especially as none of the sub-categories are adequately covered by World Bank/IMF/BIS statistics. However, their influence on the rescheduling process is not very great. The legal committee is a formality. The private sector committee does not bring new money to the private sector: indeed its main purpose seems to be to ensure that the debtor government guarantees all of the private sector debt. The trade credit and interbank line committees are rare in African reschedulings, and have done little or nothing to restore flows of finance.

The formation of these sub-committees also reflects the obsession of the London Club with data. In several initial rounds of negotiations, the poor quality of the data presented has soured the atmosphere and delayed agreement by several months. However, most African governments have made dramatic improvements in data collection and debt management systems in the 1980s, although many do not have the expertise, the time or the manpower to develop comprehensive systems. This should be a priority, and systems such as the Commonwealth Secretariat's computerized debt management system, which aim to train local personnel to use them rather than imposing outside technical assistance, should be used more extensively.

Yet why should the sole responsibility for compiling debt data rest on the debtor? There is no logical reason why the Bretton Woods institutions should not be responsible for preparing constantly updated databases, mutually agreeable to creditors and debtors. They already produce debt figures, some public and some confidential, but an 'impartial' comprehensive database would remove much of the acrimony and delay from initial rounds of London Club negotiations, and would improve the capacity of the IMF/World Bank to design programmes based on realistic projections of foreign exchange availability.

The negotiating meetings

Negotiating meetings between the African government and the committee are interspersed with further information-gathering, and with consultations with smaller banks by members of the committee. As many as ten meetings may be necessary (Nigeria's total is now well over twenty) before even a draft agreement can be reached. Each meeting is divided into two sessions: the 'Plenary' and the 'Closed'. At the Plenary Session, the debtor presents its request for rescheduling, and the supporting description of its economy and statistical material, and outlines the terms it wishes. As in the Paris Club meeting, the onus is on the debtor to begin the proceedings. Though this is justified by the creditors on the grounds that it is the debtor who wishes to change the original contract, it is accepted in negotiation theory that the first speaker to present his terms is at a disadvantage. This also relates to the data issue, in that the banks then get a chance to point out the faults in the debtor presentations and focus on them in the negotiation, rather than giving the debtor the chance to analyse their own often faulty presentation of the debtor economy.

The IMF role in preparing the submission of the debtor also applies in London Club negotiations. The Plenary Session is followed by the Closed Session at which banks withdraw to consider the request and prepare their answer. It is highly unlikely that they will agree to the terms asked for at the first plenary, because of the need to spend time reconciling their own differences. Most of the formal meeting-time is taken up by this closed bankers' session, often lasting more than fifteen hours, only to be repeated a few months later.[12] The main purpose of these closed sessions is to ensure comparability of losses from rescheduling between the committee members, and to reconcile different views about the creditworthiness of the debtor. It has often been necessary for either major Paris Club creditors or the IMF (or both) to step in with a combination of incentives and threats, in order to 'bang a few heads together' and get the bankers to agree.[13]

Between draft and signing

The steering committee is then responsible for convincing all of the smaller creditor banks to accept the terms of the deal. This can take several months, and if the objections of the minor banks are strong enough, they will necessitate renewed negotiations between the committee and the debtor. This is very rare, though, because the committee's reputation will be severely damaged if it repeatedly negotiates revisions of draft agreements. The usual practice is for a draft agreement to be delayed until sufficient creditor banks have been consulted to ensure that the agreement will not unravel. Again this process causes problems for the debtor, including the fact that even when the heads of the banks have been banged together over the major issues, tiny procedural matters can delay the signing for months. In the Zambian case, a delay of four months was caused by the question of who should sign the final document, the central bank or the finance ministry: the banks insisted on both. This delay can have serious implications for the debtor economy, and for the sustainability of IMF programmes and Paris Club deals. In addition, the cost to the debtor can also be increased. Several bankers have told me that they calculate the costs to them of contacting and convincing smaller banks (those costs they are not already charging to the debtor), and then pass them on to the debtor by way of higher fees or higher interest rate margins over LIBOR.

Why more MYRAs would help[14]

When bankers talk of a multi-year rescheduling (MYRA), they do not mean a postponement for ten years of debt payments due over one year. They mean the postponement for ten years of debt payments due over two years or more. The Cote d'Ivoire gained the first Paris Club and London Club MYRAs in May–June 1986, but all other agreements and the relief they provide remain temporary, and more MYRAs are vital for several African economies, especially Nigeria, Sudan and Zambia. Paris

Club reschedulings have been made somewhat less temporary by the growth in recent years (to the point where it is now standard procedure) of the practice of 're-rescheduling'. This is done by a 'goodwill clause', which states that the nation may apply for rescheduling again the following year provided it is still on target with its IMF programme. However, it remains very time-consuming, expensive and bureaucratic for all sides to go through the process again the next year, and a rolling annual rescheduling is an inadequate basis for medium-term economic planning to restore credit worthiness.[15]

Some interviewees have argued that there will be more delays and disagreements among bankers during the negotiation of a MYRA, citing Latin American examples. But these would be more than cancelled out (provided the MYRAs were sustainable, through safeguards proposed below) by saving the time, energy and money now spent by both sides on annual negotiations. The debtor must also be facing imminent default before a Paris Club re-rescheduling can be agreed. This is ludicrous, as it means that the resulting arrears and shortage of foreign exchange can cause the breakdown of the whole rescheduling package/IMF deal before the Paris Club is permitted to do anything about it. The Paris Club argues, and some bankers express a similar opinion, that African economies are notoriously difficult to forecast and vulnerable to external shocks, and that only a short-term approach will guarantee that adjustment policies are maintained in the face of these shocks. This argument is fallacious, given that the IMF will suspend the programme if adjustment is not carried out. It would be much more logical to organize the multi-year rescheduling and write in a clause which suspended it if the IMF programme was not fulfilled, and if subsequent negotiations failed to restart the programme or agree a new one.

A far better way to guard against external shocks efficiently, and make the management of debt sustainable, is to build certain automatic safeguards against commodity price falls, natural disasters, and delays in disbursement of aid/loans into the agreement (the first of these has been included in the latest Mexican agreement with relation to oil). If the arrears are due to external shocks, there should be an automatic adjustment of terms or re-rescheduling built into the agreement. If they are due to bad design of the programme, or to failure to commit (or delay in disbursing) funds to support the programme, then the programme should be redesigned on the basis of different conditionality or lower financing. It should be made clear that to the extent that the arrears are due to mismanagement by the recipient government or failure to implement the IMF programme, there will be no compensation or redesign. With the guaranteed compensation, the commitment of the debtor government to the deal would be much greater: indeed it might be possible to convince it to adjust more readily, subject to the availability of enough external finance. External finance would then be more likely to be committed by investors and governments, more confident of the long-term economic future of the African country. In turn, these new funds would decrease the uncertainty of the future course of the African economy, and give better guarantees of sustainability and profitability for the creditors.

The wider picture: linked negotiations, new finance and coordination

The two sets of negotiations are formally linked. The Paris Club requires the debtor, by way of the 'most-favoured creditor clause', to negotiate all other debt on terms no more favourable to the other creditors than those given to the Paris Club.[16] This is to prevent Paris Club money being used to pay other creditors. The London Club agreements demand priority for the repayment of their debts, or at least comparability with the Paris Club. The interests of the commercial banks are also served by having those of their debts which are insured by an export credit agency rescheduled at the Paris Club.[17] The Paris Club governments protect their African allies by intervening in the London Club negotiations. This intervention is generally due to the close political alliance between the debtor and a major OECD creditor (almost always the United States) and therefore could not be publicized at an open general negotiation in one forum. But there is no reason why this pressure could not be exercized behind the scenes at such a meeting. The drafting of possible terms for an agreement by a neutral party such as the World Bank at the meeting would also help to ensure comparability between all creditors, including those outside the Paris and London Clubs.

The present semi-coordinated process is also supposed to encourage new inflows of finance to the African country. Does it? This question is best answered by looking at the various dimensions.

New bank loans and investment: figures indicate continued falls after rescheduling deals. The few new loans are due to the commitment of individual banks to their operations in certain countries (for example, Standard Chartered in Ghana[18]) or the political pressure of a Western sponsor (France in Côte d'Ivoire[19]).

Bank trade credit lines: restoration of these after rescheduling is haphazard. When a bank feels committed to a country, they restore them fast, but otherwise they usually remain severely reduced and may even fall further. A MYRA would help banks feel more secure of the creditworthiness of the country, and therefore encourage rapid restoration.

Restoration of ECA cover/credit lines: this is not a condition of Paris Club reschedulings, and to date the restoration has been selective, determined by competition among Paris Club nations for lucrative export contracts, and by pressure on their governments from creditor country banks and exporters. ECA representatives explain the delays and variations in restoration as due to different assessments of the creditworthiness of the African country, but privately say that they are leaving countries off cover because they will soon need another rescheduling. A MYRA would solve this uncertainty and bring comprehensive restoration.

Coordination with future aid flows: (through consultative group (CG) meetings arranged by the World Bank) the aid levels asked for by the government at the CG meeting are not simply a negotiating tactic by the government, pitching its request higher than its needs, but have been worked out with the World Bank as the lowest realistic figure. Inevitably the pledges of aid donors fall short of the request, even when the recipient country is complying fully with the rescheduling process and IMF conditions (such as Ghana). This lack of coordination (with the notable exception of Mauritania in 1985) has brought protests from the Bank, especially over Zambia in 1984.[20] The whole package frequently collapses because of this lack of coordination. Falls in aid, necessitating further rescheduling, reflect bureaucratic rivalries between different agencies in creditor governments, or the wish by the creditor government to reduce its net transfer to the African country and to concentrate aid on political allies or economic favourites. If the former of those courses for the fall in aid was the case, one forum (or even prior negotiations between export credit agencies/finance ministries/aid agencies in each donor country) would resolve this inefficiency. If the latter were true, at least these wishes should be made explicit and publicized at one forum, so that other donors can make up the shortfall, rather than forcing the World Bank to rush from donor to donor trying to find more money, and probably ending up having to fill the gap itself.

Conclusion

The present system seems to give African governments all the disadvantages of coordination (rapid and self-reinforcing falls in creditor confidence and new money, delays in negotiation of reschedulings because of concern over comparability, collapse of complete packages because of faults in one element), without any of the advantages (efficient early warning systems to prevent delay, universally agreed databases, rapid resolution of reschedulings, immediate inflows of new funds, restoration of creditor confidence, predictable and stable foreign capital inflows on which to base medium-term economic planning). There is no doubt that one forum, in which all the data problems were cleared up by the International Monetary Fund and the World Bank, in which all sides committed themselves to a stable amount of net capital inflow to the African economy (based on projections of the balance of payments by the Bank and Fund) would be much more efficient; yet the Paris Club and London Club prefer to stay with the present system. What are the reasons for this inefficiency?

It is impossible to consider the process of rescheduling African debt without looking at how seriously the creditors take the process. The official creditors seem to be spending far more time finding more lucrative markets (mostly outside Africa) for export credits than looking at the rescheduling process to see what effects it has on African economies. When they do think about Africa, it is to demand that African economies 'adjust' by way of IMF or World Bank programmes, before they can receive significant amounts of new aid, seemingly without any awareness that more flexible reschedulings are vital to the sustainability of these programmes. Bankers are preoccupied with writing down existing loans to African countries, with establishing loan loss reserves to guard against defaults, with selling their loans to other banks at a heavy discount (of 70–80 per cent of the original loan). Some do think about reforms in the rescheduling process, but most are happy to make large profits out of rescheduling by chairing steering committees, and by advising creditors or debtors.

Though the Paris Club and the London Club are linked very closely, they both have their reasons for wishing to remain separate. The Paris Club wants the freedom to hide politically motivated concessions in bilateral agreements, and the London Club wants the freedom to charge higher interest rates and fees, and to continue to refuse to reschedule interest payments. In practice this insistence on comparability, while maintaining separate fora for negotiations, leads to long delays in rescheduling, and mistrust among the creditors.

Meanwhile, the debt service burden is forcing many African countries to jeopardize both the present and the future well-being of their people, and to forfeit their prospects for recovery and growth. None of the development plans sketched out by international agencies or by African governments themselves in the *Lagos Plan of Action* or at the UN Special Session in May–June 1986 are feasible without a solution to this debt crisis. Whether they aim at self-reliance or encouraging foreign investment, whether they aim at 'getting the prices right' or ensuring redistribution of income, they all assume that net inflows of foreign finance into Africa will be needed. Without reforms in the debt rescheduling process, however, net inflows will be impossible for most countries. For many African governments, debt is the main short-term obstacle to their development.

There is little sign that the IMF or World Bank are prepared to provide anywhere near enough finance to enable African economies to overcome the debt crisis, or to push the creditors to adopt more efficient methods. The only way to make the process fit the supposed aims of the creditors (that is, the restoration of economic health to African economies) is for the African governments themselves to push bilaterally, regionally through the ECA and AfDB, and multilaterally through the G24 and the IMF and World Bank, for these reforms. Changes in the rescheduling process are not a panacea, promising instant recovery, but they will provide badly needed stability and coordination to help over the next ten years. It is better to ensure that African governments do not suffer the consequences of short-sighted debt rescheduling in the 1980s for the rest of the century.

Notes

1. All references to Africa are to sub-Saharan Africa, not including South Africa.

2. The process varies with almost every nation, and there is not the space for detailed case studies. Several nations have avoided debt crises, emphasizing the point that no generalizations are possible. This article is inevitably a stylized version of the rescheduling process.

3. For explanations of these varying estimates, and discussion of data inadequacy, see Lancaster, C. and Williamson, J., (eds), *African Debt and Financing* (Institute for International Economics Special Report no. 5, Washington DC, May 1986), pp. 11–46.

4. These figures apply to publicly-guaranteed medium-term and long-term debt at the end of 1985. They are based on World Bank and IMF staff estimates. Green and Griffith-Jones suggest that the total debt to commercial banks (including unguaranteed debt, short-term debt and arrears) may be over US$40 billion.

5. These ratios refer only to publicly-guaranteed medium-term and long-term debt service, and to principal payments on short-term debt and arrears. They are therefore underestimates, but it should be noted that the ratios may also be reduced by rescheduling and further accumulation of arrears. They are IMF and World Bank staff estimates, based on data available at the end of 1985.

6. The 1982 figure is from Agarwala, R. *et al.*, *Financing Adjustment With Growth in Sub-Saharan Africa, 1986–90* (World Bank, Washington, DC, April 1986); the 1986 figure is from projections based on articles in *African Economic Digest*.

7. There is no room for dealing with the many other fora in which negotiations take place—with the OPEC nations, individual bilateral commercial rescheduling deals, or individual cancellations of debts owed to some OECD governments, or the complex process of rescheduling trade debts, except in passing. Nor is there room for examining the management of debt by individual creditors or debtors, as again this varies too much to be able to do it justice in such a short article.

8. Brau, E. and Williams, R., *Recent Multilateral Debt Restructurings* (IMF Occasional Paper no. 25, 1983); Burke Dillon, K. *et al.*, *Recent Developments in External Debt Restructuring* (IMF Occasional Paper no. 40, 1985); Milivojevic, M., *The Debt Rescheduling Process* (London, Frances Pinter, 1985); Plan, R., *External Debt Rescheduling* (Vienna, Manzsche Verlaas-und Universitätsbuchhandlung 1985); Suratgar, D., *Default and Rescheduling* (London, Euromoney Publications, 1984).

9. Many details of the rescheduling process are highly confidential and there are no written sources. Where no source is given for a negotiating detail,

238	MATTHEW MARTIN

the information is from confidential documents or non-attributable interviews.

10.	For Côte d'Ivoire, see *AED Banking and Insurance Special Report*, September 1984, p. 22; for Sudan, confidential sources, and Brown, R., 'International Responses to Sudan's Economic Crisis: 1978 to the 1985 Coup d'État, *Development and Change* (**17**, no. 3, July 1986), pp. 487–512.

11.	For more on the Institute of International Finance, (IIF), see Milivojevic, M., op. cit., Appendix 10, pp. 204–11.

12.	For more detail on the London Club process, especially the conflicts among banks, see Lipson, C., 'Bankers' Dilemmas: Private Cooperation in Rescheduling Sovereign Debts', *World Politics* **38**, no. 1, 1985), pp. 200–25.

13.	For a detailed description of this intervention with reference to Mexico, see Kraft, J., *The Mexican Rescue* (New York, Group of 30, 1984). For African cases, see Brown, op. cit.; Ghosh, J., 'Foreign Debt and the Economic Development of Zaïre', *Development and Change* (**17**, no. 3, July 1986), pp. 455–86; and Sampson, A., *The Moneylenders* (London, Hodder and Stoughton, 1983).

14.	It is not the aim of this article to go into the terms granted in reschedulings in detail, but the MYRA issue is vital to the process as well as the terms. Details of the terms can be found in IMF Occasional Papers nos. 23 and 40. Criticisms of these terms have been made by others: see Green, R.H., and Griffith-Jones, S., *African External Debt and Development* (report for UNCTAD/ACMS, 1984, mimeo); Green, R.H. and Griffith-Jones, S., 'External Debt: Sub-Saharan Africa's Emerging Iceberg', in Rose, T., ed., *Crisis and Recovery in Sub-Saharan Africa* (Paris, OECD, 1986); Hardy, C., *Africa's Debt Burden* (Washington, DC, ODC Policy Focus no. 5, 1985); Krumm, K., *The External Debt of Sub-Saharan Africa* (World Bank Staff Working Paper no. 741, 1985).

15.	See the debate between Brau and Nyirabu in Helleiner, G.K., *The IMF and Africa in the 1980s* (Princeton, N.J., International Finance Section, Dept. of Economics, Princeton University, 1983).

16.	Plan, R., op. cit., p. 39.

17.	Milivojevic, op. cit., p. 43.

18.	*African Economic Digest*, 11 October 1986, pp. 16–17.

19.	*AED Banking and Insurance Special Report*, op. cit.

20.	On Zambia, see Jaycox *et al.* in Lancaster and Williamson, op. cit., pp. 60–2; on Mauritania, *Financing Adjustment With Growth*, op. cit., p. 45; for general comments on the CG and aid coordination process, see *Financing Adjustment With Growth*, pp. 35–47.

Select bibliography

This bibliography aims to provide the reader with a selection of recent titles which are representative of studies on the theme of African development. Some items we have included are considerably older, but we consider these important for those attempting to understand the development process in Africa. We have also drawn attention to those journals which have a direct interest in the developmental element of international African affairs. Needless to say this bibliography is *not* exhaustive.

Aboyade, O., *Issues in the Development of Tropical Africa* (Ibadan, University of Ibadan Press, 1976).

Adedeji, A., 'Foreign Debt and the Prospects for Economic Growth in Africa during the 1980s', *Journal of Modern African Studies* (**23**, no. 1, 1985).

———— and Shaw, T.M., eds, *Economic Crisis in Africa: African Perspectives on Development Programs and Potentials* (Boulder, Colo., Lynne Rienner Publishers, 1985).

African Development Bank, *African Development Assistance: Background and Prospects* (Abidjan, ADB, 1983).

———— *Annual Report* (Abidjan, ADB, Annual).

Agarwala, R. *et al.*, *Financing Adjustments with Growth in Sub-Saharan Africa 1986–90* (Washington, DC, World Bank, 1986).

Ahluwalia, M., 'Inequality, Poverty and Development', *Journal of Development Studies* (**3**, 1976).

Ake, C., *A Political Economy of Africa* (Harlow, Longman, 1981).

Almond, G.A. and Coleman, J.S., eds, *The Politics of the Developing Areas* (London, Oxford University Press, 1960).

Aluko, O. and Shaw, T.M., eds, *Southern Africa in the 1980s* (London, George Allen & Unwin, 1985).

Amin, S., *Impérialisme et Sous-Développment en Afrique* (Paris, Anthropos, 1976).

———— *Unequal Development: An Essay on the Social Formations of Peripheral Capitalism* (New York, Monthly Review Press, 1977).

———— *Accumulation on a World Scale* (2 volumes) (New York, Monthly Review Press, 1978).

Arab Bank for Economic Development in Africa, *Annual Report* (Khartoum, ABEDA, Annual).

Ayres, R., *Banking on the Poor: The World Bank and World Poverty* (Cambridge, Mass., MIT Press, 1983).

Bairoch, P., *Diagnostic de l'Evolution Economique du Tiers-Monde depuis 1900* (Paris, Gauthier-Villars, 1967).

Bangura, Y., *Britain and Commonwealth Africa: The Politics of Economic Relations 1951–75* (Manchester, Manchester University Press, 1983).

Bauer, P.T., *Equality, the Third World and Economic Delusion* (London, Weidenfeld and Nicolson, 1981).

———— *Dissent on Development: Studies and Debates on Development Economics* (London, Weidenfeld and Nicolson, 1971).

———— and Ward, B., *Two Views on Aid to Developing Countries*, Occasional Paper 9 (London, Institute of Economic Affairs, 1986).

Baulin, J., *Conseilleur du President Diori* (Paris, Eurafor-Presse, 1986).

———— *La Politique Africaine d'Houphouët-Boigny* (Paris, Eurafor-Presse, 1980).

Bayart, J., *La Politique Africaine de François Mitterrand* (Paris, Karthala, 1984).

Bedjaoui, M., *Pour un Nouvel Ordre Economique International* (Paris, Publications de l'UNESCO, 1979).

Bell, M., *Contemporary Africa: Development, Culture and the State* (London, Longman, 1986).

Bell, T., 'The Role of Regional Policy in South Africa', *Journal of Southern African Studies* (**12**, no. 2, April 1986).

Bénot, Y., *Les Indépendances Africaines* (Paris, Maspero, 1975).

Berg, E., *Accelerated Development in Sub-Saharan Africa: An Agenda for Action*, Report Prepared by Elliot Berg (Washington, DC: World Bank, 1981).

Bhagwati, J.N., *The New International Economic Order: The North–South Debate* (Cambridge, Mass., MIT Press, 1977).

Bird, G., *World Finance and Adjustment: An Agenda for Reform* (London, Macmillan, 1985).

Bissell, R.E. and Radu, M.S., eds, *Africa in the Post-Decolonization Era* (New Brunswick, NJ, Transaction Books, 1984).

Borgin, K. and Corbett, K., *The Destruction of a Continent: Africa and International Aid* (San Diego, Harcourt Brace Jovanovich, 1982).

Braillard, P. and Djalili, M., *The Third World and International Relations* (London: Frances Pinter, 1986).

Brandt Commission, *North–South: A Programme for Survival* (London, Pan Books, 1980), First Report.

Brandt Commission, *Common Crisis: North–South Cooperation for World Recovery* (London: Pan, 1983), Second Report.

Brandt, W. and Manley, M., *Global Challenge—From Crisis to Cooperation: Breaking the North–South Stalemate* (London, Pan Books, 1985).

Browne, R.S., and Cummings, R.J., *The Lagos Plan of Action vs. the Berg Report: Contemporary Issues in African Economic Development* (Lawrenceville, Va, Brunswick, c. 1984).

Carlsson, J., *South–South Relations in a Changing World Order* (Uppsala, Scandinavian Institute for African Studies, 1982).

Carter, G.M. and O'Meara, P., eds, *African Independence: The First Twenty-five Years* (Bloomington, Indiana University Press, 1985).

Cassen, R., *Does Aid Work?* (Oxford: Clarendon Press, 1986).

—— Jolly, R., Sewell, J. and Wood, R., eds, *Rich Country Interests and Third World Development* (London, Croom Helm, 1983).

Chan, S., 'Young Women and Development in Africa—Some Generally Unconsidered Considerations', *Community Development Journal* (**18**, no. 3, 1983).

Chenery, H.B., *Studies in Developmental Planning* (Cambridge, Mass., Harvard University Press, 1971).

Cohen, S., and Smouts, M., eds, *La Politique Extérieure de Valéry Giscard d'Estaing* (Paris, Presses de la Fondation Nationale des Sciences Politiques, 1985).

Commonwealth Secretariat, *Towards a New Bretton Woods: Challenges for the World Financial and Trading Systems*, Report by a Commonwealth Study Group (London, Commonwealth Secretariat, 1983).

Corbett, E.M., *The French Presence in Black Africa* (Washington, DC, Black Orpheus Press, 1972).

Daedalus (Special Issue), *Black Africa: A Generation After Independence* (**3**, no. 2, Spring 1982).

de Bemis, G., *L'Afrique de l'Indépendance Politique à l'Indépendance Economique* (Paris, Maspero, 1975).

Deboeck, G., and Kinsey, B., *Managing Information for Rural Development: Lessons from East Africa*, World Bank Staff Working Paper no. 379 (Washington, DC, World Bank, March 1980).

Deniau, X., *La Francophonie* (Paris, Presses Universitaires de France, 1983).

de Vries, M., *The IMF in a Changing World 1945–85* (Washington, DC, International Monetary Fund, 1986).

Diouf, M., *Integration Economique: Perspectives Africaines* (Paris, Publisud, 1985).

Donaldson, P., *Worlds Apart: The Development Gap and What it Means* (Harmondsworth, Middx: Penguin, 1986).

Edgren, G., *The Role of Labour Ministries in National Development Planning* (Geneva, International Institute for Labour Studies, 1973).

Elliot, C., *et al.*, *Real Aid: A Strategy for Britain* (London, Independent Group on British Aid, 1982).

Emmanuel, A., *Unequal Exchange: A Study in the Imperialism of Trade* (London, New Left Books, 1972).

Faaland, J. and Parkinson, J.R., eds, *The Political Economy of Development* (London, Frances Pinter, 1986).

Falola, T., and Ihonvbere, J., *Critical Perspectives on Third World Integration* (Oguta, Zim Pan, 1987).

Fanon, F., *The Wretched of the Earth* (Harmondsworth, Middx: Penguin, 1985).

Food and Agriculture Organization, *FAO in Africa* (Rome: FAO, 1986).

Fieldhouse, D.K., *Black Africa 1945–80: Economic Decolonization and Arrested Development* (London, Allen & Unwin, 1986).

Fields, G.S., *Poverty, Inequality and Development* (Cambridge, Cambridge University Press, 1978).

Franck, A.G., *Capitalism and Underdevelopment in Latin America* (Harmondsworth, Middx: Penguin, 1971).

Freyssinet, J., *Le Concept de Sous-développement* (Paris, Mouton, 1966).

Friedland, E.A., 'The Southern African Development Coordination Conference (SADCC) and the West: Cooperation or Conflict?', *Journal of Modern African Studies* (**23**, no. 2, 1985).

Gauhar, A., (ed.), *The Rich and the Poor—Development, Negotiation and Cooperation: An Assessment* (London, Third World Foundation, 1983).

Geldenhuys, D., *The Diplomacy of Isolation* (Johannesburg, Macmillan, 1984).

Ghai, D., and Radwan, S., eds, *Agrarian Policies and Rural Poverty in Africa* (Geneva, International Labour Office, 1983).

Ghosh, K., (ed.), *Foreign Aid and Third World Development* (Westport: Conn., Greenwood Press, 1984).

Gorman, R.F., 'Soviet Perspectives on the Prospects for Political and Economic Development in Africa', *African Affairs*, (**83**, no. 331, 1984).

Green, R.H., 'Consolidation and Accelerated Development in Africa: What Agendas for Action?', *African Studies Review* (**27**, no. 4, 1984).

——— and Griffith-Jones, S., *African External Debt and Development*, Report for UNCTAD/ACMS (mimeo., 1984).

Griffith-Jones, S., and Green, R.H., *African External Debt and Development: A Review and Analysis*, Report for the African Centre for Monetary Studies (IDS, Brighton, Sussex, 1984).

Gruhn, I.V., *Regionalism Reconsidered: the Economic Community for Africa* (Boulder, Colo., Westview Press, 1979).

Grundy, K., *The Militarisation of South African Politics* (London, I.B. Tauris, 1986).

Gutkind, P.C.W. and Wallerstein, I., eds, *The Political Economy of Contemporary Africa* (Beverley Hills, Calif./London, Sage Publications, 1977).

Hanlon, J., *Beggar Your Neighbours: Apartheid Power in Southern Africa* (London, CIIR, 1986).

Hayter, T., *Aid as Imperialism* (Harmondsworth, Middx: Penguin, 1971).

Heyer, J., Roberts, P., and Williams, G., eds, *Rural Development in Tropical Africa* (New York, St Martin's Press, 1981).

Hirschmann, A.O., *The Strategy of Economic Development* (New Haven, Yale University Press, 1958).

Hyden, G., *No Shortcuts to Progress: African Development Management in Perspective* (London, Heinemann, 1983).

Hymans, J.L., *Leopold Sedar Senghor* (Edinburgh, The University Press, 1971).

Kakonen, J., (ed.), *Technology and African Development: Proceedings of an International Seminar* (Turku, Finnish Peace Research Association, 1979).

Keohane, R.O., *Beyond Hegemony: Cooperation and Discord in the World Political Economy* (Princeton, NJ, Princeton University Press, 1984).

———— 'Reciprocity in International Relations', *International Organization* (**40**, no. 1, 1986).

Killick, T., *Development Economics in Action: A Study of Ghana* (London, Heinemann Educational, 1978).

Kreuger, A.O. and Ruttan, V.W., *The Development Impact of Economic Assistance to LLDCs* (University of Minnesota for USAID, 1983).

Lall, S., *Developing Countries as Exporters of Technology* (London, Macmillan, 1982).

Lancaster, C. and Williamson, J., eds, *African Debt and Financing* (Washington, DC, Institute for International Economics, 1986).

Langhammer, R.J., *EEC Trade Policies Towards Associated Developing Countries—Barriers to Success* (Kiel, Kieler Studien, 1985).

Laszlo, E., *Co-operation for Development—Strategies for the 1980s* (Dublin: Tycooly International Publishing Limited, 1984).

Lavroff, D.G., *La Politique Africaine de General de Gaulle 1958–1969* (Paris: Centre D'Etudes d'Afrique Noire, Bordeaux and Institut Charles de Gaulle with A. Pédone, 1980).

Lawrence, P., (ed.), *World Recession and the Food Crisis in Africa* (London, Currey for the *Review of African Political Economy*, 1986).

Léca, J., 'Idéologies de la Coopération', *Etudes Internationales* (Quebec) (**5**, no. 2, 1974).

Lecaillon, J., Paukert, F., Morrisson, C. and Germidis, D., *Income Distribution and Economic Development* (Geneva, International Labour Office, 1984).

Legum, C., *et al.*, *Africa in the 1980s* (New York, McGraw-Hill, 1979).

Lewis, W.A., *Racial Conflict and Economic Development* (Cambridge, Mass., Harvard University Press, 1985).

———— *The Theory of Economic Growth* (London, Allen & Unwin, 1955).

Leys, C., *Underdevelopment in Kenya: The Political Economy of Neo-Colonialism, 1964–71* (London, Heinemann, 1975).

Lipset, S.M., *Political Man* (London, Heinemann, 1959).

Luke, D.F. and Shaw, T.M. eds, *Continental Crisis: the Lagos Plan of Action and Africa's Future* (Lanham, Md, University Press of America; [Halifax, N.S.], Centre for African Studies, Dalhousie University, 1980).

Mabogunje, A.L., *The Development Process: A Spatial Perspective* (London, Hutchinson University Library for Africa, 1980).

Matthews, A., *The Common Agricultural Policy and the Undeveloped Countries* (Dublin, Gill and Macmillan, 1985).

Mazzeo, D., (ed.), *African Regional Organizations* (Cambridge, Cambridge University Press, 1984).

McGranahan, D., Pizarro, E. and Richard, C., *Measurement and Analysis of Socio-Economic Development* (Geneva, UN Research Institute for Social Development, 1985).

Meier, G.M., *Leading Issues in Economic Development* (Oxford, Oxford University Press, 1984).

Mende, T., *De l'Aide à la Recolonisation: Les Leçons d'un Echèc* (Paris, Editions du Seuil, 1972).

Meredith, M., *The First Dance of Freedom: Black Africa in the Post-war Era* (London, Abacus, 1985).

Mikesell, R.F., *The Economics of Foreign Aid* (Chicago, Aldine Publishing Co., 1968).

—— *The Economics of Aid and Self-Sustaining Development* (Boulder, Colorado, Westview Press, 1983).

Morrison, K.C., 'The New International Economic and Order', *African Development* (9, no. 1, 1984).

Mosley, P., *Overseas Aid: Its Defence and Reform* (Brighton, Wheatsheaf Books, 1987).

Mutharika, B.W.T., *Towards Multilateral Economic Cooperation in Africa* (New York, Praeger, 1972).

Myrdal, G., *Economic Theory and Underdeveloped Regions* (London, Duckworth, 1957).

Ndegwa, P., *Africa's Development Crisis and Related International Issues* (London, James Currey, 1985).

Nelson, N., (ed.), *African Women in the Development Process* (London, Cass, 1981).

Nobe, K.C. and Sampath, R.K., eds, *Issues in Third World Development* (Boulder, Colorado, Westview Press, 1985).

OAU, *Africa's Priority Programme for Economic Recovery 1986–1990* (Addis Ababa, OAU, 1985).

—— *The Lagos Plan of Action for the Implementation of the Monrovia Strategy for the Economic Development of Africa*, adopted by the Second

Extraordinary Assembly of the OAU Heads of State and Government devoted to economic matters (Lagos, 28–9 April 1980).

Odetola, T.O., *Military Regimes and Development: A Comparative Analysis of African States* (London, Allen & Unwin, 1982).

Offiong, D.A., *Imperialism and Dependency: Obstacles to African Development* (Washington, DC, Howard University Press, 1982).

Ojo, O.O., *Monetary and Other Financial Obstacles to Intra-African Trade: A Case-Study of the Economic Community of West African States (ECOWAS)*, A Report Prepared for the African Development Bank (Abidjan, ADB, 1986).

Onwuka, R., *Development and Integration in West Africa* (Ile-Ife, University of Ife Press, 1982).

Pavlic, B., *et al.*, eds, *The Challenges of South–South Cooperation* (Boulder, Colorado, Westview Press, 1983).

Pearson, L.B. (Chairman), *Partners in Development: Report of the Commission on International Development* (New York, Praeger, 1969).

Perroux, F., *L'Economie des Jeunes Nations* (Paris, Presses Universitaires de France, 1962).

Phillips, A., 'The Concept of Development', *Review of African Political Economy* (8, January–April 1977).

Polshikov, P.I., *Capital Accumulation and Economic Growth in Developing Africa* (Moscow, Progress, 1981).

Price, C., *Britain and Tanzania: The Search for Real Aid* (London, Independent Group on British Aid, 1986).

Ravenhill, J., *Collective Clientelism: The Lomé Convention and North–South Relations* (New York, Columbia University Press, 1979).

——— ed., *Africa in Economic Crisis* (Basingstoke, Macmillan, 1986).

Renninger, J.P., *Multinational Cooperation for Development in West Africa* (Toronto, Pergamon Press, 1979).

Reynolds, L.G., 'The Spread of Growth in the Third World', *Journal of Economic Literature* (21, 1983).

——— *Economic Growth in the Third World: An Introduction* (London, Dickens, 1986).

Riddell, R.C., *Foreign Aid Reconsidered* (London and Baltimore, James Currey, ODI, Johns Hopkins University Press, 1987).

Rimmer, D., *The Economies of West Africa* (London, Weidenfeld and Nicolson, 1984).

Rodrigues, J., *Brazil and Africa* (Berkeley, Calif., University of California Press, 1965).

Roemar, M., 'Economic Development in Africa: Performance Since Independence, and a Strategy for the Future', *Daedalus*, (3, no. 2, 1982).

Rose, T., (ed.), *Crisis and Recovery in Sub-Saharan Africa* (Paris, OECD, 1985).

Rostow, W.W., *Eisenhower, Kennedy, and Foreign Aid* (Austin, Texas, University of Texas Press, 1985).
—— *The Stages of Economic Growth: A Non-Communist Manifesto* (Cambridge, Cambridge University Press, 1971).
Runnalls, J.D. and d'Anjou, L., eds, *The Widening Gap* (New York, Columbia University Press, 1971).
Sanderson, W.C. and Williamson, J.G., *How Should Developing Countries Adjust to External Shocks in the 1980s? An Examination of Some World Bank Macro-economic Models* (Washington, DC, World Bank, 1985).
Seidman, A., *Comparative Development Strategies in East Africa* (Dar es Salaam, East African Publishing House, 1972).
—— *Planning for Development in Sub-Saharan Africa* (London, Praeger, 1974).
Sen, A., 'Development: Which Way Now?, *Economic Journal* (93, no. 372, 1983).
Senghor, L.S., *Liberté 1: Negritude et Humanisme* (Paris, Editions du Seuil, 1964).
Shand, R.T., and Richter, H.V., eds, *International Aid: Some Political, Administrative and Technical Realities* (Canberra, 1979).
Shaw, T.M., *Towards a Political Economy for Africa: The Dialectics of Dependence* (London, Macmillan, 1985).
—— (ed.), *Alternative Futures for Africa* (Boulder, Colo., Westview Press, 1982).
—— and Aluko, O., (eds), *The Political Economy of African Foreign Policy: Comparative Analysis* (Aldershot, Gower, 1984).
—— (eds), *Africa Projected: From Recession to Renaissance by the Year 2000?* (London, Macmillan, 1985).
—— and Heard, K.A., (eds), *The Politics of Africa: Dependence and Development* (New York, Africana Publishing Company for Dalhousie University Press, 1979).
—— and Ojo, S., eds, *Africa and the International Political System* (Washington, DC, University Press of America for the Department of International Relations, University of Ife, Ile-Ife, Nigeria, 1982).
Stevens, C., eds, *EEC and the Third World* (six volumes), (London, Hodder and Stoughton, 1981–6).
Stevens, P., (ed.), *The Social Sciences and African Developing Planning* (Waltham, Mass., African Studies Association, 1978).
Strange, S., (ed.), *Paths to International Political Economy* (London, George Allen & Unwin, 1984).
Summers, R. and Heston, A., 'Improved International Comparisons of Real Product and its Compopsition, 1950–80', *Review of Income and Wealth* (Series 30, no. 2, June 1984).
Turok, B., (ed.), *Development in Zambia: A Reader* (London, Zed Press, 1979).

United Nations Department for Disarmament Affairs, *Conference on Security, Disarmament and Development in Africa: Meeting of Experts* (New York, United Nations, 1986).

Viatte, A., *La Francophonie* (Paris, Librairie Larousse, 1969).

Wallerstein, I., *The Modern World System: Capitalist Agriculture and the Origins of the European World-Economy in the Sixteenth Century* (London and New York, Academic Press, 1974).

Warren, B., 'Imperialism and Capitalist Industrialisation' *New Left Review*, no. 81, September–October, 1977, pp. 3–44.

White, D.S., *Black Africa and de Gaulle* (Pittsburgh, Pennsylvania State University Press, 1979).

White, J., *The Politics of Foreign Aid* (London, Bodley Head, 1974).

World Bank, *World Development Report* (New York, Oxford University Press, annual).

———— *Accelerated Development in Sub-Saharan Africa: An Agenda for Action* (Washington, DC, World Bank, 1981).

———— *Sub-Saharan Africa: Progress Report on Development Prospects and Programs* (Washington, DC, World Bank, 1983).

———— *Towards Sustained Development in Sub-Saharan Africa* (Washington, DC, World Bank, 1984).

———— *Financing Adjustment with Growth in Sub-Saharan Africa, 1986–1990* (Washington, DC, World Bank, 1986).

———— *Recovery in the Developing World: The London Symposium of the World Bank's Role* (Washington, DC, World Bank, 1986).

Wright, M., (ed.), *Rights and Obligations in North–South Relations: Ethical Dimensions of Global Problems* (London, Macmillan, 1986).

Yansané, A., (ed.), *Decolonization and Dependency: Problems of Development of African Societies* (Westport, Conn., Greenwood Press, 1980).

Young, C., *Ideology and Development in Africa* (New Haven, Conn., Yale University Press, 1982).

Zulu, J. and Nsouli, S.M., *Adjustment Programs in Africa: The Recent Experience* (Washington, DC, International Monetary Fund, 1985).

Useful journals

Actuel Développement (Paris)
African Affairs
Africa Development/Afrique et Développement (Dakar)
Africa Research Bulletin
African Review
Africa South of the Sahara

African Statistical Yearbook, in 4 volumes: North Africa, West Africa, East and Southern Africa, Central Africa and Others (United Nations)

African Studies Review

Afrique Contemporaine (Paris)

Année Africaine (Bordeaux)

Bulletin of the Institute of Development Studies

Cooperation South (UN)

The Courier: Africa-Caribbean-Pacific (EC)

Daedalus

Development and Change

Development Policy Review

Economic Journal

Econometrica

Entwicklungspolitische Korrespondenz (Hamburg, BRD)

Etudes Internationales (Quebec)

Europe-Outremer (Paris)

Finance and Development (World Bank)

Géopolitique Africaine (Paris)

International African Bibliography

International Organization

Internationales Afrikaforum (Köln, BRD)

IPW Berichte (Berlin, DDR)

Jeune Afrique (Paris)

Le Journal de l'Economie Africaine (Paris)

Journal of African Studies

Journal of Commonwealth and Comparative Politics

Journal of Developing Areas

Journal of Development Planning

Journal of Development Studies

Journal of Modern African Studies

Library Services Development Index (ODA)

Marchés Tropicaux et Méditerranéens (Paris)

Mois en Afrique (Paris)

Mondes en Développement (Paris)

ODU: A Journal of West African Studies

Orbis

Peuples Noirs/Peuples Africains (Paris)

Politique Africaine (Bordeaux)

Politique Etrangère (Paris)

Politique Internationale (Paris)

Public Administration and Development

Rapport Annuel Mondial sur le Sustème Economique et les Stratègies (Paris)

Relations Internationales (Paris and Geneva)

Review of African Political Economy
Revue Tiers Monde (Paris)
Round Table
South
Survey of Economic and Social Conditions in Africa (UNECA)
Third World Planning Review
Third World Quarterly
Trade and Development (UNCTAD)
Vierteljahrsberichte: Probleme der Entwicklungshilfe (Bonn, BRD)
West Africa
World Development
World Development Report (World Bank)
World Debt Tables: External Debt of Developing Countries (World Bank)
World Economic Outlook (IMF)
La Zone Franc (Paris)

Statistical appendices

Appendix 1

Country*	Average annual growth rate of GDP % 1973–84	GDP per capita 1984 (US$)	1983–84 GDP growth in %	GDI† as % of GDP 1984	Average annual growth rate of GDI % 1973–84
Angola (O)	—	—	2.5	—	—
Benin (L)	4.6	270	2.7	7	10.3
Botswana (M)	10.7	910	20.1	21	14
Burkina Faso (L)	2.9	120	−0.9	14	−3.3
Burundi (L)	3.6	200	−6.0	21	15.7
Cameroon (L)	7.1	780	5.7	26	10.6
Cape Verde (L)	—	—	9.3	—	—
Central A. Rep. (L)	0.7	250	8.7	12	−4.7
Chad (L)	—	120	3.1	—	—
Comoros (L)	—	—	—	—	—
Congo (M)	8.1	1,180	−0.7	35	6.3
Côte d'Ivoire (M)	3.7	760	−2.4	13	2.9
Djibouti (M)	—	—	0.0	—	—
Ethiopia (L)	2.3	110	−6.7	11	2.6
Equatorial Guinea (L)	—	—	0.0	—	—
Gabon (O)	—	3,140	13.1	—	—
Gambia (L)	—	240	−8.7	—	—
Ghana (L)	−0.9	330	9.5	6	−5.4
Guinea (L)	3.1	—	5.0	14	−1.5
Guinea-Bissau (L)	—	280	10.4	—	—
Kenya (L)	4.4	280	2.3	22	1.2
Lesotho (M)	5.0	210	2.0	—	—
Liberia (M)	0.2	380	−0.8	20	1.5
Madagascar (L)	—	240	1.5	14	−0.5
Malawi (L)	3.3	200	4.7	16	−2.6
Mali (L)	4.1	140	1.1	17	4.2
Mauritania (M)	2.3	390	−2.7	22	4.8
Mauritius (M)	3.6	1,020	11.3	18	−3.7
Mozambique (L)	—	—	−3.8	—	—

Appendix 1—*cont.*

Country*	Average annual growth rate of GDP % 1973–84	GDP per capita 1984 (US$)	1983–84 GDP growth in %	GDI[†] as % of GDP 1984	Average annual growth rate of GDI % 1973–84
Niger (L)	5.2	230	16.5	25	3.5
Nigeria (O)	0.7	700	−3.2	12	−2.0
Rwanda (L)	5.4	250	−5.7	—	—
São Tomé and Príncipe (L)	—	380	4.4	—	—
Senegal (M)	2.6	350	−3.6	15	−0.7
Seychelles (M)	—	2,100	0.0	—	—
Sierra Leone (L)	1.8	250	−5.3	9	—
Somalia (L)	—	—	−3.7	—	—
Swaziland (M)	—	750	0.3	—	—
Tanzania (L)	2.6	230	−7.6	—	—
Togo (L)	2.3	230	−0.6	23	−0.2
Uganda (L)	−1.3	—	4.1	8	—
Zaïre (L)	−1.0	90	3.0	—	—
Zambia (M)	0.4	400	−1.6	14	−13.7
Zimbabwe (M)	1.7	580	1.3	13	—

* Economic classification of African states (World Bank): O = Middle Income Oil Exporting Countries; L = Low Income Countries; M = Middle Income Non-Oil Exporting Countries.
† GDI = Gross Domestic Investment

Sources: United Nations, *Survey of Economic and Social Conditions in Africa, 1984–85* (Addis Ababa, UNECA, Document E/ECA/CM.12/15, April 1986); World Bank, *World Development Report 1986* (New York, Oxford University Press, 1986).

Appendix 2

Country*	Population (1984) (millions)	Average annual growth rate of population % 1973–84	Literacy rate as % of population (1985)	Average index of food production per capita 1982–4 (1974–6 = 100)
Angola (O)	8.8	3.1	41.0	81
Benin (L)	3.9	2.8	25.9	97
Botswana (M)	1.1	4.4	70.8	61
Burkina Faso (L)	6.7	1.8	13.2	94
Burundi (L)	4.6	2.2	33.8	106
Cameroon (O)	9.4	2.1	56.2	83
Cape Verde (L)	0.3	—	47.4	—
Central A. Rep. (L)	2.5	2.3	40.2	94
Chad (L)	4.9	2.1	25.3	95
Comoros (L)	0.4	—	—	—
Congo (M)	1.8	3.1	62.9	96
Côte d'Ivoire (M)	9.6	4.5	42.7	110
Djibouti (M)	0.3	—	10.0	—
Ethiopia (L)	42.5	2.8	55.2	100
Equatorial Guinea (L)	0.3	—	37.0	—
Gabon (O)	1.1	—	61.6	—
Gambia (L)	0.7	—	25.1	—
Ghana (L)	13.1	2.6	53.2	73
Guinea (L)	6.3	2.0	28.3	93
Guinea-Bissau (L)	0.9	—	31.4	—
Kenya (L)	19.8	4.0	59.2	82
Lesotho (M)	1.5	2.4	52.0	78
Liberia (M)	2.1	3.3	35.0	91
Madagascar (L)	9.7	2.8	67.5	89
Malawi (L)	6.8	3.1	41.2	100
Mali (L)	7.8	2.6	16.8	101
Mauritania (M)	1.8	2.1	17.0	95
Mauritius (M)	1.0	1.4	82.8	88
Mozambique (L)	13.6	2.6	38.0	73
Niger (L)	6.1	3.0	13.9	113
Nigeria (O)	90.4	2.8	42.4	96
Rwanda (L)	5.9	3.3	46.6	112
São Tomé and Príncipe (L)	0.1	—	—	—
Senegal (M)	6.6	2.8	28.1	66
Seychelles (M)	0.1	—	75.0	—
Sierra Leone (L)	3.3	2.1	29.3	95
Somalia (L)	5.5	2.8	11.6	69
Swaziland (M)	0.6	—	67.9	—
Tanzania (L)	21.2	3.4	79.0	100
Togo (L)	2.9	2.8	40.7	92

Appendix 2—*cont.*

Country*	Population (1984) (millions)	Average annual growth rate of population % 1973–84	Literacy rate as % of population (1985)	Average index of food production per capita 1982–4 (1974–6 = 100)
Uganda (L)	15.2	3.2	57.3	98
Zaïre (L)	29.8	3.0	61.2	92
Zambia (M)	6.5	3.2	75.7	74
Zimbabwe (M)	8.6	3.2	74.0	69

*   See notes to Appendix 1.

Sources: United Nations, *Survey of Economic and Social Conditions in Africa, 1984–1985* (Addis Ababa, UNECA, Document E/ECA/CM.12/15, April 1986); World Bank, *World Development Report 1986* (New York, Oxford University Press, 1986).

Appendix 3:   External debt: sub-Saharan Africa, 1970–85, US$ billion

	1970	1975	1980	1981	1982	1983	1984	1985
Long-term debt	5,752.9	14,929.9	43,910.2	49,189.7	55,393.3	61,461.6	62,046.1	67,979.2
Use of IMF credit	106.4	648.1	1,966.8	3,428.5	3,997.3	5,088.6	5,258.7	6,008.3
Short-term debt	n.a.	n.a.	9,480.0	10,498.7	8,628.3	10,343.9	10,914.4	11,603.3
Total external debt	—	—	55,357.0	63,116.9	68,018.9	76,894.1	78,219.2	85,590.8
External debt as a % of GNP	—	—	29.8	35.7	39.7	46.2	49.1	55.1

n.a. = Figures not available.

Source: World Bank, *World Debt Tables: External Debt of Developing Countries 1986–87* (Washington, DC, World Bank, 1987).

Notes on contributors

Olusola Akinrinade teaches in the Department of History, University of Ife, Nigeria. He has contributed chapters to a number of books and published articles in journals on African studies. He is currently completing a doctoral thesis on international organizations and foreign policy-making in developing states in the Department of International Relations at the London School of Economics.

J. Kurt Barling is a former Editor of *Millennium: Journal of International Studies* and is currently an Associate Editor of the journal. He is working on a comparative study of French and British foreign aid policies for his doctorate in the Department of International Relations at the London School of Economics where he also teaches part-time.

Ekei U. Etim is Lecturer in the Department of Political Science, Bendel State University, Nigeria. She is a research student, working on the Economic Commission for Africa and development, in the Department of International Relations at the London School of Economics.

Toyin Falola is a Senior Lecturer in the Department of History at the University of Ife. He has published many works on African affairs, his most recent publications include *Britain and Nigeria Exploitation or Development?* (ed.) (1986), *Transport Systems in Nigeria* (edited with S. Olanrewaju) (1986), and *The Rise and Fall of Nigeria's Second Republic 1974–84* (with J. Ihonvbere) (1985).

Matthew Martin has worked as a researcher at the Overseas Development Institute and the World Bank and is currently writing a thesis on the rescheduling of African debt, in the Department of International Relations at the London School of Economics.

S.A. Olanrewaju is a Senior Lecturer in the Department of Economics at the University of Ife. He has published widely on the area of underdevelopment in Africa. His most recent publication is *Transport Systems in Nigeria* (1986) (edited with Toyin Falola).

Mark Simpson is a Research Associate at the Centro de Estudos Afro-Asiaticos, Rio de Janeiro, Brazil. He is Teaching Assistant and doctoral candidate, working on the evolution of Marxist regimes in Africa, in the Department of International Relations at the London School of Economics.

Christopher Stevens is currently based in Brussels as a Research Fellow at the Institut d'études européenes, Université Libre de Bruxelles, and is also on the staff of the Overseas Development Institute and the Institute of Development Studies. He has acted as adviser to the ACP and OAU secretariats, and to the UN Economic Commission for Africa. His books include *EEC and the Third World: A Survey* (1981–86) (six volumes); *Nigeria: Economic Prospects to 1985* (1985), (Economist Intelligence Unit); *Food Aid and the Developing World: Four African Case Studies* (1979), and *The Soviet Union and Black Africa* (1976).

Scott Thomas was a Visiting Lecturer at the University of Cape Town, and is researching on the ANC diplomacy of liberation for his doctorate at the London School of Economics.

Kaye Whiteman is Editor-in-Chief of *West Africa* and has published many articles on African affairs.

Index